Th   ie was

thr   e was

the   uanian

an

Sh   English

int   nguage

wh   20, she

ca

Af   gy and

18   finally

ga

UNDERSTANDING ENGLISH SPELLING

Masha Bell

Understanding
English Spelling

PEGASUS EDUCATIONAL

PEGASUS EDUCATIONAL

A CIP catalogue record for this title is
available from the British Library
ISBN 1 903490 12 X

*Pegasus Educational is an imprint of
Pegasus Elliot MacKenzie Publishers Ltd.*
www.pegasuspublishers.com

First published in 2004

**Pegasus
Sheraton House Castle Park**

Cambridge England

Printed & Bound in Great Britain

Index

Acknowledgement

Profound thanks are due to:

Steve and Jill Cooper who concurred that English spelling might be an educational impediment when I first mooted this idea over a curry in February 1995;

Elizabeth Kuizenga in California and *Allan Campell* in NZ who read the early drafts of most chapters and have continually provided moral support;
Angela Tolley who thoroughly proofread the first manuscript;
Dr. John Gledhill who made copious critical comments on the penultimate version;

Last but foremost, *my husband Lew* who was often book-widowed over the last eight years, who repeatedly read and re-read all the chapters, who ruthlessly censored sloppy writing and superfluous adjectives and challenged everything that did not make sense easily, and especially, for regularly curbing my tendency to become work-obsessed.

Masha Bell

Introduction

Learning to read and write English is difficult. Large-scale surveys in both the USA and in Britain have repeatedly found that at least 20% of English-speaking adults cannot read well enough to be called literate. This means that around 40 million Americans and 7 million Britons have such problems.

Spelling is mastered adequately by even fewer. No more than half of all English speakers can spell accurately and confidently. Chief Inspectors for Schools in England have reported again and again that half of all children leaving primary school are very poor spellers. After 6 years in full-time education, most English 11 year olds cannot spell many everyday words correctly, including: *family, friends, holiday, picture, beautiful, believe, disappeared*. Most Italian children can spell such words faultlessly by the age of 8.

Even well educated English-speaking adults remain uncertain about the spelling of words like *accommodate, yacht, receive, practice, practise, fulfil, diarrhoea*, and hundreds more like them. Many people would even have trouble finding words like *'yacht'* and *'diarrhoea'* in the dictionary. If you have ever wondered why so many people find it difficult to learn to spell English and why some don't even manage to learn to read properly during all those years they spend at school, then you will find this book enlightening.

I came to realise that English spelling is exceptionally difficult because I had already learned a couple of languages with more regular spelling systems by the time I met up with English. Since my arrival in England in 1964 I have been repeatedly surprised to find that most native English speakers are not aware just how learner-unfriendly English spelling is, or what makes it so, although it has been causing trouble for several centuries.

As long ago as 1551, John Hart wrote about *'the vices and faults of our writing, which cause it to be tedious, and long in learning; and learned hard, and evil to read'*. Most of the *'vices and faultes'* that he complained about are still with us today. This book sets out and analyses them. It explains why learning to read and write English is difficult, and why teaching these skills can be so frustrating.

Confident mastery of English spelling requires a fairly high level of general intelligence – much higher than for many other languages. This ensures that English spelling proficiency is beyond the intellectual capabilities of many children, but many clever and talented people have been poor spellers too. Even Shakespeare is believed to have suffered from this malady.

The simplest way to make literacy acquisition in English easier is undoubtedly to make its spelling more regular. Many countries have successfully streamlined their spelling systems during the last two centuries and raised the literacy levels of their populations. The clearest evidence for the difference that spelling reform can make is provided by Denmark and Sweden. These countries educate their children in very similar ways: allowing young children to learn mainly through play and delaying formal schooling until seven. They also have very similar languages. Yet many Danish pupils leave school unable to read, while in Sweden this problem is far less common.

The main educational difference between Denmark and Sweden stems from their spelling systems. Danish spelling is highly unpredictable, as Swedish used to be before it was made much more learner-friendly at the beginning of the 20th Century. This explains why nearly all Swedish pupils learn to read and write with little effort, while many Danish ones struggle. There is every reason to believe that the same remedy would work just as well in English-speaking countries. But reform of the English spelling system does not appear to be imminent, and teachers and pupils have to continue struggling with it as best they can.

It is hoped that this book will help to make teachers and learners more effective by improving their understanding of what needs to be learned and what the main learning problems are. It should also provide some help and comfort to the millions who have tried hard to come to grips with English spelling, but have never quite managed to master it and have been baffled by their inability to do so.

This book shows what the English learning burden amounts to – by providing the word lists which learners have to cope with. They range from phonically simple reading lists to those that frequently cause reading difficulties (in Appendix R) and those which are likely to cause spelling errors (in Appendix S). As well as explaining the English spelling system, these lists provide material for reading and spelling practice.

Normally children do not learn to read by means of lists. They use a reading scheme – a series of books which becomes progressively harder. Children who cope easily and develop a love of reading move through such schemes rapidly. They go on to acquire the more sophisticated, higher order recognition and speed-reading skills by dint of their own efforts.

This book will be of help predominantly to teachers and parents of children who fail to get off to a quick start at the age of five; and to older and foreign students who generally have to learn to read and write in less time than the ten years that English-speaking children normally take to acquire these skills. They should all benefit from a clearer understanding of what makes learning to read and write English difficult, and what needs to be given special attention.

The hardest part of learning to read English boils down to learning to read roughly 2000 words in which commonly occurring letter combinations have to be pronounced in unexpected ways (e.g. laid, maid, paid – *said*). Spelling difficulties are caused by approximately 3700 words which disobey the basic rules of the English spelling system and have to be memorised individually (e.g. fake, lake, make – *steak*). This book sets out all such commonly used rogue words that are hard to read (Appendix R) or difficult to spell (Appendix S), as well as explaining the difficulties and their origins in Chapters 1 – 10.

Please note the following three explanations:

1). Since this book is aimed mainly at ordinary readers, technical vocabulary has been kept to an unavoidable minimum, apart from the use of the term *'grapheme'*. – This means a letter, or string of letters, which is used for spelling a sound. For example, in the word *'said'* the E-sound is spelt with the grapheme *'ai'*.

2). Because many English letters are used to spell different sounds (e.g. l<u>o</u>st p<u>o</u>st), linguists normally use special symbols to refer to sounds. These can be found in all bigger dictionaries with pronunciation guides, but most people find them incomprehensible. This book therefore refers to English sounds by the most common way of spelling them in English, i.e. EE-sound, AI-sound, CH-sound, AR-sound.

However, there are two sounds for which English has no easily recognisable spelling patterns:

   a) the <u>short OO-sound</u> of *'g<u>oo</u>d'*, *'sh<u>ou</u>ld'* and *'p<u>u</u>t'* and

   b) the <u>ZH-sound</u> of *'vi<u>s</u>ion'*, *'a<u>z</u>ure'* and *plea<u>s</u>ure'*.

These sounds are therefore referred to as the *short OO-sound* (as distinct from the *long OO-sound* of *'f<u>oo</u>d'*) and the *ZH-sound*.

3). Words which contain graphemes with unpredictable pronunciations are spelled out phonetically in square brackets, using recognisable English spelling patterns. The words *'treat'* and *'threat'*, for example, would have their pronunciations spelt out as [treet] and [thret].

Chapter 1

How I became interested in taking a closer look at English spelling

As a result of falling in love, with London, England and an Englishman, I became a naturalised Englishwoman in 1968. I now pose a bit of a puzzle to people who pride themselves on their ability to identify a person's country of origin. Nobody has yet come close to guessing that I was born in Germany to a Lithuanian refugee near the end of the second world war, that my mother moved back to Lithuania when I was a small child, then returned to Germany when I was a teenager, and that I came to England as an au-pair when I had turned twenty.

I developed a desire to learn English properly when I first read a Lithuanian version of Shakespeare's *'Hamlet'* at the age of 13. But as soon as I began to learn it, I started to wish that I didn't have to. I liked the language, but English spelling infuriated me as soon as I became acquainted with it at 14, and it has bothered me intermittently ever since.

I spent five years, from 18 to 23, learning English very intensively. After leaving school in Germany at 17, I began to work in an office and started to study English seriously in evening classes. Then I came to England as an au-pair and foreign student of English, before going to University. During that time English spelling was naturally never far from my mind.

What really surprised me, however, when I first came to London as an au-pair in 1964, was that it featured so prominently in the lives of native English speakers as well. It seemed to be of tremendous importance to the three boys aged 6, 10 and 14 whom I helped to look after, as well as their 16 year old brother who came home during school holidays, and their parents too. Constantly, a spelling test seemed to be looming for one of them, and either their parents or I were forever preparing and testing them.

Before coming to England I had lived for a while with relatives in Germany who also had 3 young boys. I often read poems and stories to them or listened to them read, but I never tested their spelling. We sometimes rehearsed their times tables, but spelling was something they learned at school. It caused no special anxiety and needed no more attention than other school subjects.

I eventually obtained my Certificate of Proficiency in English and studied Psychology and Philosophy at the University of Exeter. By then English had become the language I used every day, the one I also thought and dreamt in, but I still felt that I had not yet conquered English spelling properly. I was still not as confident about it as I had been with Lithuanian and German when those had been the languages which I normally used. I tended to keep my lecture notes covered up, for fear of the embarrassing thought that my neighbours might happen to glance over and spot a spelling mistake. I fervently hoped that I did not disgrace myself too much in examinations.

I got married while I was still a student. I quickly came to realise that my husband who had already graduated was, nevertheless, occasionally still uncertain about the spelling of fairly common words (which I invariably could spell). This made me nervous. I hoped that this was not an indication that I had married someone a bit dim!

I was puzzled how an intelligent, well-educated person could ever be uncertain about the spelling of any word in their own language. I had been convinced that this was a problem which affected me because I was a foreigner. I believed that my erratic education had prevented me from finding the key that unlocked the mysteries of English spelling, that I had somehow failed to understand the system properly.

Several years later I became a teacher of German, English and Russian in a secondary school for academically able girls, a grammar school. I had naively expected that these girls, who were at least 11 years old, would have already become proficient spellers. I had assumed that all bright English children would be able to spell their native language as confidently as I had spelt Lithuanian at that age. I had thought my job as their teacher of English would be mainly that of teaching them to appreciate good writing, to write clearly and imaginatively themselves and to think clearly. I was shocked to realise that the majority of 11 year olds were still a very long way short of adult spelling proficiency, and that many of the older ones were as yet not really close to it either. I never ceased to be amazed that at parents' evenings the girls' spelling ability was always the main point of concern and discussion. Other communication skills worried their parents far less. My au-pair family had not been as unusual as I had assumed at the time.

Teaching also brought me a pleasant surprise. I discovered that my own spelling had become as good as, or even better than that of most English adults. Even the very highly educated teachers of that school occasionally still made spelling mistakes. As a form teacher, I had to check reports before the headmistress was asked to sign them and they were sent home. Whenever possible I corrected errors myself, but each time some reports needed to be rewritten. Whenever I have related this to colleagues on exchange visits from Germany or France, they found this incredible.

Educated German adults certainly cannot imagine themselves making spelling mistakes in that situation, or being unsure about the spelling of any word in their active vocabulary. They occasionally still consult dictionaries for the meaning of words, but not their spellings. If they can use a word, they know how to spell it. They never need reassurance from a dictionary or a spellchecker as many English speakers so often do.

Ill health forced me to leave teaching when I was 49. After a few years of doing very little, I had recovered sufficiently to want to learn again and to pursue interests which teaching had left me no time for. One thing I had always wanted to look into, was exactly how irregular English spelling was. This was partly in response to people who claimed that English spelling can't be that much more difficult than that of other languages. My own experiences had firmly convinced me that they were wrong.

I had learned to spell Lithuanian and Russian accurately by the age of 14, without knowing exactly how long I had spent on each. I had learned them both between the ages of 7 and 14. After that it took me only 3 years to become a confident speller of German, starting from scratch and without a great deal of effort. In English, I was unable to achieve the same degree of spelling confidence in the course of 12 years, despite trying much harder.

If I had not gone on to learn other languages after learning English, I might have been persuaded that learning to read and spell English had taken me so long because it had been the last language I tackled and because I continued to learn it well into my early twenties. I had heard it said that learning a foreign language becomes increasingly difficult as one gets older and that some new foreign sounds become virtually impossible to acquire beyond one's teens. It was partly to test such theories that I decided to have a stab at learning French as I was nearing 40. I wanted to get acquainted with that major European language for other reasons as well; but seeing if, and how quickly, I could learn it was a major impetus for getting started.

I found French spelling quite difficult too, but still far less daunting than English. In 1983, after two years of spare-time study, I took the examination normally taken by 16-year-olds in England, alongside pupils in the school where I taught. I passed with an "A" grade. French had turned out to be another language that I could learn more easily than English. Learning to read French, especially, was far easier than English.

I continued to learn French on and off for another 7 years, but never very intensively. Full-time teachers in England have not had much spare time since the mid-eighties, when their workload began to expand relentlessly. I learned mainly through reading and listening to French radio while driving to and from work.

I will probably never become as fluent in French as I am in English, partly because I am not prepared to invest more time or effort on improving further. The level of proficiency which I have achieved serves me well enough. I have no problem coping with the usual tourist requirements, I can read the great French novelists and can converse on most topics easily enough. When booking a hotel in France, I have occasionally even been mistaken for a French woman. My leisurely attempts to learn French have left me certain that it is possible to achieve native-level fluency in French in far less time than in English.

It was neither my late start, nor learning English after learning other languages, that made it so difficult for me to master English. The chief barrier to faster progress in English had been its chaotic spelling.

I have since also learnt some holiday Spanish and a smattering of Italian. Those languages merely confirmed what previous experiences had already taught me several times before: a regular spelling system makes learning to read and write much easier than an unpredictable one like English. My experiences with learning several languages have left me in no doubt that English spelling is far more difficult than Italian, Spanish, German, Russian, Lithuanian or French.

I have also read many letters in newspapers from parents who have lived abroad with their children and who reported the same experience with several other languages. These parents had first watched their children struggle with English spelling and had subsequently been surprised to find how little trouble they had learning the local language. The spelling of Swedish, Dutch, Finnish, Norwegian, Hungarian, Turkish, Welsh and Japanese have all been found to be easier than English by those who have had opportunities to compare them closely.

I knew that learning to spell English accurately had absorbed much of the time and effort which I had spent on learning the language. I also knew that learning to spell English had essentially amounted to internalising long lists of words with irregular spellings. But exactly how long a list had I memorised? I wanted to know, *how many English words cannot be spelt accurately by simply mastering English phonics?* I had become convinced that only by seeing the pages of words with irregular spellings which pupils are expected to learn in the course of their education could anyone fully appreciate just how difficult English spelling really was, and why it took so long to learn.

Native English speakers absorb the conventions of English spelling over a very long time. They generally also begin to learn them at a very young age. In England, as in other English-speaking countries, the official school starting age is five. In practice most English infants now start formal education closer to four, whereas in most of Europe children start school at six and in several countries as late as seven (Sweden, Norway, Denmark and virtually all of Eastern Europe).

The very early start, followed by the long time during which spelling is learnt ensure that native speakers of English end up not appreciating how much effort they had to spend on learning to read and to spell. They begin to be initiated into the conventions of English spelling at an almost preconscious age. They then go on to absorb them by the drip-feed method over 10 or 11 years, via a succession of different teachers, with the difficulties of the task almost never clearly presented. Even those who master the skill therefore end up with little idea of the total amount of work that learning to write English really involves.

Chapter 2

Getting to grips with the size of the problem

Astonishingly, there have been very few attempts to get an accurate measure of the learning task and to present it clearly. Despite millions of words written about teaching methods and how children learn to read and write, I could not find a clear exposition of what school leavers at the age of 16 are expected to master.

For foreign language courses examination boards produce word lists, grammar rules and common phrases which should be taught. I could not find a single comprehensive list of words with irregular English spellings that English children are expected to learn. The learning task has never been made fully obvious to either teachers, parents or pupils. In 2000 the Department of Education for England compiled a list of 600 *'difficult'* words which it wanted to be taught to all pupils aged 11, but by that age they will already have encountered several thousand words which are also anything but easy.

Before the invention of computers it would have been extremely time-consuming to get an accurate measure of what learning to spell English involves. It is difficult to appraise such chaos. In the last five decades there have been some attempts to measure English spelling irregularity. A team led by P.R. Hannah at Stanford University in the 1960s calculated that around 50% of all English words have unpredictable spellings. This result was recently confirmed by E. Carney in the UK from an analysis of 25 000 words. His *Survey of English Spelling* was published in 1997.

My own investigations have also confirmed that around half of all English words have some spelling irregularity in them. I first analysed a small corpus of the 3000 most common English words and then a bigger one with nearly 7000 words, and obtained very similar result with both.

Presenting the results as percentages or ratios is, however, insufficient to give a clear picture of the learning burden. The only way that teachers, parents and learners can really understand what needs to be learned is by seeing the lists of words with irregular spellings which students have to memorise.

Several books provide list of words for learning. I found some with as few as 1000 words and some with as many as 8000 words listed in alphabetic order, but they made no distinction between words which follow basic English spelling rules and those which don't. In other words, such books fail to differentiate between easy-to-spell and difficult words.

Among books which supposedly *'explain'* the English spelling system, I could not find a single one which provided comprehensive lists of words to be learnt. Such books tend just to give the most common ways of spelling particular sounds. They show, for example, the 7 most usual ways of spelling the EE-sound (ea, ee, ei, ie, e-e, i-e, e), with a few examples of each (tr*ea*t, str*ee*t, s*ei*ze, th*ie*f, th*ese*, pol*i*ce, w*e*) but without a comprehensive list of words which have to be learnt. Such books on spelling almost invariably advise learners to start a notebook for writing down *'difficult'* words which need special attention. I wanted access to an inclusive list of such *'difficult'* words. Since I could not find one anywhere, I decided to compile one myself.

My first task was finding a satisfactory list of most common English words. I found several *'My first 1000 words'* collections aimed at younger children, but each containing a slightly different list. There was even less overlap between adult vocabulary collections and those for children. I therefore ended up building my own collection by comparing several children's dictionaries and a couple of adult vocabulary listings. I omitted all word forms which can be derived in a regular way. I listed *'work'* but not *'work<u>ed</u>, work<u>ing</u>'* or *'work<u>s</u>'* as well, as dictionaries commonly do. I tried to include only unpredictable derivatives like 'paint*er*, work*er*, sail*or*, visit*or*'. My final corpus contains 6800 words.

I then spent 2 years identifying those with irregular spellings and ended up with a list of 3695 words (listed at the end of this book). They are the words that cannot be learnt to spell accurately by simply mastering basic English spelling rules. Those 3695 words all require the memorising of *something in addition to phonics* for their spelling. Often this is just one surplus letter (frie**n**d, dou**b**t, infinit**e**, mor**e**, appl**y**). Others spell a sound with letters that are not commonly used to spell that sound in English (central – cf. [*compared with*] send, sense...; system – cf. sit, sister...; **ai**m – cf. came, same...). Several hundred words break the basic English consonant doubling rule, by *not* doubling a consonant after a short stressed vowel (bo**d**y – cf. sho**dd**y, li**l**y – cf. si**ll**y, le**p**er – cf. pe**pp**er).

The 3695 words which I identified are the minimum which any reasonably competent speller has to master. They represent the learning burden which an average English-speaking school leaver would be expected to have learned. Highly educated and literate spellers will have learned many more. One can safely round that figure up and say that for reasonable adult spelling proficiency a student of English needs to learn at least 3700 words with irregular spellings, in addition to mastering the 90 basic English spelling rules. This figure does not include any specialist or technical vocabulary, just the ordinary range of English words.

I next tried to get at least an approximate idea of how English spelling irregularity compares with that of Italian, Spanish and German. In 1998 the UK's Qualifications and Certification Authority (QCA) had sent primary schools a list of 45 very frequently used words. It described them as *'essential high frequency words which pupils will need, even to tackle very simple texts'*. The QCA recommended that infant teachers should make their classes familiar with this list as early as possible.

I enlisted the help of foreign linguist friends, and we translated those words into Italian, Spanish and German. We agreed to include grammatical inflections and all possible common meanings in our translations, to ensure that we did not miss any irregular spellings. This meant that we ended up with lists of 63 words in German, 61 in Spanish and 79 in Italian. Of those words, German has 7, Spanish 5 and Italian 4 with some spelling unpredictability. The rest all follow the basic spelling rules of those languages. Among the 45 English words we identified 23 for which there are no completely reliable spelling rules. This becomes evident by comparing them with other words (in brackets):

all *(crawl)*, **are** *(far)*, **my** *(tie)*, **come** *(sum)*, **get** *(guess)*, **he, me, she, we, see** *(tea, ski, key, quay)*, **said** *(bed)*, **look** *(put)*, **go, no** *(blow, toe)*, **going** *(growing)*, **to** *(too)*, **is** *(quiz)*, **of** *(have)*, **they** *(play)*, **this** *(miss)*, **yes** *(less)*, **was** *(because)*, **you** *(use)*.

In percentage terms this means that German has 11% irregularly spelt words, Spanish 8% and Italian 5%, whereas in English at least half of all words turned out to have some spelling unpredictability. In terms of lists of words to be memorised, this means that instead of the 3695 words with spelling problems which I identified for English, a similar analysis of about 7000 words in German, Spanish and Italian is likely to produce, at most, only 800, 600 and 400 irregularly spelt words in those languages.

It is not surprising therefore that Italian children can spell nearly every word in their language after just 2 years at school, while so many English speakers leave school at 16 still unable to spell many common words accurately. In the course of their education, English children have to memorise at least 8 times as many irregular spellings as those in Italy. It is the need to memorise vast numbers of words with irregular spelling which makes English spelling not just difficult, but *too* difficult for too many. Could this also be one of the main reasons why large numbers of English-speaking pupils become disaffected and reluctant to learn by the time they reach secondary school?

Chapter 3

Understanding the alphabetic principle and learning to read and write English

In languages that adhere to the alphabetic principle closely, grasping the idea that words are made up of sounds and that letters are used to represent them is much easier than in English. I can best illustrate this by describing how I learned to read.

I had been unfortunate in starting school in Lithuania 2 months later than the rest of my class. I began school in November, while normal practice was to start in the September after a child's 7th birthday. By the time I joined the class, my classmates were already reading short sentences. They had already been through the pages of our reading book which taught them all the basics of Lithuanian phonics – they had already learnt which individual letters, or combinations of them, are used for spelling Lithuanian speech sounds. They had learnt how the Lithuanian alphabet works.

In our reading books, printed very clearly at the top of each even page were 1 or 2 letters which represented a particular sound. Below them were just a few words containing those letters, with pictorial illustrations beside them. At the bottom of each page, the same words were printed in the style of copper-plate handwriting, as models for us to copy. The opposite page contained a few simple sentences with more illustrations. Near the end of the book, the print became smaller, the sentences more numerous and the illustrations fewer.

Because of my late start, I was plunged straight into reading whole sentences. Being blessed with a reasonable memory, I had no trouble remembering them. I could recite the page without hesitation when it was my turn to read. But one day the teacher spotted that I was 'reading' while looking at him and not at the page. When he pointed to a word and asked me to read it, it became obvious that I had no idea what reading was all about, nor did I understand what I had been doing wrong.

I managed to suppress my tears until I was back home, when my grandmother quickly reassured me that this was nothing to worry about. She helped me to fix the problem in a few days. First she took me back to the beginning of the book and explained how letters work. To speed things up, she wrote out a few at a time on the margin of her newspaper and taught me the sounds of those. She did the same the following afternoon. By the end of the week we had been through the whole Lithuanian alphabet and speech sounds, and I had learned the basics of learning to read Lithuanian. I could read any word she pointed at, in my reading book as well as her newspaper. Learning to write simply took the basic idea one step further.

In a language like Lithuanian (or Italian, Spanish, Russian, German, Dutch, Swedish, Hungarian, Serbo-Croat or Welsh) it is possible to lay a solid foundation for the whole acquisition of literacy by learning to read and to write just a small number of words really well. A few sentences which contain all the sounds of the language can serve as reliable reference points for all further reading and spelling. This is because each letter, or combination of letters, *consistently* represents a single sound.

By learning to read and write just a few very basic words, a Lithuanian child acquires a reference point for the regular representation of all Lithuanian speech sounds. For example, the five simple words *'my mother, brother and sister'* (mano motina, brolis ir sesuo) already contain the normal spellings for 12 Lithuanian sounds: M, A, N, O, T, I, B, R, L, S, E, UO.

Furthermore, as with all languages which have a common, usual or dominant way of representing their speech sounds, learning to read and write Lithuanian are two mutually supportive aspects of becoming literate. Pupils learn the sounds which letters stand for and immediately start to practise representing those sounds in simple words, mumbling the sounds to themselves while writing them.

In English this is only possible with the 50% of words which are spelt phonemically, like *'a fat cat sat'*. With variable spellings like *'slept – leapt'*, or *'leap – peep'*, learning to read and learning to spell inevitably become more disparate processes, and grasping basic phonics becomes more difficult.

From the words 'my mother, brother and sister' English children can learn just 5 reliable reading and spelling rules:

M as in **m**y and **m**other, **B** in **b**rother, **N** and **D** in a**nd**, **T** in sis**t**er.

For 3 spellings in those five simple words they will later encounter different pronunciations:

mo**th**er – **th**ink, An**th**ony;
br**o**ther – b**o**ther, b**o**th, m**o**ve, dr**o**ve;
and – f**a**ther, t**a**ble.

For 5 sounds in those words pupils will later come across several different spellings:

m**y** – b**ye**, b**uy**, l**ie**, h**igh**;
m**o**ther – m**u**ch, c**ou**ntry, fl**oo**d;
broth**er** – visit**or**, burgl**ar**, cent**re**, flav**our**;
sister – **c**ity, **sc**ience;
s**i**ster – s**y**stem, pr**e**tty, b**u**sy, w**o**men.

My first English lesson made it obvious to me immediately that English was very different from the two languages which I had initially learned to read and write, i.e. Lithuanian followed by Russian. Our teacher explained to us at the very beginning that in learning the English alphabet we had to differentiate between the names of letters and the sounds which they stood for. – In Lithuanian and Russian this had all been one thing. The letter names *were* the sounds which they represented.

Because so many English letters can spell several different sounds (e.g., *cat, father; moth, both*), and large numbers of words also have silent letters which spell nothing at all (*who, when, have, although, show*), it is impossible to refer to English letters simply by *the sound* which they represent. The English spelling system therefore requires an *additional layer of learning* from the very beginning, i.e. the learning of letter names *in addition to* the sounds which they represent.

Yet this difficulty is not the hardest part of learning to read English. The greatest problem is the recurring need to learn different pronunciations for identical letters, even in the same position of a word (e.g. *great – treat, daughter – laughter, do – go, how – slow*). This is particularly trying for foreign learners; but native speakers from linguistically poor backgrounds find many unpredictable pronunciations troublesome too.

Learning to read English is much easier when you already have some idea what the written word that you are trying to decipher sounds like. For all who are learning to read English, while also still learning the pronunciation of words and their meanings, the process is very teacher-dependent.

Most English-speaking children also need to hear many words, like *appal, avalanche, cyclical* and *latitude,* pronounced for them before they can read them with confidence, just as non-native learners do; but the latter have to rely on their teachers more heavily because they need to hear even such common words like *bread, meat* or *great* read to them before they can pronounce them correctly.

If this happened only occasionally, it would be less of a problem, but English has vast numbers of words which simply cannot be *'read'* in the sense of confidently deducing the pronunciation of a word from the letters which are used for its spelling. (Including the word *read*!) A substantial component of learning to read English is therefore *learning to guess*, and this *is far more difficult than simply learning to read* in the sense of working out the sounds of words from their letters.

As children move on to longer texts, they meet numerous identical letter combinations which have to be pronounced in different ways: *said - paid, come - home, break - freak, road - broad, horse - worse, few - sew, doll - roll, cow - low, shall - call, shoe - foe, lose - rose, flood - mood, give - drive, have - shave, get - gem, giddy - giraffe, finger - danger, enough - cough - through - though - plough,* and many more. Such words make the process of learning to read difficult and slow.

The inconsistencies of English spelling pose problems for teachers too. In most of Europe any literate adult can teach a child to read, with any text at hand, just like my grandmother taught me. In Spain it is quite normal for children to be introduced to reading by helpful members of the family before they start school.

English literacy, on the other hand, is best taught by professionals, and in a carefully planned way. To save children from total cognitive confusion and bewilderment, at least at the outset, the vocabulary used in early reading schemes needs to be carefully chosen. To give beginners a reasonable chance of grasping the alphabetic principle, it is best to introduce them only to selected, more regular spellings like *'the fat cat sat on the mat'* and to shield learners from puzzling inconsistencies.

In the early stages of learning, English reading and spelling are still best taught as James Dun recommended in 1766, in his book *'The Best Method of Teaching to Read and Spell English'*:

"...begin with words that are absolutely regular, in the sense that they are pronounced in the way children would expect;"

"...build into the exercises material that unobtrusively revises earlier work;"

"...give special emphasis to the pronunciation of c and g, the first big difficulty..."

"...introduce other difficulties progressively."

Unfortunately, it is not possible to expose children only to *"words that are absolutely regular"* for very long. Once they move from reading isolated, carefully chosen words to tackling simple sentences, they are bound to meet spellings which are *irregular*.

Every sentence contains one or two of the 12 most often used English words:

a, *a*nd, th*a*t - w*a*s;   *i*n, *i*s, *i*t - *I*;   th*e* - h*e*;   *o*f - t*o* .

They are the most fundamental sentence-building blocks and make up a quarter of all written texts. It is almost impossible to read anything without being able to read them. Yet this short and much-used list already contains four words with unexpected pronunciations which diverge from basic phonic patterns: *he, I, to* and *was*.

As children progress from reading sentences to reading simple stories, opportunities for phonic confusion become ever more numerous. As already mentioned, the Department of Education's Literacy Strategy in the UK advises reception class teachers to familiarise children aged four with 45 high frequency words "*which pupils will need, even to tackle very simple texts*" (the words on List One, as sent to schools by the QCA in 1998).

Between the ages of 5 and 7, children will meet another list of high frequency words. The Literacy Strategy recommends that in Years 1 and 2 a further 151 commonly used words should be taught (comprising List Two).

On List Two are:

110 simple common words (e.g. *about, after, again*….)

16 number words (i.e. *numbers 1 - 20*, but the words for 16 - 19
        are merely compounds which require no new learning.)

7 common colours

7 days of the week

11 months (as the word *'may'* is already one the 110 simple words).

By looking at the much-used words on the two lists of more closely, one can see why *exposure to confusing, irregular spellings becomes inevitable even in early reading* – and why *making sense of English phonic rules is difficult from beginning to end*. Only 42 words out of 196 on those two lists are phonically completely simple: 15 of the 45 on List One, and 27 out of 151 on List Two (as can be seen below).

Table 1. 42 phonically simple words on the first two lists of the UK's Literacy Strategy.

List One	a	the	big	dog	mum	
	and	went	in	for	up	
	am		it	on		
	at					
	dad					
List Two	an	bed	did	from	but	March
	had	help	dig	got	jump	
	man	red	him	not	just	her
	ran	ten	sister		must	September
	than	them	with			
	that	then				

Another 36 words also use clearly established English phonic patterns, but these are already more difficult to grasp. They contain several elements that go beyond simple sound to letter correspondences. They use positional spellings and require additional explanations of various kinds. Many children find learning to read these challenging, especially when their spelling patterns are contradicted in other very frequently used words, like *'our'* and *'your'*, for example.

Table 2. 36 high frequency words with regular but quite complicated English phonic patterns. (*'Away', 'day'* and *'play'* in column 1 are from List One, the rest from List Two.)

1.		2.	3.	4.	5.	6.
away	came	ab*ou*t cf. y*ou*	twelve	li*tt*le	October	*wa*nt
day	made	*ou*t		o*ff*	December	*wa*ter
play	make			wi*ll*	ba*ck*	
m*ay*	name	*ou*r cf. y*our*			bla*ck*	
Sund*ay*	take				ne*xt*	
w*ay*	Fri*day*				si*x*	
s*o*	n*i*ne					
b*oy*	t*i*me					
	h*o*me					
b*y*	No*v*ember					
twent*y*	J*u*ne					

The words in each *numbered* column share the following complications:

1). Many long vowel make use of positional spellings which require the decoding of letter strings like *'-ame'* or *'-ine'* instead of just single letters. Some letters are also pronounced differently at the end of short and long words (e.g. by - twenty).

2). The OU-sound is predominantly spelt *'ou'*; but the *'ou'* grapheme can be read in several different ways: as in *'out'*, *'you'*, *'your'*, *'could'* and *'country'* .

3). At the end of words, the V-sound is spelt *'-ve'*, irrespective of whether the preceding vowel is long or short (e.g. *five – give*). Vowels before *'v'* can therefore never be just decoded; they always require part-guessing.

4). Some consonants have to be doubled in word endings, while many others don't (e.g. da*d*, tha*t*, hi*m*, ma*n*). This is mainly a spelling problem, but such doublings are not helpful to young learners whose phonic sense is still uncertain.

5). The pronunciation of *'c'* (which is predominantly used to spell the K-sound) depends on the letters which follow it. It has an S-sound before *'e'* and *'i'* (e.g. De*c*ember); but before consonants and the vowels *'a'*, *'o'* and *'u'*, *'c'* spells the K-sound (e.g. 'O*c*tober', '*c*an'). - The spelling of the K-sound is controlled by several complex rules. One of them dictates that after a short, stressed vowel the K-sound is spelt *'ck'* (e.g. 'ba*ck*', but cf. 'comi*c*' and 'bi*k*e').

6) After *'w'*, the letter *'a'* tends to spell an O-sound, but not always (e.g. *wa*g).

The six rules listed above make learning to read considerably more complex than the decoding of phonically simple words like *'dad'*, *'did'*, *'him'*, *'man'* or *'but'*. They also ensure that learning to read and learning to write become increasingly separate processes, instead of just mutually supportive aspects of literacy acquisition.

The remaining 118 high frequency words to which the UK's Literacy Strategy draws attention are listed in the next three tables. They all contain complications and contradictions which make grasping the basics of English phonics difficult:

1) The 63 words in table 3 (19 from List One and 44 from List Two) can be used to teach children regularly occurring graphemes for reading, but not any reliable spelling rules, because many other words spell identical sounds differently (e.g. s*ee* - m*e*, th*ey* - pl*ay*).

2) Another 39 words can teach neither reliable reading patterns or spelling patterns (e.g. *said*, cf. *paid* and *bed*).

3) Sixteen more words are spelt predictably but are problematic for readers (e.g. a*s*, ha*s* - u*s*, thi*s*)

Table 3. Many of the sounds occurring in the very frequently used English words on List One and List Two of the UK's Literacy Strategy are spelt differently in other common words.

List One words	different spellings for same sound	List two words	different spellings for same sound	List two words	different spellings for same sound
see - me	*sea*	after (in UK	*laughter*	grey	*play*
		half English)	*scarf*	eight	*late*
I	*eye*	last "	*graph*		
my	*lie*	can't "	*aunt*	Tuesday	*June*
they	*play*	ball	*crawl*	house	*December*
		call	*halt, fault*		
go	*slow*			when	*went*
no	*toe*	much	*hutch*	what	*want*
going	*showing*	another	*mum*	white	*with*
		brother	*run*		
to	*too / blue*			August	*awful*
		or	*four*	February	*lottery*
all	*crawl*	door	*more*	January	*surgery*
		saw	*soar*		
can	*kite*			again*	*children*
cat	*kick*	don't	*alone*		
come	*queue*	old	*coal, stole*	three*	*tea*
like	*local*	yellow	*so*	tree	*key*
this	*miss*	if	*sniff*	here	*near*
yes	*mess*	night	*white*	these	*geese,*
is	*quizz*				*fleece*
was	*buzz*	first	*her*		
		girl	*learn*	their*	*there, care,*
of	*have*	thirteen	*turn*		*fair*
		Thursday		blue*	*flew, do*
				too	*flu*
		because	*was*	new*	*cue*

* See top of next page for explanations.

Table 4. 39 common words with graphemes which are *pronounced and spelt differently* in other words.

	sound spelt with **grapheme** (underlined, in bold)	the grapheme is **more commonly** read as in:	the same sound is more commonly spelt as:	
List One	are	care, fare	car, far	English has no uniform way of marking a hard *g* before 'e' or 'i'.
	get	gentle, gesture	guess / gherkin -->	
	he, me, she, we*	the	tree / tea*	
	look	spooky	put, push	
	said	paid	bed, get	
	you*	out	too / blue / blew*	
List two	Saturday	nature	scatter	* See explanations above.
	many	lane	penny	
	very	here	(merry)	
	Wednesday	wedding	went	
	be	the	three	
	people*	geography	(peep, leap)*	
	good*	school	*	
	could, should*	shoulder	*	
	would*	"	*	
	pull, push, put*	but, dull	*	
	do, two, who	go	too*	
	Monday, once	on	Sunday	
	one, some	home	fun	
	down	shown	count	
	there, where,	here	air, care, bear*	
	were	"	"	
	four, fourteen	our	or, forty	
	your	"	"	
	door	poor	"	
	laugh	caught	scarf, craft	
	school	chop	scoop	

Table 5. 16 words which obey dominant English spelling patterns are problematic for readers. This can be seen when the used graphemes (underlined) are set against other common words.

f<u>ive</u>	give	a<u>s</u>	this
l<u>ive</u> *		ha<u>s</u>	
		hi<u>s</u>	
h<u>ave</u>	gave		
		u<u>s</u>	fuss
l<u>ove</u>	drove		
<u>ov</u>er	oven	h<u>ow</u>	slow
		n<u>ow</u>	
s<u>eve</u>n	even		
el<u>eve</u>n		t<u>oo</u>k	sp<u>oo</u>ky
		<u>A</u>pril	<u>a</u>nd, <u>a</u>bout
		Jul<u>y</u>	man<u>y</u>

* 'live' has two possible pronunciations

The information contained in the five tables above can be summed up as follows. Of the **196** high frequency words in the UK's early years literacy programme,

- **42** are phonically simple,
- **36** <u>have more difficult but still phonic spellings,</u>
- **63** contain teachable reading patterns, but their spellings are unpredictable,
- **39** contain unpredictable graphemes for reading and spelling,
- **16** contain elements which cannot be read phonically.

In other words, just **78** of the **196** most commonly used English words obey English phonic rules in a straightforward manner; the other 118 all contain complications of some kind.

These figures make it clear that even in the early stages of reading pupils have to become adept at partially guessing the sounds of quite a few words. Over a quarter (28 %) of the most frequently used English words (55 out of 196) require part-guessing. They cannot be simply phonically decoded from their letters.

The figures also show that learning to spell these high frequency words is much more difficult than learning to read them. Many learners will find 138 words on that list of 196 hard to spell. The 36 words with regular but complex positional spelling patterns already overstretch the abilities of quite a few pupils (e.g. came - may, black - October). The 102 words with unpredictable spelling patterns cause difficulties for almost everyone. Only pupils with a very strong visual memory have no trouble in coping with phonic contradictions like 'd*o* - t*oo* - t*wo* - y*ou*'.

As children move up through the school years, reading becomes more and more dependent on intelligent guessing. Learning to spell makes ever growing demands on memory. These non-phonic impediments also make holding on to the basic rules of English phonics progressively more difficult.

Children who are not mature enough, or those who don't have the requisite brain power or sufficient home support for these intellectual challenges, can easily become overwhelmed by them. It is often said that a good beginning wins half the battle. The irregularities of English spelling increase the likelihood of a bad start in learning to read and write. For some children they make it highly probable that the battle with literacy is lost altogether.

The difficulties which stem from English spelling inconsistencies also pose several methodological conundrums:

---

1) When should schools begin to teach reading and writing?

2) Should children be assessed for reading and writing readiness and only subjected to these intellectually demanding tasks when they are mature enough for them?

3) How long should children practise with just phonically simple words and remain shielded from phonic inconsistencies?

4) Is it perhaps best to delay writing until much later? - Or do children have a better chance of memorising the 3700 common English words which are spelt unpredictably if they start early?

5) Should infants perhaps be set according their reading readiness? (This would almost certainly mean teaching boys and girls separately in the early years.)

Educational research has so far failed to provide clear answers to these questions, and changes in teaching methods appear to make little difference. During 1990's carefully planned phonics teaching was adopted in nearly all primary schools in the UK, but this has not led to any marked improvements in the reading or writing of 11-year-olds.

Several teaching methods, have been tested and then discarded again during the past century. Phonics has been tried many times before, but in the 1960's many teachers opted for the whole-word method instead, because they had been dissatisfied with the results of that strategy.

In the late 1960's and early 1970's many schools across the whole English-speaking world experimented with shielding their youngest learners from the inconsistencies of English spelling in a really drastic way, by first introducing them to reading and writing with the Initial Teaching Alphabet (i.t.a. - a more consistent method for spelling English, as explained more fully in chapter 9). This was done in the hope that children would cope with normal English spelling much better once they had learned how the alphabetic principle operates with i.t.a..

By this method infants learned to read and write very easily - but only for as long as they used i.t.a.. Many pupils came completely unstuck when they had to switch to normal English spelling after first learning to read and write with i.t.a.. Perhaps the same can happen when pupils are initially exposed predominantly to just phonically spelt words? Perhaps this is also a poor preparation for the later encounters with the harsher realities of English spelling?

For as long as English spelling remains as it is, it is probably better to expose pupils to the prevailing English spelling inconsistencies progressively, but from the beginning, rather than start them off in a fools paradise of regular spellings, like phonics can do, or like i.t.a. did. The i.t.a. experiment proved that sudden exposure to numerous spelling contradictions is too much of a shock for some children.

Understanding the alphabetic principle (i.e. grasping phonic rules) is the easy part of learning to read and write English. The much harder part is coping with the thousands of words that contain elements which disobey the rules, which cannot be decoded or spelt by reference to a reliable system.

Most children master the regular aspects of English spelling in two to three years. Even weaker learners can manage this reasonably well, but during the next 8 - 10 years of schooling many of them become hopelessly confused by the unphonic exceptions which assail them from every subject. This makes it increasingly difficult for them to hold on to the phonic sense which they initially acquired, and quite a few pupils end up leaving education at 16 almost illiterate.

Preventing weaker learners from sinking into phonic confusion is probably the biggest challenge for teachers. They are unlikely to do this effectively without a proper understanding of what learners may find difficult. Perusal of this book, and especially the lists of words with phonic inconsistencies in Appendixes R (reading lists) and Appendix S (spelling lists), should provide them with a clearer appreciation of the English spelling system.

The lists in the two appendices can also be used for reading and spelling practice, even though children generally learn to read in context, beginning with captions to pictures, then short and longer stories, novels and other texts, rather than lists of words. Teaching reading by means of word lists alone would probably become unbearably boring for most young children, but regular bouts of short reading practice with lists of words which cannot be phonically decoded might well help many students make better progress.

Moreover, it has often been suggested that learners cope very much better with their learning tasks when they understand what is required of them. The word lists in this book set out what has to be mastered. They remove much of the psychological obfuscation in which learning to read and write English is often shrouded. They expose the alphabetic imperfections which have become an integral part of English spelling in the course of the past six centuries. They should also enable learners to see how many of their problems with reading and writing are due to flaws in the spelling system rather than their own laziness or stupidity.

Chapter 4

The main sources of spelling difficulties

Learning to spell any language is much harder than learning to read it. Reading involves mere recognition of the sounds or words which the letters on the page represent, whereas spelling requires the active production of them by the writer. Learning to recognise that the graphemes 'o-e' and 'oa' both spell the same sound (e.g. *stole, coal*) is far easier than memorising which one has to be used in a particular word. Just as identifying a face in an identity parade is much easier than drawing one, learning to read a word is easier than to spell it.

Learning to spell English is much more difficult than learning to spell many other languages for the following 3 reasons:

1. **English often uses positional spelling** (e.g. *shop - station*) **and therefore has more basic spelling patterns than most other languages.**

2. **Nearly all dominant English spelling patterns have many exceptions**:
   ale, gale, stale - *frail, nail*...;
   mole, pole, stole - *coal, soul, roll*...;
   say, day, play - *they, weigh*..;
   ace, face, grace - *base, chase*....;
   phase, phrase - *gaze, braise*....;
   fence, hence, pence, - *dense, tense*...;

3. **For several sounds English has no clearly identifiable spelling pattern at all.**
   The long OO-sound, for example, is spelt with the letters *'oo'* at the end of 18 common short words (e.g. *too, zoo*) but in 34 other words it is spelt in a variety of unpredictable ways (e.g. *do, blue, flew, through, shoe*). This means that hundreds of English spellings simply have to be learned individually.

Each difficulty will be discussed separately.

4. 1. Positional spellings

All languages have around 40 basic speech sounds, or phonemes, and
English has 44. It has

24 consonants:
*b, ch, d, f, g, h, j, k, l, m, n, ng, p, r, s, sh, t, v, w,
y, z, voiced th* (*this*), *unvoiced th* (*think*), and *zh* (as in *vision*);

19 vowels:
6 short vowels as in - b*a*t, b*e*t, b*i*t, h*o*t, c*u*t, b*oo*k;

9 long vowels as in - s*ay*, s*ee*, t*ie*, t*oe*, d*ue*, t*oo*, *ou*t, *au*tumn, *oi*l;

4 blends with r as in - c*ar*t, t*er*m, f*or*t and f*air*,

and a *half-vowel as in - *a*band*o*n, cert*ai*n, crit*i*c*a*l, ev*i*d*e*nce, *a*ccept*a*nce.

*Only stressed English vowels can be heard clearly. Unstressed ones tend
not to be pronounced at all (when they occur at the end of words as in *'certain',
'critical'* and *'often'*); or they become a mere hint of a vowel sound, which is
not quite a short *'e', 'i'* or *'u'* (e.g. *abandon, acceptance, critical, evidence*).
As can be seen in these examples, this indistinct, unstressed English half-
vowel is spelt in several different ways.

If English had just one spelling pattern for each phoneme, it would have
only 44 spelling patterns, instead of the 96 basic graphemes which it has
(and which are summarised pages 47-8). The use of positional spellings
inevitably results in more spelling patterns which need to be learned.
    Using just one spelling for a particular sound, irrespective of its position
in a word (e.g. *mayday, solo*), makes learning to spell easier than the use of
two or more different graphemes which depend on the sound's position in a
word (e.g. *mile, fly*). - [The long I-sound in *'mile'* is spelt predominantly
as *-i-e* when it occurs in the middle of words, but as *-y* at the end of
words, e.g. *'fly'*.]
    A few English sounds, like the K-sound and SH-sound, have rather
complex positional spellings, which can only be mastered with substantial
amounts of practice. What makes them even more difficult to master are the
*exceptions which need to be learned, in addition to the basic rules for
spelling them.*

37

The spelling of the **K-sound** is tricky. There are altogether 10 rules which need to be mastered for spelling the K-sound. They apply as follows:

1. At the beginning of words, we use *k* before E and I *[kerb, kiss, kind]*,

2. but *c* before A, O and U *[cat, cod, cup, couple]*.

3. At the end of *short, one-syllable* words the K-sound is spelt *-ck* after a short vowel *[smack, peck, lick, shock, duck]*,

4. but *k* when a vowel sound is spelt with two letters
   [leek, speak, oak, spook, look, stake, like, poke].

5. At end of *longer* words we always use *c*
   [comic, dramatic, fantastic, music].

6. Before consonants we use *c* *[clap, crib]*,

7. after consonants *k* *[dark, milk, market]*
   and between consonants things become uncertain *[ankle, uncle]*.

8. In the middle of a word, after a short, stressed vowel the K-sound is mostly spelt *ck* *[bucket, rocket]*.

9. The KW-blend is spelt *qu* *[queen, quit]*.

10. The KS-blend is spelt *x* *[tax, taxi, exit]*.

The spelling of the **SH-sound** takes some learning too. It has four different spellings: *sh, tio, ssio, ci.*
1. It is spelt *sh* at the beginning *(ship)* and the very end of words *(cash)*.

2. In words which end with a **SHN**-sound, the **SH**-sound is spelt predominantly *-tio-*, as in *action, station, pollution* or *ignition*,

3. and *-ssio-* after a short vowel, as in *session* and *discussion*.

4. Endings which sound *-shos* or *-shan* tend to be spelt predominantly *-cious* or *-cian* (e.g. *vicious, musician*).

4. 2. Exceptions to English Spelling Patterns

Most young children take several years to learn spelling rules like those on the page opposite for the K-sound and SH-sound. Even so, mastering them would still be relatively easy *if it was not for the many words which do not follow them*. For example:

kept - *chemistry*, cat - *karate*, peck - *trek*, bivouac - *attack*, dark - *monarch*, crop - *chrome*, rocket - *occupy, crocodile*, quit - *choir*, exit - *accident, except*;

potion - *ocean*, impression - *discretion*, passion - *fashion, ration*, malicious - *ambitious*, optician - *gentian*.

English spelling is, nevertheless, not completely chaotic - 69 of its 96 graphemes are dominant. They represent clearly identifiable ways of spelling sounds in defined positions of a word. There are 44 spelling patterns for consonants and 25 patterns for vowel sounds which are used in well over half of all words in which those sounds occur. Each of them is also used in *at least 20 words*, with most of them being far more numerous than that - but nearly all of them have some exceptions as well.

For only two spelling patterns could I find *no real exceptions*:

1. The **B-sound** is invariably spelt with *b* - although the letter *b* can sometimes be silent, as in 'de*b*t' or 'dou*b*t'.

2. At the beginning of words, before *a, o* and *u*, the **J-sound** does appear to be spelt consistently with the letter *j*. I could find no exceptions to the *'jab, job, jug'* rule, apart from the archaic spelling of *'gaol'* for *'jail'*.

The main source of English spelling difficulties is the constant need to memorise spellings which do not comply with basic, phonic English spelling patterns. Nevertheless, the regular aspects of English spelling are still worth teaching and learning.

Consonant graphemes in particular are fairly reliable. They have far fewer divergent spellings than those used for vowels. The rules learnt for spelling consonants will not be very frequently contradicted or undermined by the need to learn alternative spellings. The regular graphemes for spelling consonants, and exceptions to them, will therefore be presented and discussed first.

4. 2. 1. -   Consonant spellings and exceptions to them

Consonant spellings can be learnt more easily than graphemes for vowels for the following reasons:

1) The total number, as well as percentage, of irregular consonant spellings, is far lower than for vowels.

2) Many consonants are spelt identically in different positions of words (e.g. *bib, dad, mum*) - see table 1 below.

3) English words generally contain more consonants than vowels, sometimes many more (e.g. *plot, splash, sprint, strength)*. This means that from the very beginning learners get more practice with the regular consonant spellings than the more unpredictable vowel ones.

The next three tables show all 44 clearly dominant English spelling patterns for consonants. The first lists the easiest and most reliable ones.

Table 1. The left-hand column shows the 15 simplest consonant spellings and their recorded occurrences in 6800 common words. The right-hand column contains the figures for recorded exceptional spellings and some examples of them, with figures for the more frequently occurring divergent spellings given after the words which exemplify them.

Consonants as in the words below	Occurrences in 6800 words	*Exceptional spellings* - (These are fully listed in Appendix S, tables S 1 - 17)	
		no.	*examples*
bib	784	*0*	
dad	1010	*1*	*blonde*
film, if	580	*52*	*photo 35, puff 12, rough 5*
gag	198	*40*	*ghost, guess, guilt, league*
hand	237	*4*	*who, whom, whose, whole*
mum	1128	*17*	*bomb, limb 9, autumn 6*
net, ten	2312	*35*	*knee 15, gone 13, gnat*
ring	40	*1*	*meringue*
pop	1220	*1*	*hiccough*
rat,	1670	*26*	*write 20, rhubarb 6*
this (voiced)	61		
thing (unvoiced)	142		
willow	216	*33*	*when, where, white*
you	31	*5*	*uniform unite, universe, university, union*
vision (zh-sound)	19	*9*	*pleasure 7, azure, fissure,*
total occurrences	**9 650**	*232*	

Nine English consonants use positional spellings. These are spelt with 29 different patterns, but 10 of them apply just to the K-sound.

Apart from presenting all the dominant positional spelling patterns, the next two tables also show that *most positional spelling patterns for consonants are relatively predictable.* In comparison to vowel spellings, they have only small numbers of exceptions.

Table 2. This shows the 19 positional spellings used for 8 English consonants. (Spellings for the K-sound are shown in the next table.)

Pattern	Occurrences in 6800 words	*Exceptions* no.	*examples*	(fully listed in Appendix S tables S 1 - 17)
chip, spee**ch**	155	*1*	*cello*	
ba**tch**	23	*4*	*much, rich, such, attach*	
ja**b**, **j**o**b**, **j**u**g**	78	*0*		
ur**ge**	115	*2*	*spinach, sandwich*	
a**g**ent	71	*8*	*subject, inject*	
le**g**, fee**l**	1945	*0*		
we**ll**	43			
send	138	*47*	*centre 18, city 18, science*	
fen**ce**	137	*56*	*sense 35, base 21*	
an**c**estor	62	*29*	*consider, counsel*	
shu**sh**	162	*12*	*chef; sure, moustache*	
sta**ti**on	580	*34*	*diversion 19, ocean, fashion*	
to**t**	1398	*5*	*debt, doubt, subtle, two, pterodactyl*	
separa**t**e	156	*11*	*favourite 7, democrat*	
van	411	*0*		
dri**ve**, gi**ve***	120		**English words do not end with '-v'* *(cf. have - shave)*	
ne**v**er	55	*3*	*chivvy, navvy, skivvy*	
wi**se** (final z-sound)	91	*22*	*blaze, size, seize, froze* *US another 16: advertize, agonize*	
ab**s**orb (med z)	94	*16*	*citizen, gazelle 16, possess*	
	5 834	*250*		

41

Table 3. This shows the 10 spelling patterns for the K-sound and numbers of exceptions to them. These patterns take some teaching and learning, as explained on pages 37-9, but they are nearly all strongly dominant nevertheless, i.e. each has relatively few exceptions.

Pattern	Occurrences	Exceptions - (fully listed in Appendix S, table S 4, page 204)
kid, kept	124	7 *chemistry, architect*
cat, cod, cup	1022	18 *chaos 11, karate 4, queue*
deck	62	6 *spec, trek, yak*
peek	36	5 *unique, antique*
comic	89	9 *barrack, anorak, kayak, stomach*
clap	192	10 *chlorine, chrome*
milk	86	10 *disc, mollusc, mosque, monarch*
rocket	25	21 *second 10, occupy 6, liquor 4, echo*
queen	78	4 *acquaint, acquire, acquit, choir*
taxi	98	14 *accent 7, except 5, exhaust, exhibit*
1812		*104*

4. 2. 2 - Dominant Spelling Patterns for Vowels and '*weak*' graphemes

The tables on the next four pages list all the main graphemes for English vowels, as well as spellings which diverge form them. They show that in contrast to consonant spellings, which are predominantly regular, nearly all vowel spellings have large numbers of exceptions. There are also fewer clearly dominant spellings for vowels - just 25, as opposed to 44 for consonants.

This is because eleven English vowel spellings are unreliable. They are *'patterns'* only in the sense that they are the most common way of spelling those sounds in certain positions. But there are numerous alternative spellings for the same sound.

A grapheme for a particular sound is not really much of a *'pattern'* if it is used in just a little more than half of all words in which that sound occurs (like *oo* for the long OO-sound in *spoon*). It can be seen in table 4 that the OO-sound is spelt with *'oo'* in 72 words, but in another 57 words it is spelt differently (e.g. *group, move, rude*).

A pattern that is used in even less than half of all words, is still weaker. The short OO-sound of *'wood'*, for example, is spelt with *'oo'* in 15 words, but in another 21 words it is spelt differently. This means, that for every word with the short OO-sound in it, learners have to memorise exactly how it is spelt. In other words, *the spelling of the English short OO-sound is completely unpredictable*. In this book such patterns are referred to as *'weak'*.

Table 4. This lists the **17 _weak_ English spelling patterns**. The graphemes which are used most often for these 17 sounds, in these particular positions, are shown in bold and underlined in the left-hand column. The occurrences of these graphemes among 6800 common English words are given next to them.

The right-hand column shows how often a different spelling pattern was encountered and gives examples of them. For frequently occurring alternative spellings, the number of recorded alternatives is also given (after the word which demonstrates the alternative spelling).

Patterns	Occurrences in 6800 words	_Exceptions -_ no.	examples	(fully listed in Appendix S, tables S 43 - 62, pages 228-43)
11 vowel patterns				
l**ea**p *	152	_304_	_sl**ee**p 133, h**e**r**e** 86, rec**ei**ve, bel**ie**ve, pol**i**c**e**,_	
w**oo**d *	15	_21_	_p**u**t 15, w**o**uld, w**o**man_	
sp**oo**n	72	_57_	_r**u**d**e** 31, s**ou**p 13, m**o**v**e**, fr**ui**t, shr**ew**d_	
t**oo** *	18	_34_	_fl**ew** 12, bl**ue** 8, d**o**, tw**o**, thr**ough**, c**ou**p, sh**oe**_	
f**au**lt *	39	_64_	_d**aw**n 17, **a**ll 14, sh**aw**l 8, s**a**lt 10, n**ough**t_	
c**a**r**e**	31	_27_	_**air** 15, **ae**rial, th**ere**, th**ei**r_	
t**er**m *	70	_125_	_f**ur** 65, f**ir** 36, **ear**n 11, w**or**k 8, w**ere**, jo**ur**ney_	
hast**en** *	73	_131_	_aband**on** 68, urb**an**, cert**ain**_	
ordin**ary** *	37	_55_	_batt**ery** 25, carpent**ry**, lux**ury**_	
fl**y**	17	_14_	_d**ie** 5, h**igh** 4, b**ye**, b**uy**_	
d**ue** *	20	_22_	_f**ew** 19, vi**ew**, men**u**_	
Vowel totals:	**544**	_854_		
6 consonant patterns				
gem	20	_19_	_**j**et, **j**ig_	
le**dge**	24	_21_	_le**g**end, pi**ge**on, ma**j**esty_	
for**t**re**ss** *	11	_44_	_men**ace**, lett**uce**, ba**s**i**s**, practi**ce**, practi**se**_	
mu**sh**room*	5	_17_	_an**ci**ent, pre**ss**ure, ma**ch**ine, con**sci**ence_	
essen**ti**al	20	_15_	_commer**cial** 14 controver**sial**_	
vi**ci**ous	20	_15_	_preten**tious** 12, lu**scious**_	
Consonant totals:	**100**	_131_		
TOTALS:	**644**	_985_		

*Ten of the patterns in table 4 are marked with an asterisk. They all spell the sound which they represent in less than 50 % of words in which this sound occurs. When such weak spelling patterns are used for sounds which occur in large numbers of words, the learning burden becomes especially heavy, as is the case with long EE , as can be seen in the next table.

Table 5. **The long EE-sound** occurs in 456 common words (listed Appendix S, tables S 43 - 48, pages 228 - 31), but not one of its several spelling patterns is used for more than 1/3 of the words in which it occurs:

---

1. _ea_ is used in 152 words (e.g. _stream_) - 33 %
2. _ee_ in 133 words (e.g. _street_) - 29 %
3. the pattern of _here_ or _legal_ in 86 words - 20 %
4. _ie_ in 31 words (e.g. _chief_),
5. _ei_ in 12 words (e.g. _receive, weird_),
6. the pattern of _police_ or _trio_ in 29,
7. 7 words use _e_ _(be, he, she, me, we, cathedral, secret)_;
8. 6 words have assorted unpredictable spellings (_key, quay, people, ski, debris, souvenir_).

This means that the spelling of the EE-sound can simply not be learnt or taught phonically. Learners have to memorise how this sound is spelt in each of the 456 words in which the EE-sound occurs. During the learning stage the different spelling alternatives constantly compete with each other in students' minds.

The fact that the _ea_ grapheme can spell the short E-sound (e.g. _bread, dead, threat_) as well as the EE-sound complicates matters still further. Consequently, mastering the spelling of just this one sound takes much time and effort. If, instead of using the several, unpredictable graphemes which are shown in the table above, the EE-sound was always spelt with just one of them, this learning burden would not exist.

It can be seen in table 4 on the previous page that for all 17 weak patterns there were a total of just 644 _'regular'_ occurrences, but 985 spellings which diverge from them. In other words, the various exceptions far outweigh the rules. This means that _all 1629 spellings have to be learnt individually._

Six of the weak spellings in table 4 are consonant spellings; but these occur in only 231 common words, as opposed to 1398 words with similarly unpredictable vowel spellings. _The majority of exceptional spellings that learners have to memorise are vowel spellings._ The next table shows that nearly all of the dominant vowel graphemes have large numbers of exceptions as well.

Table 6. This shows the **25 dominant spelling patterns for vowels**. The patterns are shown in the words in the left-hand column, followed by the numbers of common words in which they were found to occur.

Numbers and examples of alternative spellings for the same sounds are given on the right.

Patterns	Occurrences in 6800 words	*Exceptions* no.	examples (They are all fully listed in Appendix S, tables S 18 - 41)
5 short vowels			
c**a**t	466	3	*salmon, meringue, plait*
p**e**t	300	64	*head 49, said, friend*
b**i**t	421	53	*system 45, pretty, women*
p**o**t	375	35	*want, what 30, gone, cough*
b**u**t	308	68	*some 50, country 14, blood*
4 long vowels			
c**a**k**e**	338	108	*main 90, weight 10, break*
b**i**t**e**	278	79	*bright 18, cycle 26, kind 12*
st**o**l**e**	170	96	*coal 37, bold 24, roll, bowl*
t**u**n**e**	137	21	*beauty, feud 6, jewel 6, nuclear, nuisance*
4 vowel blends			
out	74	23	*brown*
b**oi**l	29	1	*oyster*
cart	138	4	*are, heart, hearth, sergeant*
		88	*(in UK) banana, aunt, calm, fast, bath*
for	188	62	*more 22, your, door, oar - UK also: saw 13*
2 stressed endings			
pl**ay**	35	19	*they 7, duvet 7, weigh, café, matinee*
g**o**	106	59	*blow 42, toe, though*
8 unstressed endings			
dadd**y**	602	51	*monkey 26, movie 8, taxi 12, coffee*
bett**er**	340	136	*visitor 75, grammar 34, harbour 18*
		87	*future 42, data 45*
pertin**ent**	137	39	*dominant*
evid**ence**	39	19	*acceptance*
critic**al**	195	33	*towel 28, civil, pistol*
amb**le**	93	17	*kernel, stencil*
love**able**	33	17	*credible*
blizz**ard**	22		
2 vowels in prefixes			
d**e**cide	57	28	*divide*
induce	73	28	*endure*
total:	**4 954**	**1 238**	

45

4. 2. 3. - Ten Small Spelling Patterns

In addition to the 69 dominant spelling patterns and 17 weak patterns presented so far, there are another 10 patterns which are used only in very small numbers of words. The 98 words which obey those patterns, and their 16 exceptions, are perhaps better regarded as just another list of 114 spellings which learners need to memorise.

One of them is unique: *'to'* as an infinitive marker, as in *'to do'*, *'to go'* or *'to see'*, has an unstressed final **'o'** which occurs in no other English word. It is a barely audible half-vowel. We really say just*: t'do, t'go, t'see.* (In *'to London'* by contrast, the *'to'* sounds much more like *'too'*.)

Table 7. This shows the 10 very small English spelling patterns and their exceptions. - (The complete word lists can be found on pages 225-7.)

Patterns	Occurrences	Exceptions			
6 vowel patterns					
always	9	1	*all right*		
warm	17	1	***wore**, (worn)*		
quarter	4	0			
now	11	4	*bough, **plough**, **slough**, thou*		
toy	12	1	*buoy*		
to	1				
	(54)	(7)			
4 consonant patterns					
agen**cy**	16	5	*controversy,*	*courtesy,*	*gypsy,*	*topsy-turvy,*
			embassy		
musi**cian**	12	1	*gentian*		
zip	14	1	*xylophone*		
bu**zz**	2	2	*quiz, whiz*		
	(44)	(9)			
	98	**16**			

This section of the book concentrates predominantly on *spelling difficulties*, but Appendix R lists many words on pages 124-39 which have straightforward phonic spellings - for vowels as well as consonants.

The tables in this chapter also give only a few examples of divergent spellings. Appendix S lists all the common words in which they occur.

The next two pages list all the 96 main English spelling patterns which have been discussed. There is, however, *one further spelling convention* in which vowels and consonants are both involved jointly, and which learners find particularly hard to master - *consonant doubling*. This will be discussed separately, after the summaries of basic English spelling patterns.

Table 8 on this page lists the main graphemes for all English vowels and table 9 on the next page those for consonants. The tables contain only the most often used patterns. Examples of words which spell the same sounds differently have been shown in the tables above. Appendix S provides comprehensive lists of all words with divergent spellings.

Table 8. This lists the 42 basic **spelling patterns** for English **vowel sounds**.

(Weak and small patterns, as set out in tables 4 and 7 above, are printed in italics and marked with (w) or (s), after the words which exemplify them.)

<u>6 short vowel spellings</u>	<u>7 endings with</u>
cat	<u>stressed vowels</u>
pet	play
sit	go
pot	*fly (w)*
mum	*now* (s)
wood (w)	*due (w)*
	too (w)
<u>12 long vowel spellings</u>	*toy (s)*
mate	
bite	<u>11 endings with</u>
bone	<u>unstressed vowels</u>
tune	daddy
scout	better
oil	blizzard
mean (w) [EE-sound]	believable
spoon (w)	pertinent
autumn (w)	evidence
always (s)	musical
water (s)	sample
quarter (s)	*hasten (w)*
	ordinary (w)
<u>4 vowel blends with r</u>	*to (go, do) (s)*
cart	
dormouse	<u>2 unstressed vowels</u>
term (w)	<u>in prefixes</u>
care (w) [AIR-sound]	decide
	include

Table 9. The 54 basic **spelling patterns** for all 24 English **consonants**.
(For vowel patterns see previous page.)

bob

| chip |
| catch |

dad
film
gag

| jab, job, jug |
| agent |
| cage |
| *gentle (w)* |
| *badge (w)* |

hand

| kept |
| cat, cod, cup |
| rock |
| peek |
| comic |
| clap |
| milk |
| rocket |
| queen [Kw-sound] |
| taxi [Ks-sound] |

| leg |
| well |

mum
net, ten
ring
pop
rat

| send |
| fence |
| decide |
| *fortress (w)* |
| *agency (s)* |

| shop, rush |
| station |
| *mushroom (w)* |
| *essential (w)* |
| *vicious (w)* |
| *musician (s)* |

| tot |
| separate |

this (voiced)
thing (unvoiced)

| van |
| have |
| never |
| (v is usually not doubled) |

willow

you

| wise |
| absorb |
| *zip (s)* |
| *buzz (s)* |

vision

4. 3.   Consonant doubling - the most difficult aspect of English spelling

The greatest number of errors committed by students in examinations or spelling tests is caused by uncertainty about consonant doubling. They often fail to double a consonant where this is required - or they insert a doubled letter where this is not necessary.

When to double or not to double a consonant requires more learning than any other aspect of English spelling, and is never completely mastered by most people. The question, 'One ... or two?' makes even well-educated adults reach for the dictionary more often than any other spelling uncertainty.

The basic idea is simple enough. Consonant doubling and 'the magic -e' / 'open vowel' concept are devices which were invented to *mark vowel length*. Children are taught to double   the   final consonant   *when adding the suffixes -ing, -ed, -en, -er, -y* or *-ish* to the 233 one-syllable words below (e.g. chat - *chatting, chatted, chatty, chatter*; red - *redden, reddish*) to *keep the preceding <u>stressed vowel short</u>*. Only about 270 new words can be formed in this way from those below. Not all the suffixes can be added to all of the following words:

> *bag, bat, can, cap, cat, chat, clam, clan, clap, crab, dab, dam, drab, drag, fad, fan, fat, flap, flat, gag, glad, grab, gran, ham, hat, scrap, scan, sap, sag, sad, rat, rap, ram, prat, plan, pat, pan , pad, nag, mat, map, mad, lap, lag, jam, jab, sham, slam, slap, snap, span, spat, stab, strap, tag, tan, tap, trap, wag, wrap, yap, zap,*
>
> *bed , beg, bet, fret, get, hem, jet, leg, let, net, peg, pen, pet, red, set, stem, step, trek, vet, web, wet,*
>
> *bid, big , bin, bit , brim, chip, clip, crib, dig, dim, dip, drip, fit, flip, flit, grim, grin, grip, grit, hip, hit, jig, kid, lid, lip, pig, pin, pip, quit, quiz, rib, rid, rig, rim, rip, shin, ship, sin, sit, skid, skim, skin, skip, slim, slip, slit, snip, spin, spit, split, strip, swim, thin, tin, tip, trim, trip, twig, twin, whiz, win, wit, zip,*
>
> *blot, bob, bog, chop, cop, crop, dog, don, dot, drop, flog, flop, fog, frog, grog, hog, hop, hot, job, jog, jot, knot, lob, log, lop, mob, mop, nod, plod, plot, pod, pot, prod , prop, rob, rot , shop, slog, snob, sob, spot, stop, throb, top, tot , trot,*
>
> *but, club, cub, cup, cut, drug, drum, fun, glum, grub, gun, hug, hum, jug, jut, lug, mud, mug, nun, nut, plug, plum, rug, run, scrub, shrub, shrug, shun, shut, slug, slum, strum, strut, stud, stun, sum, sun, thud, thug, tug, up.*

The dominant English method for spelling the *long* vowel sounds AY, IE, OE and UE is with *'magic e'*, as in *'make', 'fine', 'pole'* and *'tune'*, or as *'open vowels'*, as in *'mason', 'tiny', 'polar'* and *'tunic'*. When the letters *a, i, o* and *u* are followed by a single consonant and another vowel they should, according to this spelling principle, be pronounced as long vowels.

Sometimes this method is used with the letter *e* as well (e.g. *even*) although the long EE-sound is more often spelt differently (e.g. dr*ea*m, red*ee*m).

Consonant doubling, as a means of keeping stressed vowels short, and the *'open vowel'* method are meant to be interdependent aspects of English vowel spelling. This system was invented in the 15th century and is supposed to operate on the model of *ma*s*o*n - *ma*ss*ive*, *tin*y *- tin*n*y*, *po*l*ar - po*ll*en* and *tu*n*ic* - *tu*nn*el*. The purpose of consonant doubling is *to close open vowels* and to ensure *a short pronunciation for them* (e.g. *dine - dinner, diner).*

If the method was used consistently, few people would have much trouble understanding it or applying it. Even young children grasp the logic of this system quite easily, as their early *'misspellings'* often demonstrate. When they are first taught the consonant doubling rule, many children begin to apply it logically and write: *boddy* for *body*, *holliday* for *holiday*, *verry* for *very* - following examples like *shoddy, jolly* and *merry*.

Young learners take a while to master this rule for the *suffix '-ed'*, because in the resulting longer words, the *e* is sounded only after *d* and *t*, (e.g. *plodded, patted*). After all other consonants, the *e* is usually *silent* (e.g. *grabbed, begged, hummed, stunned, hopped, stirred*). Such words are pronounced simply as *grabd, begd, humd*, etc.. Learning to spell them as their correct longer versions requires extensive practice, but since this spelling pattern is totally consistent, most children cope with it in the end.

Spelling difficulties are caused by *multi-syllable words which disobey the English consonant doubling principle.* Many words, which are not formed through the addition of suffixes, contain unpredictably doubled consonants which do not follow a *short and stressed* vowel (e.g. *accommod*a*tion, imm*e*diate, arr*e*st*), and several hundred more fail to double a consonant after a short, stressed vowel (e.g. *m*o*dern, h*a*bit, s*a*lad*).

One cannot decide whether a consonant after a short, stressed vowel in a multi-syllable English word should be doubled or not, simply by applying phonic sense. When in doubt, one has to resort to a dictionary or a spell-checker. Hundreds of uninflected base words which rhyme and sound much the same are spelt differently:

doddle - model; attitude - latitude, sorrel - laurel, mischief - bailiff.
This means that learners have to memorise:

380 multi-syllable words with regularly doubled consonants
    (e.g. *ladder, pepper, letter*)
    and
556 words with *'missing'* or *'surplus'* doubled consonants
    (e.g. *radish, leper, petal* - *collect, apply*).

Table 10 provides a detailed analysis of the problem by consonant.

Table 10. This summarises the use of regularly doubled consonants and the use of *tch, dge* and *ck* after short vowels. It also enumerates departures from the English consonant doubling principle. The last three columns give numbers and examples of the different ways in which the consonant doubling principle is not applied.

The majority of words with **missing** consonants (312 out of 397) are simply a letter short (e.g. g*a*laxy cf. g*a*llery, v*e*ry - m*e*rry, l*i*ly - s*i*lly). In others the doubling rule is disapplied differently:

47 words have a *single consonant and an unpredictably spelt short vowel*,
  (e.g. **any** cf. *penny, jealous - jelly, syrup - stirrup*),
22 have *c* or *sc* where one would expect *ss* (e.g. *acid* - cf. *passive*),
16 have *s* where one would expect *zz* (e.g. *chisel* - cf. *blizzard*).

All the words which are summarised in this table are listed in Appendix S, tables S 63 - 79, pages 244 - 57.

Regularly doubled consonants			The consonant doubling rule is not applied in one of three different ways:			
	Example	No. of words	No.of words in which the rule is not applied	**Missing** doubles	**Irregularly** spelt vowels *and* missing doubled letters	**Surplus** doubled consonants *(stressed vowel is underlined)*
				no example		
bb	ho*bb*y	14	**15**	*13 robin*	*2 double*	
(cc)			**14**			*14 acc*u*se*
dd	da*dd*y	17	**28**	*21 radish*	*4 ready*	*3 odd*
ff	o*ff*er	19	**22**	*6 profit*	*1 heifer*	*15 affect*
gg	ma*gg*ot	11	**10**	*7 agony*		*3 aggressive*
ll	ye*ll*ow	84	**84**	*55 melon*	*6 colour*	*23 hell*o
mm	si*mm*er	24	**56**	*33 limit*	*3 women*	*20 imm*u*ne*
nn	ma*nn*er	20	**57**	*42 manor*	*8 any*	*7 anno*y
pp	pe*pp*er	18	**45**	*19 leper*	*5 leopard*	*21 app*e*ar*
rr	pa*rr*ot	51	**76**	*48 parish*	*9 nourish*	*19 arr*a*nge*
ss	le*ss*on	25	**43**	*22 acid*	*2 sausage*	*19 dess*e*rt*
tt	la*tt*er	52	**42**	*28 lateral*		*14 attr*a*ct*
zz	di*zz*y	4	**29**	*22 wizard*	*7 dozen*	
tch	ki*tch*en*	8	**2**	*2 lichen*		
dge	bu*dg*et*	8	**12**	*12 logic*		
ck	po*ck*et*	25	**21**	*20 document*		*1 cockat*o*o*
	totals	**380**	**556**	*350*	*47*	*159*

* Before *ch, ge* or *k/c* a vowel is usually kept short by means of *tch, dge or ck*.

The number of multi-syllable words which disobey the basic English consonant doubling rule rises from 556 to 588 if one also includes the 32 words which have a short vowel before *v*, as in *never* and *river*. This is, however, a *'regular spelling pattern'* which merely gives the reader no indication whether the vowel is short (as in *clever, liver*) or long (as in *lever, driver*). [For more on this see Appendix R, table R 58, page 179.]

4. 3. 2 Additional undermining of the consonant doubling principle

The consonant doubling concept is further diluted by 244 one-syllable words which end in *-ff, -ll, -ss, -zz* and *-ck* and *-tch,* and in which consonant doubling serves no phonic function. We rarely double *b, d, g, m, n, p* or *t* at the end of short words (e.g. *grab, bad, bag, rum, run, shop, shot*). Such words show that a single vowel in a one-syllable word, ending with a consonant is automatically short.

Many doubled consonants at the end of short words are at least *entirely predictable:*
> 62 words with *-ck* (e.g. *back, neck, brick, clock, duck*),
> 42 with *-ll* (e.g. *ball, bell, bill, doll, bull, dull*),
> 23 *-tch* (e.g. *catch, sketch, ditch, notch, hutch*)
> and
> 17 ending in *-dge* (e.g. *badge, edge, fridge, lodge, smudge*)

Of these 144 regular doublings, only *-dge* (or *d* before a final *-ge),* serves a useful function. The *d* indicates a short pronunciation for the preceding vowel, rather than a long one, e.g. *cadge - cage, fridge - oblige*.
[All the words with predictably doubled consonants in word endings are listed in tables S 80 - S 83, pages 258-59.]
The purpose of doubling a final *-l* is complex and frequently contradictory. Only *e, i* and *u* before *ll* are invariably short (e.g. *bell, bill, bull*), but *-ull* has two different pronunciation (e.g. *dull* - with the dominant sound for *u,* and *full* - with the short OO-sound of *wool*); and an *a* or an *o* before *ll* can be *long (call* [caul], *roll* [role]) *or short (shall, doll)*.
In UK English, *l*-doubling is made even harder to master by regular doubling of a final *-l* in longer verbs when adding the suffixes *-ed* or *-ing,* even if the vowel before it is not stressed (e.g. *cancel - cancelled, cancelling, label - labelled, labelling*).
The usual pattern for longer words is as in *permit -permitted, prefer - preferring,* i.e. the final consonant is doubled only when the preceding vowel is stressed. After an unstressed vowel the consonant is generally not doubled (e.g. *summon - summoned, summoning*).

It is even harder to grasp the logic of doubling *f, s* and *z* *at the end of just some one-syllable words.*

FF: 10 short words with a short vowel end with *-ff*

> cliff, cuff, duff, gruff, off, puff, sniff, stiff, stuff, whiff

but 8 do not

> cough, rough, slough, tough, trough,   if, chef, of

and *staff* is pronounced with a long vowel sound before the *ff* in standard English.

SS: 22 one-syllable words with a final S-sound after a short vowel end in *ss* (e.g. *less, miss, loss, fuss*), but 6 extremely common words don't

> gas, yes, this, bus, plus, us   (also *pus*)

and in 6 others the vowel before *ss* is long

> brass, class, glass, grass, pass, gross .

S-doubling is further complicated because 12 longer words mark unusual stress with *ss* (e.g. *confess, regress*), while 12 other words use *ss* after an unstressed vowel (e.g. *carcass, fortress*), and 71 others with identically sounding endings use *s, ce* or *se* (e.g. *atlas, crisis, office, palace, promise*) - see table S 61, on page 242.

ZZ: A *z* is doubled at the end of two common words, but not two others:
> buzz, jazz - quiz, whiz ,

and in four very frequently used words the same sound is spelt with *s*:

> as, has, is, was .

A further 83 one-syllable words have cumbersome but fairly predictable short vowel markings in their endings, e.g. *babble, peddle, sniffle, goggle, buckle, apple, cattle* and *puzzle*. (They are all listed in table S 84, page 260.)

The pattern of endings with doubled consonants and *-le*, as in *little*, is contradicted by 38 exceptions.

a) Words with the consonants **m, n** or **r** never follow the pattern of *babble, fiddle* or *settle*. They are spelt as the 11 words below.

pommel	channel	funnel	panel		barrel	squirrel
pummel	flannel	kennel	tunnel		quarrel	

b) When such endings contain an **S-sound**, their spellings are unpredictable: 11 words spell the ending as *-stle*, but 6 don't.

apostle	gristle	rustle	whistle	hassle	tassel	
bristle	hustle	thistle	wrestle	tussle	vessel	
bustle	jostle	trestle			mussel	muscle

c) A further 12 words diverge from the dominant pattern in various unpredictable ways.

nickel	camel	chisel	treble	couple	subtle
	chapel	laurel	triple	double	
	model			trouble	

In words like *apple, giggle* and *muddle* the *doubled consonant and the final e are both redundant.* Their final *e* is now as superfluous as the *e* of *atte* (for *at*), or that of *hadde* and *shoppe* once was. In those words the *e* stopped being pronounced several centuries ago and was eventually dropped in writing too, and the doubled consonants were reduced to singles.

All the words on the pattern of *apple, bristle* or *flannel* could be spelt more simply as *apl, brisl* and *flanl* on the pattern of *best, stamp,* and *milk*. To suggest that *best, stamp and milk* should be spelt as *besste, stammpe* and *millke* would now seem ridiculous, but *apple* and *huddle,* and 81 other words like them, are still very much like that. Children are invariably taken aback when they first see simple words like *apl* and *litl* spelt as *apple* and *little*.

Consonant doubling in words like **apple** and **little** was probably introduced in order to distinguish them from a few similar-looking words with long vowels. This perceived need may have arisen because a handful of words (like those opposite) were not made to conform to the newly developing English spelling system in the 15th century. They were allowed to

able	cable	cradle	fable	gable	stable	table		noble
bible	bridle	disciple	rifle	stifle	title	trifle		bugle

keep their original French spellings, or had their English spellings remodelled on French lines.

If those few words had been made to conform to the more English pattern of *label* and *libel*, then the consonant doubling in 100 words like *babble, rabble* and *channel* would probably not have occurred, or would have been abolished by now.

Moreover, according to the open vowel rule, a vowel is supposed to have a long pronunciation *only when it is followed by a single consonant and another vowel.* Before two consonants, it is meant to be short (e.g. *banter, gladly, minted, sprinted*). This means that *aple, batle* and *catle* should really serve well enough, even with the redundant final *-e* after *l*.

If the 161 one-syllable words with short vowels, which currently end in *-ck, -ll, -tch, -ff, -ss* and *-zz*, were spelt with just *-c, -l, -ch, -f, -s* or *-z*, they would undoubtedly all be pronounced exactly as they are now (e.g. *pac, bel, cach, puf, mes, buz*). This is evident from already existing simpler spellings like *mac, rec, sac, trek, yak; fulfil; attach, us, bus, plus; quiz* and *whiz*. These, and words like *mad, bet* and *spin*, prove the total superfluity of short vowel marking at the end of one-syllable words.

This is also confirmed by words like *music* and *traffic* which had a surplus *-k* until relatively recently. They used to be spelt *musick* and *traffick*, ending with the equivalent of a doubled *k*. Yet we now use just the *-c* ending in nearly all such words (*basic, classic, electric*) and read them just as easily in their simpler forms. These show that words like *brick, stick* and *truck* could easily go the same, less cumbersome way (i.e. *bric, stic, truc*).

Redundant doubled consonants that follow well-established patterns, like *back, bell* and *catch*, can be taught systematically, but they absorb much teaching and learning time. Most young children find them puzzling and hard to master; but worst of all - they help to aggravate the already difficult area of consonant doubling even further.

In conclusion, the main difficulty of English consonant doubling is erratic adherence to the doubling principle. The derivatives which can be obtained by adding suffixes to one-syllable words like *bid, beg* and *cut* (i.e. *bidding, begged, cutter*) may appear to be based on sound logic, but a closer look at the use of doubled consonants in multi-syllable words proves otherwise. The chief difficulty in mastering English spelling lies in memorising the exceptions which diverge from basic spelling patterns. Consonant doubling is especially difficult because it necessitates the memorising of particularly large numbers of words with random spellings. This makes it *the most difficult aspect* of English spelling.

Chapter 5

Heterographs

(different spellings for identical pronunciations like *there / their / they're)*

English spelling often operates like a system of mathematics which has no axiom that *'one always equals one'* and that in algebra *x cannot* at the same time *be equal to 2, 5 and 10.* Instead of *1 = 1* or *x = 1,* English spelling allows *x = 1 = 2 = 5, or whatever.* Such lack of logical consistency causes what psychologists call *'cognitive confusion'* - children lose sight of what they are trying to learn. It may even impede their development of logical thinking.

Having to choose between alternative spellings for identical sounds is a constant difficulty for learners, but the majority of different spellings can at least be linked to different words as in *tree, tea* or *key.* These are difficult enough to cope with, and their mastery takes much time, but when parts of *identically sounding words* are *spelt differently, for different meanings,* as is the case with heterographs (e.g. *see / sea,* **meet** / **meat,** **fair / fare**), learning to spell becomes almost impossibly hard. The frequent errors which even well-practised adults commit with **their /there /theyre, to, too, two** and **its / it's** provide ample evidence for this.

Heterographs epitomise English indifference to the alphabetic principle. This principle demands that speech sounds should be represented in a consistent and reliable manner, in the same way that musical sounds are represented by notes and numerical values by figures. Similarly, words which sound the same should look the same. Heterographs clearly do not, by definition.

Most were created *quite deliberately* by Dr. Johnson. When he started to compile his famous dictionary which was published in 1755, English spelling had already become largely standardised, i.e. one spelling had become adopted as the *'correct'* one for the majority of English words. This had not been the case in earlier centuries.

In the 16th century, in Tudor England, many English words still had more than one spelling (e.g. *Queen /Quene, yere /yeer, first /fyrst, ready /redy).* Even printers used many different spellings for identical words, with each house using its own spelling style, but by the end of the 16th century these had been largely abandoned. By about 1600 an agreed standard spelling had been adopted for the majority of English words. Yet even in

1750 a few hundred words still had alternative spellings, and Samuel Johnson was reluctant to lose them.

For a handful of words different spellings were by then already linked to different meanings. Johnson hit on the idea of *linking all* still surviving different spellings for identically sounding words *to different meanings*. By deliberately preserving this spelling diversity in his dictionary he created an additional, gratuitous spelling difficulty for learners.

He probably did not appreciate the problems which he thus created. His own memory was phenomenal and he relished showing it off, both as a schoolboy and in later life. It is also unlikely that he envisaged a time when education ceased to be the prerogative of a relatively small and time-rich intellectual elite and millions of lesser mortals would be educated and expected to learn to write in the course of their education.

Besides, the curriculum of grammar schools in the 18th century was aimed chiefly at training the mind. Having a spelling system that could only be mastered with lots of practice may well have been seen as something desirable for keeping boys occupied. Imparting knowledge was then not a high priority. This was partly because the body of available knowledge that could be disseminated was very much smaller than it is now.

Grammar school education consisted of little more than the study of the Bible, Latin and Greek. Much time was spent making translations from classical languages into English and back again, parsing and committing long passages to memory. The chief objective of education appeared to be training the memory. This was still the case as late as the first half of the 19th century when Charles Darwin was a boy. He regarded most of his schooling as a profligate waste of time.

He could see no point in learning the grammar of dead languages or the memorising of thousands of unpredictably spelt English words which deprived him of opportunities for more relevant learning. Unsurprisingly, Darwin later became a supporter of the movement to simplify English spelling.

Apart from failing to appreciate what spelling difficulties he was creating, Dr. Johnson probably did not realise how prescriptive his choices would become. He wrote, *"the spellings which I adopt are still convertible"*. Nevertheless, his dictionary virtually set English spelling into tablets of stone. Hardly anyone has dared to meddle with his spelling choices for the last two and a half centuries.

Most people now tend to believe that heterographs are necessary. After 11 - 15 years of having been told - *'These are the correct spellings. Just get on and learn them.'* - it is easy to end up thinking that they must be right; that *there must be some good reason for having them*. Such training makes it easy to become convinced that serious misunderstandings might arise if we abolished them.

Yet in speech identically sounding words with different meanings never lead to confusion, even when we hear them on the telephone or on the radio, when comprehension cannot be aided by gestures or facial expressions. Even when the word with the sound of *'heer'* occurs twice in the same sentence, as in 'I can't *hear* you from *here*' it still fails to give trouble. Not once in 36 years using English has anyone ever asked me to spell out a heterograph because the person I was speaking to was not sure which sense applied. Children learn easily to distinguish between 'Come *here*!' and 'I can't *hear* you!' long before they ever see those words in their written forms. People who never manage to learn to spell at all are, nevertheless, also surprisingly able to cope with such words.

What proves most clearly that we do not really need to spell any words differently for different meanings are the many hundreds of common English words which have just one spelling for two or more different meanings, e.g. river *bank* - *bank* account, able to do / *can* - *can* of beans, eat a *date* - *date* someone, hear a *sound* - *sound* arguments, postage *stamp* - *stamp* your foot, chocolate *bar* - *bar* food (also 'metal *bar'*, 'all *bar* one', 'called to the *bar'*).

However unnecessary heterographs may be, their spellings are exceedingly hard to master. Students first need to learn to associate the different spellings with different meanings. Then, when using such words in their own writing, they need to stay aware of the meaning of the whole phrase or sentence which they are composing, in order to make the correct spelling choice. These words cannot be spelt accurately outside the phrase or sentence in which they are used. (*Their* house was near the end of the road. / *There* was no one around.)

Getting such spellings right is a vastly more complex accomplishment than just representing speech sounds with letters. It is also a constant distraction in writing. It imposes an extra layer of spelling difficulty, in comparison with more phonemic spelling systems.

Heterographs always require the memorising of unpredictable spellings. In a pair of heterographs, at least one member inevitably has to diverge from the regular, or more dominant spelling pattern (e.g. sum /*some*; berry /*bury*). When a word has three different spellings, then at least two of them are bound to diverge (site, **c***ite*, s**ight**), and in the worst cases all three of them are unpredictable in some way (e.g. *there* / *their* / *they're*).

Neither *there* nor *their* follows the more common patterns of *care, dare* or *hair*; and the contraction *they're*, comprises the irregular spelling of *they* which does not follow the pattern of *play, say* and *day*. It is therefore not surprising that the *there* / *their* / *they're* triplet causes more spelling errors than most. Yet this difficulty need not exist.

If Dr. Johnson had chosen just one alternative from *there* and *their* for his dictionary, spellers would not be constantly distracted or tripped up by this dichotomy. Better still, if he had amended the spelling of his choice so that it followed one of the more common spellings for the AIR-sound and settled on either *thare* or *thair,* he would have made life even easier for learners. We would not keep getting them so persistently muddled and teachers would not have to waste so much time and red ink on correcting them, over and over again.

The buckets of red ink that must have been expended on correcting just the words *there* and *their* over the centuries would probably fill a substantial sea. This has come about because one influential man, on his own admission, was simply not interested in making English spellings represent speech sounds in a reliable fashion.

German spelling fared far better. It was also fixed largely by just one person - Jacob Grimm, of fairy tale fame. Together with his brother Wilhelm he laid the foundations of German spelling and grammar. When he and his brother collected German folk tales and fairy stories, he collected the spellings which where used at the time, just like Dr. Johnson did.

However, when he came to compile a dictionary for German in the first half of the 19th century, he amended many of them to fit in with dominant spelling trends and eliminated exceptions wherever he felt able to. He tried to establish a regular, predominantly logical system for German spelling from the outset. Later others streamlined his system still further. That is why German spelling is now much more predictable and easier to learn than English spelling.

We must be grateful that Dr. Johnson did not leave us with even more spelling trouble than he did. English has at least 2000 words with different meanings but just one spelling: *bank, crank, fly, tie, tank, arm, back, neck, foot, hop, flap, flip, etc.* One could easily create more spelling misery with them. For example, on the model of the UK differentiation between the noun p*ractice* and the verb *to practise,* Dr. Johnson could easily have extended the idea to 'I *promise'* and 'I give you my *promice'.* He could also have introduced 'I *work'* and 'I go to *worke',* and much more on similar lines. Mercifully he contented himself with making only around 400 words more difficult than necessary.

The *practice / practise* pair is famous in Britain for making nearly everyone stop and think. Most people find it very hard to remember when to use which. In the US, by contrast, the distinction has been abolished, and they get by perfectly well with just the single spelling of *practice,* for both noun and verb. This proves that all other heterographs could easily go the same way. We would very quickly get used to not having them any more, and teachers would be amazed how much better their pupils can suddenly spell.

I have established that English has at least 253 common words which require the learning of 522 different spellings. Among them are 16 words which have 3 different spellings (e.g. *where - wear - ware*). Learning them all entails more practice, drilling, correction and endless repetition than anything else. They can all be seen at the end of this chapter. All learners take a long time to master them confidently. Even good spellers, after years of practice, will occasionally still misspell some of them. Should we perhaps stop and think if we really need them?

The word *bar* shows just how well we can cope with many different meanings for a single spelling: in a *bar*, behind *bars*, iron *bar*, a *bar* of chocolate, all *bar* one, to *bar* from a *bar*, to be called to the *bar*. Only the more refined discipline of ballet could not go along with such common sense, and so dancers practise at the *barre*, although in practice this is also just a wooden *bar*.

It would be possible to have different spellings for all the different meanings of *bar* as well: e.g. behind *barrs*, an iron *baar*, a *barh* of chocolate, all *bawr* one, to *bargh* from the bar, to call to the *bhar*. This idea probably seems completely ridiculous. Yet heterographs are exactly like that - deliberately created, totally unnecessary spelling difficulties.

Just how arbitrary Dr. Johnson's decisions were can be seen by looking at some of his choices more carefully. He gave us *right*, *write* and *rite*, but *right* still has several meanings which we do not differentiate in spelling: we can turn *right*, be *right*, *right* a wrong, start *right* away, defend human *rights* or lean politically to the *right*.

We would have no more trouble coping with 8 meanings for *right* than we do with the six which we already have. Furthermore, if some prestigious authority now decided that the simplest of the 3 spellings for the word, namely *rite*, will do for all of its different meanings, this particular source of confusion would disappear.

The arbitrariness and superfluousness of heterographs is demonstrated particularly clearly by several dozen words which have *identical spellings for different meanings but different pronunciations*: e.g. we *live - live* show, take the *lead - lead* weight, a good *read - read* it yesterday, loud *row - row* a boat, this is no *use - use* it now.

Since we can cope with even such an extreme lack of differentiation between spelling, meaning or pronunciation, the idea that we ever need to spell identically sounding words differently for different meanings, in order to avoid possible confusion, is very questionable indeed. All heterographs could easily be reduced to one spelling, just like the *practice / practise* differentiation which has been eliminated in the US. By preserving Dr. Johnson's heterographs we are merely perpetuating a totally gratuitous spelling difficulty which continues to waste the efforts of pupils and teachers, and trips up many spellers throughout their lives.

We have ample evidence that millions of spellers get into regular muddles with distinctions like *to / too / two*. Vast numbers of people find them very hard to learn in the first place and even more difficult to apply correctly in their own writing. Is there any point in this continuous torture?

While learners are forced to differentiate between *to, too* and *two* at enormous expense, nobody is troubled by the fact that *to* still has two quite different meanings, and slightly different pronunciations, as in 'I've decided *to* go *to* London'.

Abolishing heterographs would immediately make English spelling very much easier to learn. Instead of forcing children to memorise 522 spellings for 253 common words, more than half of which are unpredictable in some way, we could let them learn just 253 spellings for those 253 words. These would then join the list of over 2000 other words that have one spelling for different meanings without causing confusion: *count, cricket, crow, deal, dock, lean, mean, left, like, sense, sound, wag, wake, watch, wave, wax, way, well, will, etc..*

Even just simplifying a few of the best-known sources of confusion like *its / it's,   to / too / two,   their / there,   hear / here* and   *see / sea* would save many hours of learning time and irritation. We know that these cause spelling problems to children and adults, year after year, but instead of removing the difficulty, we continue to perpetuate it, at enormous cost.

This is like a having a public building with a step at its entrance which regularly trips someone up, but refusing to do anything about it. - Notices are posted about the danger, people are repeatedly trained how to negotiate it and warned to be wary, but large numbers continue to stumble or tumble down, because of a determined refusal to mend the faulty step itself.

All 253 most common heterographs are listed on the following pages as follows:

1)   On the next three pages, the 253 frequently used sets are analysed according to the sounds for which they have different spellings, beginning with the numerically largest group - those containing the EE-sound.

2) The same heterographs are also listed in alphabetical order on pages 65 and 66, followed by 80 less frequently used ones on page 67.

Learners find heterographs notoriously difficult. The different groupings might serve as better mnemonic aids for different learners.

Heterographs grouped by sound
(* Heterographs which contain several unpredictable elements are marked with an asterisk.)

48 common words have alternative spellings for the **EE-sound**.

bee/be	eve/**eaves**	leech/leach	reed/read	sheikh/chic*
beech/beach	feet/feat	leek/leak	reek/wreak*	steel/steal
been/bean	flee/flea	leaver/lever	reel/real	sweet/suite*
beet/beat	freeze/frieze	meet/meat	sealing/ceiling*	tee/tea
breech/breach	geezer/geyser	need/knead	seamen/semen	teem/team
cheep/cheap	genes/jeans*	pee/pea	see/sea	wee/we
creek/creak	Greece/grease*	peace/piece	seem/seam	week/weak
deer/dear	heel/heal	peek/peak	seen/scene*	wheel/weal*
discreet/discrete	here/hear	peel/peal	serial/cereal*	
eerie/eyrie	key/quay*	peer/pier	shear/sheer	

37 words with the **AY-sound** have alternative spellings.

ale/**ail**	gage/**gauge**	maze/maize	stake/steak	nay/**neigh**
ate/**eight**	gate/**gait**	pale/**pail**	strait/straight	pray/prey
bale/**bail**	grate/great	pane/pain	tale/**tail**	slay/**sleigh**
base/**bass***	hale/**hail**	place/plaice	vale/veil	Sunday/sundae
brake/break	lane/lain	plane/plain	vane/vain/vein	way/**weigh**
Dane/**deign**	made/maid	rain/reign	wait/**weight**	
faint/feint	male/mail	raze/raise	waste/waist	
fate/fête	mane/main	sale/sail	whale/wail*	

22 words have **'missing' or 'surplus' doubled consonants**.

ad/**add**	check/cheque/Czech	medal/me**dd**le*	pe**dd**ler/pedlar
aloud /allowed*	Finn/fin	metal/me**tt**le*	pi**dg**in/pigeon*
be**rr**y/bury*	Finnish/finish	moose/mousse*	ri**gg**er/rigor
but/bu**tt**	gel/jell*	mu**ss**el/muscle	tic/ti**ck**
canvas/canva**ss**	in/i**nn**	pallet/palate/palette	
ca**rr**ot/carat*	lap/La**pp**	pedal/pe**dd**le*	

18 words spell the **long I-sound** in different ways.

aisle/isle	mite/mi**ght**	slight/sleight	I/**aye**/eye	dryer/drier
bite/byte/bi**ght**	rime/rhyme*	stile/style	by/buy/bye	flyer/flier
knight/night*	rite/**right**/ write	time/thyme*	die/dye	
lightening/lightning*	site/si**ght**/cite	tire/tyre	hi/**high**	

13 words have alternative spellings for '-er' in endings.

alter/altar	lumber/lumbar	miner/minor	rigger/rigor	stationery/stationary
caster/castor	manner/manor	peddler/pedlar	seller/cellar*	summery/summary
hanger/hangar	meter/metre	razer/razor		

12 words have different spellings for the medial **OE-sound** and 6 for the final OE-sound.

bolder/boulder	lone/loan	road/rode	sewn/sown	doe/dough	toe/tow
broach/brooch	moan/mown	role/roll	thrown/throne	roe/row	no/know
groan/grown	pole/poll	sole/soul	yolk/yoke	so/sow/sew	oh/owe

12 words spell the **OR-sound** differently.

boar/bore/Boer	coarse/course	forth/fourth	horse/hoarse	pore/pour	war/wore
boarder/border	for/four	hoar/whore*	or/oar/ore	sore/soar	worn/warn

10 words have alternatives for the **S-sound**.

sell/cell	sensor/censor	serial/cereal*	signet/cygnet	practice/ practise
seen/scene*	sent/scent/cent	sight/cite*	council/counsel*	Greece/grease*

9 words have different spellings for the **AIR-sound**.

air/heir*	fair/fare	hair/hare	stair/stare	wear/where*
bare/bear	flair/flare	pair/pear/pare	their/there	

9 have differing '-al' / '-le' / '-el' / '-ol'   endings.

bridal/bridle	dual/duel	medal/meddle*	pedal/peddle*	principal/principle
capital/capitol	idle/idol	metal/mettle*	navel/naval	

7 words each have different spellings for **unstressed vowels,** the **short U-sound,** the **AU-sound and** the **W-sound.**

batten/baton	complement	counsel/council*	lessen/lesson
carrot/carat*	/compliment	current/currant	prophet/profit*
cum/come	nun/none	sum/some	won/one
dun/done	ruff/rough*	sun/son	
ball/bawl	Gaul/gall	maul/mall	taut/taught*
faun/fawn	haul/hall	Paul/pall	
weather/whether	wheel/weal*	wile/while *	watt/what*
wet/whet	which/witch*	wine/whine	

Several other sounds have alternative spellings in small sets of words

6 UE-endings	6 OO/ou/...	6 ER-sound	6 R-sound	6 C/K/CH/QU
blue/blew	coo/coup	berry/bury*	rap/wrap	arc/ark
cue/queue*	moose/mousse*	berth/birth	retch/wretch	bask/Basque
due/dew	root/route	earn/urn	ring/wring	cord/chord
flue/flew/flu	shoot/chute*	fir/fur	rote/wrote	franc/frank
hue/hew	threw/through	herd/heard	rung/wrung	kernel/colonel*
revue/review	troop/troupe	pearl/purl	rye/wry*	scull/skull
5 N	4 S/Z	4 -Y endings	4 -E endings	3 short E
nap/knap	braise/braze*	bogy/bogey	born/borne	led/lead
nave/knave	geezer/geyser*	caddy/caddie	cast/caste	lent/leant
new/knew	grisly/grizzly*	chilly/chilli	fiance/fiancee	red/read
nit/knit	prise/prize	story/storey	heroin/heroine	
not/knot				
3 F	3 H	3 short I	2 M	2 J
draft/draught*	hole/whole	gild/guild	dam/damn	gel/jell*
faze/phase	holy/wholly	gilt/guilt	plum/plumb	Jim/gym*
profit/prophet*	hoop/whoop	him/hymn		
2 OO	2 OUR			
to/too/two	flower/flour			
you/ewe	our/hour			
6 oddments:				
bow/bough boy/buoy hart/heart martial/marshal shoot/chute* wood/would				

64

253 common heterographs in alphabetical order - **a - l**

* Those marked with an asterisk contain more than one spelling difference, and <u>triplets</u> are underlined.

ad/**add**	capital/capitol	fiance/fiancee	hi/**high**
air/heir*	**carrot**/ carat*	fin/ **Finn**	him/**hymn**
aisle/isle	caster/cast**or**	Finnish/finish	**hoar**/whore*
ale/**ail**	check/che**que**	**fir**/fur	hole/**whole**
a**loud** /allowed*	cheep/cheap	**flair**/flare	<u>holy/wholly/holey</u>
alter/alt**ar**	**coarse**/course	flee/**flea**	hoop/**whoop**
arc/ark	complement	<u>flue/flew/flu</u>	horse/**hoarse**
ate/**eight***	/compliment	flyer/flier	
	cord/**chord**	**for**/four	<u>I/aye/eye</u>
bale/bail	counsel/council*	forth/**fourth**	idle/idol
ball/bawl	creek/cre**ak**	franc/frank	in/**inn**
bare/bear	cue/**queue***	freeze/frieze	
base/**bass***	cum/**come***		Jim/**gym***
batten/bat**on***	current/currant	gage/gauge	
be/**bee**		gate/**gait**	kernel/colonel*
beech/beach	dam/dam**n**	**Gaul**/gall	key/**quay***
been/bean	Dane/de**ign***	geezer/geyser*	**knight**/night
beet/**beat**	deer/de**ar**	gel/jell*	
berry/**bury***	die/**dye**	genes/jeans*	lane/lain
berth/birth	doe/d**ough**	gild/gui**ld**	lap/**Lapp**
<u>bite/byte/bight</u>	draft/draught*	gilt/gui**lt**	leaver/lever
blue/**blew**	dryer/drier	grate/**great**	leech/leach
<u>boar/bore/Boer</u>	dual/du**el**	**Greece**/grease*	leek/leak
border/ **boarder**	due/**dew**	grill/gri**lle**	lessen/lesson
bogy/boge**y**	dun/done	groan/gro**wn**	lightning/lightening*
bolder/bou**lder**			lone/loan
born/born**e**	earn/**urn**	hair/**hare**	lumber/lumb**ar**
boy/**buoy**	eve/**eaves**	hale/**hail**	
braise/braze*		hanger/hang**ar**	
brake/**break**	faint/f**eint**	hart/hea**rt**	
breech/breach	fair/**fare**	haul/**hall**	
bridal/bri**dle**	fate/f**ete**	heel/**heal**	
broach/bro**och**	faun/**fawn**	herd/**heard**	
but/but**t**	faze/**phase***	here/**hear**	
<u>by/buy/bye</u>	feet/**feat**	heroin/heroine	

Common heterographs m - w

made/maid	peek/peak	sale/sail	tale/tail
male/mail	peel/peal	sealing/ceiling*	taut/taught
mane/main	pedal/peddle*	seamen/semen	tee/tea
manner/manor	peddler/pedlar*	stationery/stationary	teem/team
martial/marshal	peer/pier	summery/summary	their/there/they're
maul/mall	pidgin/pigeon*	see/sea	threw/through
maze/maize	place/plaice	seem/seam	throne/thrown
medal/meddle*	plane/plain	seen/scene*	tic/tick
meet/ meat	plum/plumb	sell/cell	time/thyme*
metal/mettle*	pole/poll	seller/cellar*	tire/tyre
meter/metre	pore/pour	sent/scent/cent	to/too/two
miner/minor	practice/ practise	serial/cereal*	toe/tow
mite/might	pray/prey	sewn/sown	
moan/mown	principal/principle	sheer/shear	vale/veil
moose/mousse*	prise/prize	sheikh/chic*	vane/vain/vein
mussel/muscle*	profit/prophet*	shoot/chute*	
		sight/cite/site*	
navel/naval	rain/reign	signet/cygnet*	wait/weight
need/knead	rap/wrap	slay/sleigh	war/wore
new/knew	raze/raise*	slight/sleight	waste/waist
nit/knit	razer/razor	so/sow/sew	watt/what*
no/know	reed/read	sole/soul	way/weigh
not/knot	reek/wreak*	sore/soar	wear/where*
nun/none*	reel/real	stair/stare	wee/we
	revue/review	stake/steak	week/weak
oh/owe	rigger/rigor*	steel/steal	wet/whet
or/oar/ore	rime/rhyme*	stile/style	whale/wail*
our/hour	ring/wring	story/storey	wheel/weal*
	rite/write/right	strait/straight	which/witch*
pair/pear/pare	rode/road	sum/some	wile/while
pale/pail	roe/row	sun/son	wine/whine
pallet/palate/palette	role/roll	Sunday/sundae	won/one*
pane/pain	root/route	sweet/suite*	wood/would
Paul/pall	rote/wrote		worn/warn
peace/piece	ruff/rough*		
pearl/purl	rung/wrung		
pee/pea			

80 less frequently occurring heterographs

aid/aide	dean/dene	jam/jamb	sensor/censor
ascent/assent	dependent/dependant		sloe/slow
aught/ought	descent/dissent	lea/lee	staunch/stanch
	discreet/discrete	leaf/lief	step/steppe
barren/baron	doc/dock	lode/load	sty/stye
base/bass			sucker/succour
bask/Basque	eerie/eyrie	mantel/mantle	symbol/cymbal
beetle/betel	elicit/illicit	marten/martin	
bell/belle	ensure/insure	mean/mien	tear/tier
bloc/block	eyelet/islet	morn/mourn	tern/turn
bole/bowl		mote/moat	throe/throw
bow/beau	faro/pharao		tor/tore
	flow/floe	nap/knap	troop/troupe
calendar/calender	forgo/forego	nave/knave	tun/ton
cannon/canon	fryer/friar	nay/neigh	
canvas/canvass			wane/wain
cast/caste	gaff/gaffe	prier/prior	wave/waive
censor/censer	gamble/gambol		weever/weaver
climb/clime	grisly/grizzly	retch/wretch	whirl/whorl
colour/culler		rye/ wry	wont/want
coo/coup	hoard/horde		
core/corps	hue/hew	sac/sack	yoke/yolk
crape/crepe		scull/skull	you/ewe
crummy/crumby	inquire/enquire	seed/cede	your/yore

One could make a list of several hundred more heterographs, if one included not merely root words, as in the tables above, but also derivatives (e.g. *past/passed, copse/cops*).

Chapter 6

Disputes over teaching methods

The irregularities of English spelling don't just make becoming literate difficult. They make the teaching of literacy much harder too; and this has generated endless disagreements over teaching methods. The debate began as soon as church elementary schools became quite common in England in the 16th century, and it is still going on.

John Hart wrote in 1551 about *'the vices and faultes of our writing, which cause it to be tedious, and long in learning; and learned hard, and evil to read'*. He realised even then that English spelling was far more difficult than that of other languages. He advocated simplifying it, but in the English-speaking world the idea of making the learning of spelling easier by simplifying the spelling system has so far not caught on.

Instead of this there has been a relentless search for better teaching methods. Despite the fact that poor adult literacy rates are common to all English-speaking counties, poor teaching has been regarded as the main cause of this so widely spread disappointing performance.

Millions of words have been written about how best to teach children to read and write English. Dianne McGuinness's book *'Why Children Can't Read'*, published in1997, is one of the more recent additions to the numerous similar titles which have been produced during the past 450 years. She herself observes, quite correctly, "*...if there was a simple answer to teach children to read an English alphabet we would have found it before now*".

Expert opinion has been divided roughly into two camps: those favouring the phonic method, or 'phonics', and those supporting a 'whole word' or even a 'whole language' approach. There are different varieties of phonics, and the 'whole word' strategy manifests itself in varying forms too. Nevertheless, the various schemes used by schools tend to lean towards one or the other. The popularity of each has alternately waxed and waned, and currently the phonics method is enjoying its turn of popularity.

In essence the phonics approach advocates making pupils aware that words are made up of sounds and that we use letters to represent those sounds. It advises that children should be taught how to read sounds from letters and how to represent sounds with letters. The method was rediscovered after several decades during which the 'whole word' approach had been deemed preferable. Phonics is now widely used in the UK and the US. In some American states it is now obligatory by law.

Diane McGuinness claims that the 'whole word' method dominated virtually the whole of the 20th century. She maintains that in English speaking countries phonics has previously really never been taught, except by a few exceptional teachers. Perhaps rightly so?

McGuinness herself states "..*the structure of the language determines ...how it must be taught*". Phonics is certainly totally appropriate for teaching reading and writing with a truly alphabetic spelling system.

The advocates of phonics ignore the fact that English spelling is frequently unalphabetic. Since 1066 it has become increasingly divorced from the alphabetic principle. This makes it quite different from the many languages with which phonics can be used very successfully.

The essence of phonics is making learners aware how the alphabetic principle operates. Because so many English words contain unalphabetic elements, the phonics method cannot be used in English in the same straightforward way as in languages that have more regular spelling systems.

Any sensible teacher has always known that mastering phonics should be part of learning to read and write English. Such teachers are also fully aware that this is but the easy part of becoming literate; that spelling proficiency cannot be attained by phonics alone; that the hard and tedious part of learning to spell is mastering all those frequent departures from the alphabetic principle. Phonics is just the beginning. It is a good beginning, but no more than that.

If English did not have so many words that diverge from common spelling patterns in some way, the whole-word method would probably never have occurred to anyone. It was born out of the realisation that large numbers of English words cannot be read accurately except as wholes (e.g. *though, cough, through*) and that many words spell identical sounds in different ways (e.g. *be, bee, sea, key, ski*).

Such words have regularly made teachers aware that phonics does not take learners of English all that far. Observing the cognitive confusion which the irregular spellings of English so often create, has even made many teachers doubt whether the teaching of English phonics is not altogether a waste of time.

English has close to 100 spelling rules, as explained in Chapter 4. Many of those are also quite complicated (eg. *mat - mate - play; kit - cat - lick - traffic*). When such rules are also quite regularly broken in around half of all words, it is not so unreasonable to wonder just what use the teaching of all those phonic rules really is. To some it even seems morally wrong to pretend to young children that English is quite phonetic, knowing full well that the basic rules are frequently broken.

Unfortunately a few prominent academics drew some very unreasonable conclusions from this. They did not just advocate that the teaching of phonics should be abandoned. They began to argue that reading and writing needed no teaching at all. They recommended that children should be exposed to interesting books and then left to learn for themselves, or so the supporters of phonics like McGuinness now claim. I have never considered such suggestions worth looking at, and doubt that they were ever strictly followed by many classroom teachers. However, education in the English-speaking world did go through a phase when just making things interesting was seen as the answer to all learning problems.

I find it very hard to believe that many practising teachers were ever afflicted by this degree of lunacy. Nevertheless, the advocates of phonics often claim that the 'whole word' method resulted in many children being left to learn by themselves, instead of being taught to read and write by their teachers.

If that was really true, it immediately raises questions about the effectiveness of the phonics method itself. Children might now be achieving better test scores quite simply because they are *being taught* and *not because they are taught by a superior method. More* teaching, no matter by what method, is likely to make an enormous difference. Even with phonetically spelt languages children learn faster with some help from a teacher.

My own children must have passed through the primary stage during the height of the 'whole word' lunacy, as depicted by the current promoters of phonics. They attended two different, ordinary local first schools in England in the seventies, but they were certainly taught to read and write. They must have followed some kind of scheme, because they regularly brought home reading books. They also had little tins for words which they found troublesome. Their teachers wrote such words on small pieces of card, to take home for further practice each evening. I have no idea what the teachers would have called their methods, but they certainly taught my children to read and write.

What I could not help noticing about the words which my children brought home for additional practice was that they were *invariably ones with unpredictable spellings* (e.g. *although, any, do, through, thought, friend, one, only, said, they,* ...) The likes of *the, cat, dog, hand, sand, cave, drive, drove, stone* were never brought home. The tins were needed only for words with irregular, confusing or down-right nonsensical spellings - the ones that could not be taught by the phonic method alone.

My children's struggles with English spelling also made me realise just how much easier learning to read and write had been for me. Compared to the gargantuan hurdles facing them, becoming literate in Lithuanian had been child's play. I was first reminded of the difference when my daughter began to show an interest in learning to read at the age of 4, long before she started school. One day she asked me, *"Why is there an 'H' in 'John'?"* - Why indeed.

I could have explained that John probably has the H in it because it is related to the German name Johan, in which the H is sounded. I could have gone into the history of English spelling and etymology. Later on I sometimes did, but it always seemed such an unnecessary distraction from the business at hand - the one of learning to read and write.

Her questions multiplied, and I was repeatedly reminded of the contradictions that had once troubled me so much, but which I had forgotten during the intervening years. I was once again made aware of the vast numbers of puzzling English spellings conventions for which teachers cannot give good reasons or explanations.

Why should *'kick'* end in *'ck'*, while *'c'* is good enough for *'fantastic'*? Why does the *'l'* need to be doubled at the end of short words (*still, full, tell*...) when other letters don't (*bed, sit, swim, pun*..)? Why is there always an *'e'* after *'v'* at the end of words, even when this is totally useless (*have, give, live* ...), only making it harder to read the words where it does serve a purpose (*shave, drive, alive*..)? Exactly what is the compelling reason for still hanging on to the *'-ugh'* ending in *'although'*, other than just making life for learners vastly more difficult than it could be? What purpose does the *'i'* in *'friend'* serve? - other than making that word so hard to spell.

Teachers frequently resort to mnemonics in order to help children remember various English spelling peculiarities. E.g. *'I before E, except after C'*, although even that rule gets broken in *'weird'* and *'seize'*. - *'One collar, two socks'*, helps with the fiendishly difficult spelling of *'necessary'*, since children can relate this to the fact that we have only one neck but two feet.

Such devices are helpful, but the need for them is in itself evidence that English spelling is very hard to learn. They invariably divert children's concentration from what they are trying to communicate. For vast numbers of children keeping a grip on what they are trying to say when learning to write in sentences is hard enough. They could do without the extra layer of difficulty and distraction caused by unpredictable spellings.

'The Best Method of Teaching to Read and Spell English' is something which teachers have been trying to discover for a long time. It was the title of a book by James Dun published in 1766. In it he advocated:

1)   *"...begin with words that are absolutely regular, in the sense that they are pronounced in the way children would expect;"*

2)   *"...build into the exercises material that unobtrusively revises earlier work;"*

3)   *"...give special emphasis to the pronunciation of c and g, the first big difficulty ....introduce other difficulties progressively."*

Despite the millions of pages that have been written on the subject since then, nobody has yet come up with a better overall strategy. It is what good teachers have always used. It is also pretty much what the proponents of 'phonics' advocate, but they pay little heed the '*difficulties*' which, according to James Dun, need to be introduced *'progressively'*.

The proponents of phonics invariably minimise the difficulties caused by the unpredictability of English spelling. Dianne McGuinness, admits that young children are liable to try and apply phonic rules to all words, and that this tendency has to be corrected. However, she believes that *with controlled exposure,* the *'correct'* spellings can be attained quite effortlessly.

Reality proves otherwise. Classroom teachers invariably find that learning to spell *'correctly'*, learning *when not to use English phonic rules* is the more difficult part of literacy teaching. Learning to spell the 3695 words (listed on pages 262 - 70) which diverge from basic English phonic patterns in some way is what takes so much time and effort. No learner of average ability can achieve this in much less than 10 years, and even then only with regular practice and frequent testing.

Many foolproof teaching methods have been advocated over the years. Currently English primary schools follow the dictates of the Literacy Strategy and Literacy Hour, with much emphasis on the teaching of phonics.

After regular testing was first introduced in the mid 90's, there were dramatic improvements in children's test scores for a few years in succession, but they have remained almost completely static since the year 2000. It has been discovered, yet again, that around 25 % of learners cannot reach an adequate standard in reading and writing, especially writing.

The improved test scores may have reflected some real temporary improvement in reading and writing. The introduction of regular testing was accompanied by several measures which had previously been found to raise standards: literacy teaching was given more attention and a better time allocation; there was copious provision of new teaching materials and parents were put under pressure to read to their children and to help them more with their homework.

One other factor undoubtedly also helped to improve the test scores temporarily: teachers and pupils learned what the tests were all about. This meant they could prepare for them and even practise sitting them. Telling teachers exactly what they should teach always leads to improved scores in tests and examinations.

There is, however, a limit to the improvement in test scores which all the above-mentioned factors can bring - for as long as the chief underlying obstacle to progress remains unchanged. It was not surprising that before long children's test results proved impossible to raise any further.

What has been found once more is that, despite expending additional time and resources, around a quarter of all children simply cannot get to grips with English spelling. Even the most brilliant teachers cannot make much of a difference to this, and certainly not any particular teaching method.

For as long as English retains *'the faultes of our writing'* that John Hart pointed out in 1551, literacy acquisition will remain *'long in learning... and learned hard'*, and no teaching method can alter this. The problem has been around for centuries, and it looks as if it is going to stay with us for some time to come - unless we decide to make our outmoded spelling practices a little more logical and leaner-friendly.

Chapter 7

Spelling errors

Learning English as a foreign student, teaching it at secondary level and observing my own children learning to spell left me fairly certain as to what makes English spelling difficult. More recently, my investigations into English spelling pinpointed a few areas which were likely to give most learners trouble.

One way of finding out exactly what spellers find difficult is to see which words they misspell in their own writing, especially in tests and examinations, and to analyse their errors. I have therefore amassed and examined as many misspellings from different educational levels as I could find.

This chapter shows what kind of spelling errors students have been found to commit

1) in primary school tests,

2) at secondary school,

3) in English language examinations at the age of 16,

4) on a science course at Imperial College in London,

5) in an English examination at Oxford university.

It concludes with a brief examination of spelling errors made by secondary teachers of English.

7. 1. Primary Errors

In 1998 Ken Spencer, a lecturer in educational studies at the University of Hull, administered a 40-word spelling test to all 236 pupils aged 6 - 11 in an average primary school. After he had studied the results and used them for his own research project, Ken kindly allowed me to peruse those test papers too.

The test words had been selected from previous national literacy tests - 20 words from tests for 7-year-olds and the other 20 from lists for 11-year-olds. All children were tested with both lists. The words from the two tests can be seen in the tables below. Next to the words (in brackets) are the percentages of pupils who spelled each word correctly. The words are ranked from least misspelt to most often misspelt.

Table 1. 20 words chosen from national tests for 7-year-olds (and the percentages of pupils who spelled them correctly).

Hat(97), net(91), hand(85), fish(84), flag(83),
house(62), sock(61), boat(55), road(54),
morning(41), holiday(40), spade(39), shout(39), because(35)
smile(32) family(29) wait(27) friends(25) bucket(23)
pictures (13)

Table 2. 20 words from national tests for 11-year-olds.

Still(80), replace(72), crept(67),
heard(53), tallest(48), notice(44), silence(41),
visitors(37), disturbed(35), honest(35), piece(32),
remained(30), echoed (29), sneeze (28), uncoiled (26),
beautiful (24), shook (21), sprawling(21), slipped(17),
stretched(11).

The most striking feature of the results was that *the words which each class misspelled most often were identical*. The ranking order from least to most often misspelt word was also virtually the same for each year group.

A high proportion of children could spell the words which obeyed basic English phonic rules (e.g. *hat, net, hand, fish, flag*). The children could even cope quite well with various special rules (e.g. *still* - always doubling the final *l*; *replace* - the 'magic *e*' pattern and the final S-sound spelt mostly as -*ce*).

The results make it clear which aspects of English spelling cause learners problems. *Most errors consisted of making the wrong spelling choice, when sounds had alternative spellings*, as can be seen from some examples of pupils' misspellings in the box below.

Be**au**ti**fu**l: *buetiful, butiful, butifull*;

Cr**e**pt: *creapt, crepped*;

Di**st**u**r**bed: *disterbed, distirbed, desterbed*;

E**cho**ed: *eckoed, ecoed, ecowed, echoad*;

H**ea**rd: *heared, herd, hurd, hered*;

Hon**e**st: *onest, onist, honised*;

Not**ice**: *notise, notis*;

P**ie**ce: *peace, peice, pice, peece*;

Rem**ai**ned: *remaned*;

Sh**ook**: *shuck, shocke, shouk, shouck*;

Sil**e**n**c**e: *silance, silense, silnce*;

Sn**eeze**: *snease, sneez, sneese, snize, sneze*;

Sli**pp**ed: *slipt, sliped*;

Sti**ll**: *stil;*

Spr**aw**ling: *spralling, sprorling, sproaling*;

Str**etch**ed: *streched*;

Unc**oil**ed: *uncoyled, uncoild, uncoield*;

Visit**o**rs: *visiters*.

Even many of the simplest test words, ones which would be in most children's active vocabulary, contained sounds which were spelt differently in other common words:

bec**au**se - **was**;	b**oa**t - note, wrote;
b**u**cket - brother, c**ou**ntry;	fri**e**nds - tr**e**nd, l**e**nd;
heard - answered, feared;	holiday - holly, jolly;
hou**se** - how, mi**ce**;	m**or**ning - yawning;
pi**cture**s - pick, chair, others;	r**oa**d - rode, code;
so**ck** - park, magic;	sm**i**l**e** - style, island;
sti**ll** - until;	sp**a**d**e** - paid, raid;
w**ai**t - hate, late.	

Young children misspell because they try to spell logically, by analogy with other words which contain identical sounds. They get confused when identical sounds have different spellings. It is nearly always easy to see what their misspellings are based on.

> beautiful - *buetiful, butiful, butifull*
>   cf. **du**e, **du**tiful, **full**;
>
> crept - *creapt, crepped*
>   cf. l**eapt**, ste**pped**;
>
> disturbed - *disterbed, distirbed, desterbed*
>   cf. t**erm**, st**irr**ed, d**es**troyed.

Words with several unpredictable elements in them proved especially troublesome, as their attempts to spell the word *pictures* demonstrate:

> *pickchers, picchers, picktures, picturs, pictuers, pictrues, picters, pictres, pichures.*

Coping with the different spellings for the K-sound was clearly very difficult too:

> *beckos, buket, eckoed, ecoed, soc, sok, shoock.*

Knowing whether a verb had a regular or irregular past tense was also a problem:

> *crept - crepped, heard - heared, slipped - slipt, uncoiled - uncoild*

All the misspellings shown are taken from the children's test papers.

Table 3. Ken Spencer subsequently administered another 50-word spelling test to the same classes. After I had once again calculated the percentage of pupils who spelt each word correctly, I put all 90 words from both tests in rank order from least to most often misspelt. I also noted which elements in each word were misspelt most often. These are highlighted in the list below.

man(100),

hat(97), away(94), pond(92), net(91),

hand(85), fish(84), flag(83), named(83), coat(82), some(81), still (80), line (80),

brick(75), what(74), street(73), replace(72), lights(71), hair(71), corner (70), sunny(68), crept(67), asked(66), shopping(66), baker(64), near(64), seat(64), house(62), taken(62), white(62), first(62), sock((61), only(60),

boat(55), road(54), heard (53), wrong (52), camped (51), anything(49), tallest(48), pavement(48), weather(47), hurt(46), garage (45), notice (44), silence(41), morning(41), holiday(40),

widest(39), spade(39), shout(39), hopeful(39), carefully(38), visitors(37), disturbed(35), honest(35), because(35), almost (33), moving(33), piece(32), smile(32), quickly(31), direction(31), practice(31), creature(31), breeze(31), remained(30),

echoed(29), family(29), sneeze(28), wait(27), uncoiled(26), friends(25), beautiful (24), bucket(23), sprawling (21), shook (21),

grabbed(19), arrived(19), excluded(19), slipped(17), luckily(16) pictures (13), stretched (11), opposite (11), gradually (11),

mysterious(9), beginning(8), believe(7),

disappeared(2).

That list of 90 words shows even more clearly that spelling unpredictability causes spelling errors. The words which pupils could spell relatively well had either no unpredictable elements in them, or no more than one (e.g. man, hat, away, pond, net). Pupils misspelled predominantly those words which contained sounds which were spelt differently in other common words, e.g. *flag - egg,* *named - aimed,* *coat - note,* *some - sum, mum,* *still - until,* *line - find.*

The number of misspellings committed with a particular word was related to the amount of unpredictability within it. The word *'disappeared'* proved to have 6 sources of uncertainty (**di**/de - **s**/ss - **a**/u/e - **pp**/p - **ear**/eer/eir/ere - **ed**/d) and was consequently misspelt in some way by 98 % of pupils, i.e. all but a few exceptionally gifted spellers made some kind of error in the spelling of it.

All pupils misspelled longer words than short ones. This is partly because a long string of letters is easier to jumble up than a short one. Young spellers are especially prone to errors of transposition. The main reason, however, why longer words are more difficult to spell is because they almost invariably contain more spelling uncertainty. The four two-syllable words *'replace', 'corner', 'shopping'* and *'sunny'*, which follow dominant English spelling patterns closely, were spelt correctly by 60 % of pupils. By contrast, 7 shorter, one-syllable words which are spelt highly unpredictably were spelt accurately by only 40 % of pupils (i.e. *shook, shout, piece, breeze, sneeze, friends, wait*).

Practice made a difference. With age, pupils performed progressively better, but even the 10-11-year-olds were still a long way short of adult spelling proficiency. Only 56% of Year Six spelt more than 10 of the 20 harder words from the second list correctly. A fifth of that age group could not manage more than 5 words out 20.

7. 2 Words which secondary pupils find difficult

In the autumn of 2000 Mr. Blunkett, who was then Secretary of State for Education in England, inadvertently provided strong evidence that spelling unpredictability, rather than insufficient grasp of spelling rules, is chiefly responsible for spelling errors. His department produced a list of **600 difficult words** which he wanted secondary schools to teach more intensively.

Most the of words were listed under 14 subject areas (English, Maths, Science, History, Geography, Religious Education, Music, Drama, Personal and Social Education, PE, Art, Design and Technology, Information Technology, Library), with between 20 - 30 words for each. A few examples from each can be seen on the next page.

It is easy to see why pupils might misspell these words. (Unpredictable elements which are likely to cause spelling errors have been highlighted.)

English: advertise/advertisement, alliteration, apostrophe, atmosphere, chorus, clause…

Maths: addition, approximately, axis, decimal, enough, estimate, guess…

Science: acid, amphibian, apparatus, chemical, circulation, cycle, dissolve …

History: agriculture, bias, castle, cathedral, chronological, citizen, civilisation …

Geography: abroad, amenity, atlas, authority, climate, contour, country …

RE: Bible, Buddhist, burial, celebrate, ceremony, Christian, commandment, commitment …

Apart from the more specialised, subject-related vocabulary there was also a more general list of 150 words which teachers had collected. They knew that these were hard to learn because their pupils kept misspelling them despite their continuous efforts to remedy this.

Among them were many universally-known tricky words:
accommodation, actually, a_lot_of (written as one word), although, analyse …. believe, beneath, business … caught, chocolate, climb, column, conscience, conscious, … decide, definite, design, diary, …embarrass, environment …February, fierce, forty …guard …health, height …issue … jealous, knowledge, listening, miscellaneous, mischief, outrageous, people, queue, receive, Saturday, technique, Wednesday weight weird women.

These 10 sets of heterographs were also listed:
affect/effect, allowed/aloud, braking/breaking, course/coarse, our/are, practise/practice, sites/sights, source/sauce, threw/through, to/too/two).

(Surprisingly, two sets of heterographs which teachers have to correct ad nauseam *there/their/they're* and *it's/ its* were not among them.)

Many teachers felt insulted by Mr. Blunkett's list of 600 words. They saw it as yet another instance of blaming teachers for poor spelling standards. They already knew that these words needed special attention. They had been doing their best to enable pupils to spell them, but students kept getting them wrong, despite all their efforts. They had alerted Mr. Blunkett's department to them in the first place.

The list reminded me of Examiners' Reports for English which had repeatedly made me fume inwardly on reading them when I taught the subject. Year after year they trotted out a sentence or two on the lines of:

"It was disappointing to see so many pupils still showing confusion between some very common words. This year's crop included *'two, too, to'*, *'here, hear'....*"

Did the examiners genuinely not realise that teachers were busting a gut to prevent this? Could they really not see that the spellings were the source of all those constantly recurring errors rather than lack of effort by teachers and pupils? Most of the words on Mr. Blunkett's list are difficult to learn quite simply because they have irregular spellings.

Mr. Blunkett's list contains not just 600 but 673 words, because it does not count derivatives as separate words, although many of them have unpredictable spellings. Many are also difficult for inexperienced readers because they have shifting stress (e.g. *addict / addiction*) or changed vowel length (e.g. *Bible / biblical*) or both (e.g. *agile / agility*).

Of the whole list of 673 words, only 112 words have predictable spellings. However, most of these would be still unfamiliar to average 11-year-olds. They need to learn how to use them and not just to spell them, as they progress through their secondary education, for example,

combustion, composition, condensation, conjunction, constitution, contradiction, digestion, edition, fraction, friction, function.

561 words on Mr. Blunkett's list are liable to be misspelt because they *all contain unpredictable elements in them.* It was easy to identify five major sources of errors, with uncertainty about consonant doubling chief among them.

As explained earlier, consonant doubling is the main English spelling difficulty, because English has no reliable rules for consonant doubling in multi-syllable words. Many words which sound as if they should have doubled consonants fail to have them (e.g. *model*). Others have doubled consonants for reasons which are unrelated to their pronunciation (e.g. *apparent - with a stressed short vowel in the second syllable, not the first*). The single easily identifiable group of difficult words on Mr. Blunkett's list reflected this difficulty.

1) *Uncertainty about consonant doubling* made 163 words on Mr. Blunkett's list difficult to spell.

21 words <u>have doubled letters which follow a stressed, short vowel</u> (e.g. <u>a</u>*dd*ict, c<u>o</u>*mm*a, *e*ff*ort, m<u>a</u>*mm*al), as is meant to happen, according to the putative English consonant doubling principle;
    but
55 words with short, stressed vowels <u>do not have doubled consonants</u> after them (e.g. c<u>o</u>*lony*, <u>e</u>*lement*, <u>e</u>*nergy*, h<u>a</u>*bitat*, h<u>a</u>*zard*, l<u>i</u>*nen*, m<u>e</u>*lody*, p<u>a</u>*rable*).

47 words <u>fail to have their short, stressed vowels followed by a doubled consonant</u> *and also* contain other unpredictable elements:
    i) Some have irregularly spelt short vowels, as well as 'missing' doubled consonants (e.g. *acrylic, burial, jealous* - for what should really be *acrillic, berrial* and *jellous*).
    ii) Some words use a *c* instead of the *ss* which one would logically expect (e.g. *acid* for the word which is pronounced *assid, decimal* for *dessimal*)
    iii) Others are spelt even more unpredictability still (e.g. *discipline* rather than *dissiplin*; *synagogue* for what should really be *sinnagog*).

40 words have <u>doubled consonants, but not after a short and stressed vowel</u> (e.g. *accommod<u>a</u>tion, conn<u>e</u>ct, diss<u>o</u>lve*); some words even have a doubled consonant after an unstressed vowel, while a stressed, short vowel in the same word is not followed by one (e.g. n<u>e</u>*cessary*, p<u>a</u>*lette*, p<u>a</u>*rallel*).

2) *The EE-sound,* as in *'street'*, for which English has no dominant spelling pattern, occurs in 51 words on Mr. Blunkett's list (e.g. *achieve, athlete, beneath, keyboard, litre, metre, people, protein, region).*

3) 41 words spell *the short vowels 'e', 'i' and 'u'* unpredictably, i.e. not as in 'bet, bit, but' (e.g. *wealth, weather, Wednesday*; *dynasty, gym, system*; *country, stomach*).

4) 40 words do not follow *the 'magic e' pattern* for long vowel sounds with *'a', 'i'* and *'o'*, as in 'take', 'bite', and 'note', (e.g. *break, straight, weight; climb, design, height, lighting; control, roll*).

5) 41 words spell *the ER-sound* erratically, i.e. not as in 'mother' or 'her', (e.g. *author, binary, diary, grammar, major, murmur, survey, rehearse*).

Those five areas of inconsistency make 336 words on the list difficult to spell. Another 60 words contain either *silent letters* (e.g. chronology, parliament, rhythm), *irregular spellings of the S-sound* (e.g. citizen, scene) or *unpredictable spellings of the final L-sound* (e.g. cycle, identical, novel). The remaining 165 difficult words contain an assortment of unpredictable elements (e.g. *analysis, practice, practise*; *share, surely; choose, lose*; *harmony, simile; component, consonant; Jewish, Judaism*).

Mr. Blunkett sent out his word list mainly as an attempt to squeeze a little more measurable achievement from pupils in their first year at secondary school. British school children are now the most tested in Europe, and school tests had revealed that during the first 18 months at secondary school children did not make as much progress as they did year by year at primary level.

This does not mean that during this time children do not continue to learn a great deal. On entering secondary school pupils have to cope with the demands of making new friends, getting to know new teachers, finding their way around a much bigger complex of buildings and joining new clubs and groups of various kinds. They begin to learn several new subjects, each with their own specialist vocabulary, and perhaps even a second foreign language. In addition to this, their hormones are wreaking all kinds of havoc with their emotional and physical selves.

The move from primary to secondary school is tremendously stressful and demanding for most children. Parents almost invariably observe that for the first few months their children come home exhausted. They usually also have more homework than they were accustomed to and their lives change in other ways too. Many children have to get up much earlier than before, because they now have to travel to school, or to travel further than they did before. For those who travel by public transport there are additional social stress factors.

Alongside all this, pupils are suddenly faced with an enormous amount of difficult new spellings to learn. Just 25 words from each subject quickly add up to a list of around 600, as Mr. Blunkett's selection shows. This is a substantial extra load, even for pupils who have coped well with everything they had to learn so far. But large numbers of pupils start secondary education with only a feeble command of the spellings they were expected to have mastered at primary school.

Successive national tests in the UK have revealed that only just over half of 11-year-olds manage to reach government targets for writing. Having started secondary education ill equipped to cope with it, vast numbers of pupils also leave it still unable to spell many common words correctly by the time they reach 16.

7. 3 Spelling errors of 16-year-olds

English examination boards have amassed mountains of evidence over the years which shows that vast numbers of 16-year-olds in the UK commit numerous spelling errors. A research paper by A L Massey and G L Elliott of the University of Cambridge Local Examinations Syndicate, published in 1996 under the title *'Aspects of Writing in 16+ English Examinations between 1980 & 1994'* enables us to see the words which students misspell and how they misspell them.

The aim of the authors had been to establish whether spelling standards in the English Language examination had deteriorated over the period from 1980 - 1994. They were unable to reach firm conclusions on this for a variety of reasons, but their publication provides valuable insight into spelling.

The authors selected the papers of 30 boys and 30 girls from each grade category of already marked and graded essay papers for the years 1980, 1993 and 1994. They scrutinised the fourth sentence of each script and listed for each year, and separately for each grade, the words which pupils misspelled and how they misspelled them.

The three examinations were not identical. The exam system for 16-year-olds in the UK changed a great deal between 1980 and 1994. The 1980 and 1993 examinations were taken only by the upper end of the ability range, while the 1994 examination was open to all pupils. Therefore only data from the last exam provide information about the spelling skills of the whole ability range, and I therefore studied these more closely. Even they do not give the complete picture, because pupils whom schools deemed unlikely to gain even a G grade would not have been entered and are therefore missing from the results, so are pupils excluded from school for bad behaviour.

Nevertheless, we can be fairly certain that the results of the pupils taking the English Language examination in 1994 still give a fairly good picture of the spelling abilities of 16-year-olds in England today. There have been no significant changes in the structure of pre-16 secondary education since that time. Writing ability is also fairly resistant to change. Since the mid 1990's English primary schools have been under intense government pressure to raise literacy standards. Reading standards have consequently improved, but performance in writing has remained virtually unchanged, as evident from successive test scores since 1998.

In the 1994 GCSE English Language examination 480 pupils committed a total of 417 spelling errors in one sentence.

For each grade category the number of errors committed was as follows:

A*	-	10	D	-	40
A	-	6	E	-	63
B	-	12	F	-	120
C	-	25	G	-	141
		53			364

The least surprising result is perhaps that the pupils who were awarded A and B grades made very few spelling mistakes, since spelling accuracy has an impact on the grades which are awarded in an English examination.

Poor spelling is however not always a reliable indicator of poor writing. Some poor spellers write well and achieve high grades for other reasons, such as a wide vocabulary, a credible story line, well-sustained arguments and well-constructed sentences and paragraphs.

The 480 pupils misspelled a total of 338 words. The number of *misspelt words* is lower than the number of *errors* because several words were misspelt by more than one student. Also, for 10 errors the researchers could not identify the misspelt words, mainly because of some very poor handwriting in the grade categories F and G.

Of the total of 338 misspelt words, only 53 words (16%) followed basic English spellings patterns reliably. Even the errors committed with these words did not reveal poor grasp of basic English spelling rules. They were mainly just accidental slips, committed under examination pressure (e.g. *'a'* instead of *'and'*, *'at'* for *'that'* , *'cut'* for *'cup'*, *'it'* for *'is'*, *'is'* for *'his'*, *'lake'* for *'take'*, *'now'* for *'how'*, *'other'* for *'over'*, etc.).

Only the following words with predictable spellings were misspelled by pupils in each grade category:
A*: lantern, silence, stupid;
A : 0;
B : 0;
C : him, it;
D : coping, it, lady, living, on, opened, take, started;
E : hand, legs, may, mice, mistaken, mixed, smashed;
F : and, avoiding, but, exist, get, she, expected, his, how, lady, roses, than;
G : about, conditions, cup, drinking, for, game, gave, as, had, it, like, lot, mice, mum, November, opened, over, put, rest, rugby, sit, that, them, then, vacated.

The majority of misspellings committed in the 1994 GCSE English Language examination left little doubt why so many students keep making spelling errors in English. They misspell words with unpredictable elements in them. Even candidates who were awarded F or G grades, and probably had the poorest grasp of phonics, misspelled predominantly words that had something unpredictable in them. Only 18% percent of words which they spelled incorrectly (42 words out of 228) had reliable, phonemic spellings.

Many relatively simple words were clearly misspelt only because other common words, with identical sounds, have different spellings (e.g. *ladie* cf. budg**ie**, *leggs* cf. **egg**s, *mist**ea**ken* cf. st**ea**k, *wh**ell* cf. **wh**en, *sma**ch**ed* cf. ma**ch**ine). - Older children, just like younger ones, often fail to make the correct spelling choice, when different alternatives are on offer.

Not unexpectedly, the bulk of misspelt words had unpredictable elements in them, especially consonant doubling:
58 would normally be spelt with *doubled consonants,*
19 had *short vowels not marked by doubled consonants.*

Other clearly difficult words were:
29 which contained the long *EE-sound* (**pe**ople, p**ie**ce, rec**ei**ved)
29 with *unpredictably spelt short vowels* (**a**ny, fr**ie**nd, b**ui**ld, **o**ther),
27 with *unpredictably spelt long vowels* (c**o**ld, sh**ou**lder, sl**ow**ly),
25 stemming from 12 common sets of *heterographs*
  (been/bean, here/hear, knew/new, no/know, of/off,
  see/sea, there/their, threw/through, to/too/two,
  wear/where, weather/whether, which/witch).
24 compound*s* caused problems because of uncertainty about whether they should be spelt as *one word* (nobody), or *two words* (no one).

The remaining 74 misspelt words contained assorted elements of spelling uncertainty (e.g. **by** - bye - hi; **half** - laugh; **j**est - congest; sit - city; **you** - use).

It was noticeable that the weakest candidates, those who obtained F and G grades, were quite often affected by the *oo - ou - u - o - ow* overlap in words like *scoop - group - mould - country - fund - put - foot - woman - do - go - slow - now*. In Ken Spencer's primary tests the *'u'* in *'bucket'* and the *'oo'* in *'shook'* had also proved difficult for large numbers of pupils.

Knowing when a past tense verb was regular or irregular was also a recurring problem for weaker students (e.g. *burned, heard, played, paid*). So were the more complex English rules for adding suffixes (e.g. *comeing, dieing, enemys, geting, liveing*) and the use of apostrophes (e.g. *had'ent, it's for its, theyed*).

7. 4 Spelling errors of undergraduates and university graduates

Many pupils eventually manage to cope with memorising the thousands of unpredictable English spellings surprisingly well, in contrast to the even larger numbers who don't. Yet sadly, even after the age of 18 many very able students continue to commit spelling errors during their time in higher education. Not even university educated teachers of English are immune to this problem.

Dr. Bernard Lamb, a Genetics lecturer at Imperial College in London, and Bernard Richards, a retired lecturer of English at the University of Oxford, have both produced evidence for this. In the early 1980's each had become appalled by the spelling errors which many of their students were regularly committing and began to record them.

We can be certain that students at both of these prestigious institutions were very highly motivated and had achieved very good results in their A level examinations to qualify for entry to these colleges. The research conducted by Messrs. Lamb and Richards proves that high intelligence does not necessarily enable you to become a good speller of English. They also show that highly intelligent people commit most of their spelling errors with the same types of words as less clever ones do, apart from errors with unstressed half vowels (e.g. rele*va*nt, rel*a*vent - more detail on page 90).

Dr. Lamb became deeply interested in the spelling standards of school leavers and school teachers, as well as those of his own students. He has produced several publications on the subject. In a monograph published in 1992 he lists 83 sets of word *'confusions'* which his students were prone to commit, for example, *'whether/weather/wether', 'bred/bread'.*

Dr. Lamb has provided clear evidence that even very intelligent science students find *different spellings for identical sounds difficult to cope with.* His students were especially liable to be tripped up by different spellings for identically sounding whole words. He lists the following 30 heterographs.

Barr/bar	here/hear	sheer/shear
bare/bear	leech/leach	sight/site
boar/bore/boor	lose/loose	sow/sew
bread/bred	one/won	sun/son
by/buy	pales/pails	their/there
callus/callous/callose	pistil/pistol	to/too/two
course/coarse	principal/principle	were/where
dual/duel	pupal/pupil	when/wen
flour/flower	rite/write/wright	whether/weather
for/four	seems/seams	which/witch

Different spelling for identical sounds led to confusion in another 14 sets: beds/beads; breed/bread; sweet/sweat; nice/niece; lose/loose; slope/slop; bowel/bowl; rouge/rogue; moult/malt aseptic/asceptic, decent/descent, precedence/presidence; reenforces/reinforces; thymine/thiamine.

Difficulties with consonant doubling were evident in another 8 sets: as/ass; below/bellow; emersion/immersion; furry/fury; offspring/ofspring; strarred/stared; striped/stripped; wadding/wading.

Dr. Lamb's students also made a few slips which he considered as *absentminded*, but consonant doubling was implicated in most of those too. Some involved consonants which are unrelated to keeping a vowel short (accept/except; acceptable/expectable), others had no doubled consonant after a short, stressed vowel (forest/forage; mineral/minimal). [If the English consonant doubling rule applied consistently, these would be spelt *'forrest/forrage'* and *'minneral/minnimal'*].

A quarter of 'confusion errors' were not really just simple spelling errors: 21 sets of 'confusions' demonstrated that some science students took a while to master their new scientific vocabulary, or simply more sophisticated English vocabulary:

---

affected/infected;   amylase/amylose;   antigen/antibody;   assume/deduce; axons/exons; confirmation/conformation; denote/donate;   elevate/alleviate; fertilisation/feminisation;   infer/imply;   inferred/conferred; invariable/inviable;   nucleation/nucleotides;   prescribed/proscribed; proline/proflavin;   reverberant/revertant;   resembled/reassembled riboflavine/ribose;   stimulate/assimilate;   suspensions/solutions; temperate/temporary.

Just six sets of confusions listed by Dr. Lamb can be ascribed to obvious lapses in concentration (air/our;   laying/lying;   locus/locust; preform/perform; rape/ripe; would have/would of). The majority of genuine spelling confusions by his students (58 out of 64) can be seen to stem from difficulties inherent in the English spelling system.

As part of his investigations into spelling standards, Dr. Lamb selected 35 words for closer monitoring. They were ones which had attracted his attention because previous cohorts of his students had often misspelt them. During the academic year 1990-91 Dr. Lamb recorded systematically how 110 first year Life Science undergraduates misspelled them in their practical books.

Among the 35 words were a few names of famous geneticists and also some scientific terms, which clearly involved new learning, in addition to spelling, but 22 of them were ordinary English words. Unsurprisingly, these all contained at least one very obvious element of spelling uncertainty. Also predictably, consonant doubling turned out to be a salient problem. It is not difficult to see why many of Dr. Lamb's students misspelled the following 22 words:

---

aberration, inoculate, necessary, occurred, occurrence, occurring, effect/affect, complementary/complimentary, , its/it's, whether/weather, extreme, height, striped, airborne, environment, independent, miniature, reciprocal.

Dr. Lamb also lists 58 'terrible spellings' (in his view) which his students produced between 1986 - 1992. These also all contained easily identifiable spelling problems. Three sources of errors were especially evident, occurring in over half of the total.

Doubled consonants featured in 13 misspelt words:

abberation, allign, assexual, bakk, deciferred, clooting, godd, flamming, occured, intelegent, prosses, rippens, sorpressor.

Unstressed half-vowels in 12:

anterrhinum, negitive, charicters, charecters, disintergrates, incedants (for 'incidence'), relavent , riciprical, riquire, seperatly, simalar, segrogate.

The EE-sound in 10:

beas, desiese, extream, extreem, extreame, feading, geen, obsolite, sheats, reeding.

The remaining lapses can be traced to assorted vagaries of the English spelling system:
aline, hight, hieght, hibrid;
delt, streatching;
cirtain, firtile;
asceptically, coinsides;
shair, fushion, envoirment, groth, precortions, youthenasia, etc..

Students of English at the University Oxford can safely be assumed to be some of best spellers in the world. Yet even they misspell some quite common English words, and for much the same reasons that others do, as Bernard Richards' investigations show.

Their errors with ordinary words also stem from phonic contradictions and general disregard for the alphabetic principle evident in English spelling conventions. The 1995 cohort misspelled 61 ordinary, widely used words.

---

19 misspellings stemmed form **uncertainty about consonant doubling**:
accross, adressed, agression, attatchment, collosal, collumn, disatisfaction, embarassing, exagerated, axcelerating, melodrammatic, occassion, ocurs, padel, priviledge, revellation, ridgedly, sillouette, squallor.

16 misspellings involved **unstressed half-vowels**:
apparant, prominant, relavent, referance; definately, indefinate, comparitive, imaginitive; coincedence, devestating, dispair, gullable, monotinous, rediculous, seperate, solomn.

10 misspellings inserted **silent letters**:
angery, arguement, disasterous, develope, dosen't, inherites, twighlight,

or omitted them: *wether* (for whether), *boundries, rythm* (for **rhythm**).

4 misspellings contained the **EE-sound**:
acheived, concieted, discreet, greivious.

The remaining 12 misspellings were due to **assorted unpredictable elements of English spelling**:
endevour, gratefully, lable; abolishion, concience, conciousness, viscious; absense, critisized; fued, grusome; style(for stile).

One kind of error which was frequently committed by students in higher education but was not noticeable in the misspellings of young children or 16-year-olds was the misspelling of unstressed half-vowels. Among the misspellings of students at Oxford in their English Language and Literature examinations in 1986 and in 1995, 47% of errors were misspellings of unstressed vowels (e.g. *anomoly, imaginitive, indefinately*). This is probably because unstressed half-vowels occur mainly in more sophisticated English vocabulary, the kind which is learned predominantly at university.

After university many well-educated adults remain prone to spelling errors too. Dr. Lamb lists 26 words which teachers of English misspelled when replying to a questionnaire about the teaching of spelling which he had sent to secondary schools. In this small sample English teachers made errors with:

---

consonant doubling:
    innaccurate, proffession, apalling, targetted, accomodate, dissatisfaction;

the spelling of unstressed half-vowels:
    encorporate, grammer, independant, prosribed [for prescribed], *optomism, intergrated, contreversial, consoledating;*

silent letters:
    burocratic, govermment, moral (for morale), *therfore, loose* [for lose], *none-contact;*

and **a few assorted unpredictable elements** of English spelling:
    abismal, leftie, practise, bi-product, academea;

as well as the occasional absentminded slip: *attracitive.*

Dr. Lamb claimed that spelling standards in the UK had deteriorated during the 1980s. He believed that this deterioration was due mainly to poorer teaching and also to teachers becoming less concerned about spelling errors, often not correcting them in pupils' writing.

Mr. Richards also believed that he had evidence for a deterioration in spelling proficiency. He found more misspelt words on Oxford examination scripts of 1995 than in 1986, with 141 and 80 errors respectively, but this difference may not stem from generally worse spelling standards. The difference may be due simply to the increase in student numbers which has occurred at all UK universities over the past few decades.

The expansion of higher education means that students from a broader band of intelligence now attend university, not merely the top 5%, as was the case until 30 years ago. Since only the brightest have ever managed to spell English really well, university lecturers now inevitably encounter more scripts with spelling errors.

Even if there has been a slight deterioration in spelling ability over the last two decades, this may not be due to poorer teaching. There have been various technological and social changes which now make it more difficult for students to master the thousands of unpredictable English spellings than in the past. Students are now less exposed to the written word than previous generations. With the spread of video recorders and computers, they no longer acquire as much of their knowledge from written sources. Outside schools hours too, new forms of entertainment have come to compete with reading and writing. School curricula have also expanded a great deal between those years. Intensive and regular teaching of spelling now has to compete for time with a wider range of subjects.

The bottom line is, that with English spelling being as unpredictable as it is, to become an accurate speller requires a great deal of practice, a fairly high level of basic intelligence and a special kind of visual memory. Dr. Lamb and Mr. Richards have both provided evidence that even a university education, with its extensive note-taking and essay-writing, is insufficient to enable all intelligent graduates to spell faultlessly. Even for intelligent people learning to spell English is an endless process. As they go through life, they keep learning new spellings and forgetting some of those they learned earlier.

In the book *'Super Speller'* the late Graham King provides a list of 2000 words which have been found to give trouble to large numbers of people. Most them are not among the more common vocabulary used in this study, but the majority of them are not extremely rare or unfamiliar either: e.g. *abacus, abattoir, abbreviate, abdominal, aberration, abhorrent, abscess.*

Graham King believed that *'basic human laziness'* was the main cause of poor spelling. He does however also recognise that *"The difficulty with spelling begins with the way in which written English handles the sounds of the language."*

He is wrong about the *'difficulty'* being merely the beginning. Disregard for the alphabetic principle causes English spelling problems from beginning to end. It ensures that half of all children at primary and secondary school manage to acquire only rudimentary spelling competence. For many people in the upper half of the intelligence range spelling also remains a long-lasting bane.

Some spelling difficulties affect predominantly just young learners or weaker students, but a few deficiencies inherent in the English spelling system are particularly noisome. They give young children a hard time at the start of their education and affect many spellers ever after.

The majority of spelling errors committed by young and old alike are to due mainly to the following 5 unalphabetic elements in English spelling:

Consonant doubling,
the spellings of the long EE-sound,
divergent spellings for short and long vowels,
the various spellings for unstressed half-vowels,
silent letters.

Chapter 8

A brief history of the English language
and English spelling

or How we ended up with such a mess on our hands

All European writing systems have developed from the Sumerian script which originated in the Middle East about 5000 - 6000 years ago. Around 1000 BC the Greeks modified this by adding vowels to it. Five hundred years later the Romans adapted the Greek alphabet to suit their needs. Other European languages then developed their alphabets from the Latin one.

In the days of the Roman Empire Latin spread across most of Europe. It was brought to England in AD 43, when the Romans began to settle here almost a century after Caesar's first exploratory invasion in 55 BC. The Romans stayed in Britain for three and half centuries. When they finally withdrew in 410, England was plunged into what are now referred to as the Dark Ages, because for at least two centuries of English history there are no written records.

Latin was brought back to England by Christian missionaries, beginning with St. Augustine in 596. English writing developed from this during the 7th century. The oldest surviving English texts date from around 700. England was the first country in Europe to adapt the Latin alphabet for a writing system of its own.

When alphabets are first established, their designers usually try to ensure that the symbols which they adopt represent the speech sounds of the language in question as reliably and efficiently as possible. Those who have studied the oldest surviving manuscripts of Anglo-Saxon have concluded that English once had a very consistent alphabet too.

Unfortunately, all spelling systems get out of synch with the spoken language after a century or two, because living languages are incessantly changing. This is barely perceptible at any given moment in time, but easily noticeable over longer periods. We are now able to detect changes in pronunciation and vocabulary when listening to early radio and television programmes. Over a shorter time span these changes would have been difficult to register.

Since the end of the fifth century, when Saxon tribes from Northern Europe first brought English (or *Engle, Anglic* or *Anglisc*) to England, the English language has undergone many changes. We have no tape recordings of early Anglo-Saxon and can only trace the development of the language by studying texts which have survived from various points in its long history.

Most of us cannot gain ready access to the originals. Only a very small number of manuscripts from the earliest period of English writing are still in existence and have to be carefully protected to ensure their continued survival, but numerous books contain short extracts from them. The Cambridge Encyclopedia of the English Language, for instance, contains examples of English writing from its infancy and throughout its later development.

Copies of the hand written originals are almost impossible to read without some training. Even printed versions of them are difficult to decipher at first sight. This is because they contain many words which are no longer in use today, and those which have survived into modern English were nearly all spelt differently 1000 years ago. Moreover, from careful analysis of early poetry and its rhymes, linguists have concluded that early English would have been pronounced very differently too.

Anglo-Saxon vocabulary was almost entirely Germanic, and everyday English still contains many items from this source. German has also changed over time, but the family likeness is still unmistakable in hundreds of modern German and English words. It is not difficult to find the English cousins of the following German words:

Brot (bread), *Butter, Milch, Wasser, Suppe*;
Mutter (mother), *Vater, Bruder, Schwester, Sohn, Tochter, Mann, Weib,*
Arm (arm), *Hand, Ellbogen, Knee, Nase, Kinn, Ohr, Haar;*
Haus (house), *Garten, Feld; Tag* (day), *Nacht, Jahr;*
*bring*en (to *bring*), *sing*en, *spring*en, *trink*en, *wasch*en.

With minimal training one can see the common ancestry in many more:

Macht - might, *Licht* - light, *Furcht* - fright, *Woche* - week, *Monat* - month, *alt* - old, *jung* - young, *blau* - blue, *weiss* - white, *danken* - to thank, *denken* - to think, *essen* - to eat, *trauen* - to trust.

One major difference between Anglo-Saxon and modern English is grammatical. Anglo-Saxon grammar was far more complex than that of today's English. We now regularly add just four kinds of endings to the basic form of words:

1. **-ing** endings for ongoing or continuous action (e.g *ongoing*);

2. **-s/-es** endings for verbs in the 3rd person in the present tense
    (e.g. he *works* and *washes*, while I, you, we and they *work* and *wash*);

3. **-'s** endings to indicate possession (e.g. *mother's* milk);

4. plural **-s/-es** endings (e.g. *one book - two books, kiss - kisses*), but this pattern is not quite as systematic as the other three; it is undermined by several irregular plurals (e.g. m**ou**se - m**i**ce, wi**f**e - wi**v**es).

Several more suffixes can be added to root words to create other words, but they are not completely systematic. We *sometimes* use the **-ed** ending to form the past tense of verbs (e.g. *'worked', 'stepped')*, but the majority of the most commonly used verbs (150 in all) do not follow this pattern (e.g. 'brought', 'dreamt', 'kept', 'slept', 'took'). We *predominantly* form adverbs by adding **-ly** to adjectives (e.g. *'slow' - 'slowly')*, but again by no means always: we work *'well'* and *'fast'*, not 'goodly' or 'fastly'.

English words once had many more grammatical endings. Verbs in the present tense, for example, were very similar to those which German still has now. The verb *drehen* (to turn) takes the endings:

Ich drehe, du drehst, sie dreht, wir drehen.

In middle English this was:

I turne, thou turnest, she turneth, wee turnen.

By the 14th century, when Chaucer wrote the Canterbury Tales, the number of such endings had already diminished substantially, but he still used more than we do now.

Some linguists now think that the Vikings may be chiefly responsible for the simplification of English grammar. They began to invade the island and to settle in the Northeast at the end of the 8th century. Before long they were trading and intermarrying with local inhabitants, as well as those from adjacent regions.

It is believed that the Anglo-Saxons and Anglo-Vikings (i.e. the Saxons and Vikings who settled in England and their descendants) would have been able to communicate with each other quite easily because they spoke only slightly different versions of the same Germanic language. The main differences between them were probably just word endings. In their dealings with each other they would have soon learnt that they could understand each other best if they emphasised the main parts of the words and made little of their endings. Before long all inessential endings were dropped altogether, and English grammar became very much simpler.

Nearly all European languages first adopted grammatical systems with changing (or inflected) word endings on the model of Latin. In English only a few of them still survive (e.g. mother - mother*s*, mother*'s*; to write - he write*s*, I am writ*ing*). Several European languages continue to use many more changing word endings than English.

German, for one, has many more than just the changing verb endings already listed above. For example, '*the man*' is '*der Mann*' when used as subject (e.g. '*The man* led the way'.) When used as an object (e.g. 'I know *the man*'), '*der Mann*' becomes '*den Mann*'; when indicating possession (*the man's*) it changes to '*des Mannes*'; and '*to the man*' translates as '*dem Mann*'.

German is now also undergoing some of the grammatical simplification which occurred in English several centuries ago. *Dem Mann*, for example, used to have an -e ending (*dem Manne*) until quite recently. In spoken German some verb endings are now being eliminated. The *-e* ending, as in *ich bringe, trinke*, is generally no longer pronounced. It is still obligatory in formal writing, but is already much omitted in private correspondence.

In spoken *French* many erstwhile word endings have also been eliminated, but written French staunchly preserves them all. For example, the verb *to speak* is *parler*. It is pronounced *parl* when used with *je, tu, il/elle, ils/elles*, but is written as *je parle*, t*u parles*, *il parle*, *ils partlent*. This amounts to spelling *speak* (with *I, you, he* and *they*) as *I speake, you speakes, he speake, they speakent*, yet pronouncing the word in each case just *speak*.

The development of *English* has proved that the Latin model of grammar, with its many changes in word endings can be simplified. In this respect English is undoubtedly *the most advanced and modern European language*. Its grammar became simplified as different Germanic and Latin antecedents became fused in it. It is far more of a hybrid than most other major European languages which have developed mainly from just Germanic or Latin roots, and hybrids often flourish better than their parent stock.

The Norman invasion of 1066 also changed the English language and helped to simplify its grammar still further. After the Conquest, Norman French quickly replaced English as the official language at court and all offices of state. The ruling barons spoke French, and all those who wanted to get on in life were soon speaking it too. As a result of this, for almost 200 years English continued to be spoken predominantly just by the illiterate lower classes.

It is highly likely that if English had been left in the hands of the least sophisticated classes of Norman society for a little longer, the '-s' ending of verbs in the third person (e.g. make**s**) would probably not have survived either. We can see simpler folk still attempting to simplify English grammar to this day, as in *'he **be** here later'*, but such sensible changes have become more difficult to implement than they were in preliterate times.

English began to re-gain its status as the dominant language of England in the 13th century, when Norman supremacy began to diminish. Much of continental Normandy was gradually lost to France. The rest became property of English Kings, instead of England belonging to Norman Kings, as had been the case during the previous 150 years; but it took another 200 years before the English language was fully re-established as the official tongue of England.

The Hundred Years War between England and France which began in 1337 did much to restore the prestige of English. Edward III had to treat his nobles with some deference because he needed their soldiers and money to fight his war. He periodically had to call Parliaments to raise revenue. Since much of the nobility refused to speak French by then, the King had no choice but to follow if he was to obtain their assistance.

English was first spoken in Parliament in 1362, when it was also decided that the language used in the law courts should henceforth be English. Even more significantly, Henry IV used English instead of French when claiming the throne of England in 1399. He was the first king to do so for three and half centuries. In the 2nd half of the 14th century Chaucer also wrote the Canterbury Tales in English, and John Wyclif produced the first English Bible.

French was still used as the language of instruction in grammar schools up to the time of the first plague in 1348, but not after it (according to a written comment made by the Oxford scholar John of Trevisa in 1387). In the second half of the 14th century children who were privileged enough to be educated were learning English in its own right and were taught other subjects in their own language. Gentlemen were no longer teaching their children French at home either.

The end of the Hundred Years war with France dealt the final blow to French linguistic domination of England. As the country lost most of its territorial possession on the Continent, the people of England lost all vestiges of affection for the language of their enemy. This helped to re-instate English as the official language of England. From 1430 onwards even the *Chancery clerks*, the King's official scribes and civil servants of that time, had to stop using French and Latin and switch to English for all official documents, record keeping and correspondence.

The Chancery clerks did not merely have to abandon their old writing habits. Hurriedly, they also *had to invent a system for spelling English*; and they had to do it almost from scratch. The very small number of texts which had survived from pre-Conquest times would have been incomprehensible to them, because the English language had changed very drastically during the intervening centuries. By the end of Norman supremacy the higher strata of society had become increasingly bilingual. By the time English reasserted itself, many French words had inevitably become part of English speech, and many Anglo-Saxon words had acquired a different pronunciation or meaning. Many other old words had fallen out of use altogether.

This was partly because England itself had changed a great deal since 1066. There had, for example, been no castles in Saxon England and therefore no word for such structures in Anglo-Saxon speech. As these Norman fortifications became part of the English landscape, the French word for them became part of the English language. This would have been equally true of many other changes introduced by the Normans, especially in administration and the dispensation of justice.

English writing had first begun to reappear in the 13th century and grew steadily in the next, but the Chancery clerks of 1430 would have been unable to use much of this as a basis for a new English spelling system. For as long as all copying was done by hand, books remained expensive and scarce. What also prevented the clerks from using them as a source of English spelling rules was that each author followed his own spelling style, and even that inconsistently. Identical words were regularly spelt in several different ways - not just in the same book, but on the same page.

A further difficulty for anyone attempting to devise an English spelling system in the 15th century was that quite different varieties of English, with different vocabularies, had evolved in different parts of the country. This had already begun before the Norman conquest, but the trend intensified when French became the dominant language.

In the first half of the 15th century England did not yet have any kind of Standard English. This was still evolving in the linguistic melting pot of London, as the capital's trade and industries were attracting increasing numbers of people from all regions, but especially the East Midlands around Oxford and Cambridge. The clerks of the Chancery, by virtue of their elevated official position, were undoubtedly themselves contributing to the development of Standard English, as well as establishing conventions for spelling it.

The Chancery scribes were not academic linguists. They would certainly not have had much time for lengthy consideration of spelling issues. Suddenly they simply had to start writing English. Inevitably, they carried on using many of the French and Latin spelling conventions which they were accustomed to, especially as many words were then still pronounced identically in both French and English.

Even if the pronunciation had already become Anglicised, they were likely to continue using the French spelling conventions by force of habit. After all, the words 'couple' and 'double' have been pronounced the English way (as 'cupl' and 'dubl', instead of 'coopl' and 'doobl', as in French) for a very long time, but we still spell them according to French rules now.

The most important event in the standardisation of modern English spelling was probably *the invention of printing presses* and their importation to England in1476. When William Caxton started his business in London, he set it up only a short distance form Chancery Lane. His establishment was therefore very much influenced by the new official spelling standard which the clerks had hurriedly cobbled together. Unfortunately, Caxton and his assistants merely helped to make it more chaotic.

Caxton had lived abroad for 30 years. On his return to England he felt anything but confident about his command of the language. In the Prologue to one of his books he expresses concern about his 'sympleness and vnperfightness' in it. He wrote that the Kentish dialect which he had learned as a child had been very different from that which was spoken in London in the 1470s. The foreign assistants whom Caxton brought with him from the Netherlands to help him run his printing business were even less proficient in English than he was.

Of great significance for the eventual standardisation of English spelling was also the fact that spelling consistency was something that nobody paid much heed to when the printing of English books first began. At the end of the 15th century and throughout the 16th, the few people who could write, spelt as they pleased. Even Queen Elizabeth I, who was probably one of the most highly educated individuals of that period, regularly used several spellings for identical words.

Type-setters were certainly far more concerned with the look of the page than with spelling consistency. They happily decorated words with additional letters, like an extra -e or a doubled consonant, to avoid having too much blank space at the end of a line. Neat margins had a much higher priority than spelling regularity. In addition to this, individual compositors within a printing establishment followed their own spelling instincts. As the number of printing houses increased, English spelling became ever more varied.

Spelling discrepancies began to attract attention as the volume of printed material increased and more people learned to read. Those who taught children to read in particular, found that the proliferation of different spellings made both learning and teaching the subject difficult. They began to call for standardisation, and English spelling then became the subject of academic debate.

Some teachers like John Hart (1569) and scholars like Sir Thomas Smith (1568) immediately sought more than just the adoption of a single agreed spelling per word. They advocated that the representation of English sounds should also be made more predictable. They wanted a spelling reform which would provide one agreed spelling for each sound, as well as each word.

Others were vehemently opposed to making the English spelling system as whole more orderly. They believed that adopting just the most popular current spelling for each word would be sufficient to make teaching easier, and this view has predominated ever since.

The most prominent opponent of reform was the eminent headmaster Richard Mulcaster, one-time High Master of St. Paul's school in London. He argued that popularity should be the key determinant when a choice between alternative spellings had to be made. He was inclined to be guided by the phonetic principle only when two spellings were used equally often, and therefore genuinely competing with each other. If, for example, *'same'* and *'saim'* both occurred equally frequently, then *'same'* would be his preferred option. In less equal instances, the *'more usual'* form was the one he would recommend, even if the other was more phonetic.

Mulcaster's intellectual prestige helped the anti-reformers win the battle, but most of his influence on the future of English spelling came from compiling a list of his preferred spellings for nearly 9000 words. He appended his spelling list to a book (*The first Part of the Elementarie* , published in 1582) in which he outlined his views on the need for the standardisation of English spelling and his hostility to more fundamental reform. In it he also formulated some English spelling rules. He was, for example, the first to clarify the use of the *'magic e'* (as in *'cake'*). Ironically this eventually led to *'silent e'* being dropped from hundreds of words where it did not serve the 'magic' function (e.g. *'beene'*, *'scorne'*). He thereby effected some spelling reforms, despite being opposed to them.

His book was written as a contribution to academic debate on spelling. It was not intended to be of direct help to teachers, but it set the direction for the first generation of English text books which then came into being. The most influential of these was Edmond Coote's *The English Schoole-maister*, published in 1596. This concerned itself only with the teaching of reading and writing and consisted mainly of a list of 1400 difficult spellings for pupils to learn, as a minimum requirement for entry to a grammar school. This list was of more immediate use to teachers than Mulcaster's 9000 words.

Coote's book became very popular and had a great effect on the final standardisation of English spelling during the 17th century because it influenced generations of printers. Scholarly debates at the universities were less successful in changing their habits. This was partly at least because they were often still conducted in Latin. Even Sir Thomas Smith's book which was about English spelling and the advantages of spelling reform, was still written in Latin (*De recta et emendata lingue anglicae scriptione dialogus, 1568).*

Modern English spelling conventions were thus established chiefly by a circular process during the 16th and 17th centuries. Schoolmasters promulgated the favourite spellings of printers, although these had often been arrived at in a whimsical or haphazard manner. Printers wanted to sell books and knew that they were most likely to succeed in this by pleasing the public - by printing the spellings which people would find agreeable, i.e. those spellings which they had become familiar with in their elementary reading books. So the printers in their turn adopted the spellings which were most commonly taught. As printers gradually fell more into line with common spellings, the spelling lists which children were taught changed accordingly, and so forth. At no time, then or since, did anyone stop to examine if the spellings they were using or recommending were sensible according to alphabetic principles.

Apart from the printers and schoolteachers, there was also one group of academics who had a fairly substantial effect on the standardisation of modern English spelling. These were the 54 university scholars whom *King James I* appointed to produce a new English translation of the *Bible*, which was published in 1611. These learned gentlemen conferred with each other regularly on points of meaning and linguistic usage, and inevitably made some spelling decisions too.

Their spellings were often still inconsistent, just like the spellings of other writers of that time. In the Preface to this Bible, for example, we find *'we'* and *'wee'* used in one sentence, as can be seen in the two extracts below. (All words with spellings which diverge from modern conventions have been underlined.)

"An other thing we thinke good to admonish thee of that wee haue not tyed our selues to an vniformitie of phrasing, or to an identie of words as some peraduenture wish that we had done, that some learned men some where, haue beene as exact as they could that way...

For is the kingdome of God become words or syllables? why should wee be in bondage to them if we may be free, vse one precisely when wee may vse another no lesse fit...?"

The above short extracts from the Preface reveal that English spelling continued to change after 1611. They enables us to see, for example, that:

1) Many words which we now write as one could then be separate or not,
  e.g. *an other* or *another, our selues, some where.*

2) *u* and *v* were interchangeable, e.g. *haue, selues, vniformitie, peraduenture;*

3) many more words than now were still spelt with a *decorative final e,*
   e.g. *beene, kingdome, lesse;*

4) *y* and *ie* were used differently, e.g. *identitie, curiositie, tyed.*

It needs to be noted that the Bible's spelling style, as well as language, were conservative. For example, many writers were by then already distinguishing between *v* and *u*. The Bible translators reverted to the earlier custom of not doing so, perhaps to enhance the impression that this work was something which had been handed down from earlier generations. Their work therefore slowed rather than accelerated the modernisation of English spelling.

The spellings they used became influential because this Bible, and later editions of it, were soon placed in every church in England. It then made its way into most homes and became the most read book in the country. The spellings used in it inevitably became very familiar, and any printer with commercial sense soon adopted them.

During the 17th century academics had slightly more influence on English spelling, but again they only made it more difficult. University dons of that century had little respect for English. They held Greek and Latin in far higher esteem. Oxford and Cambridge continued to use Latin as the language of instruction long after English had come into regular use elsewhere, including Parliament and the Law.

In the 16th and 17th centuries scientific advances and the general expansion of knowledge during the Renaissance required the introduction of thousands of new words. Numerous imports from Greek and Latin were added to English vocabulary during this time. Since Greek and Latin were able to provide an almost endless stream of words for all requirements, they came to be regarded as superior languages, and attempts were made to remodel English on their lines. For example, the prefixes *'im-'* and *'in-'* were preferred to the common English *'un-'*, as in *'un*believable', and introduced wherever possible (e.g. *'im*possible', *'in*credible').

The study of the origins of words also took off as an academic interest, especially the search for Greek and Latin roots. English words which are deemed to stem from Latin but no longer showing their ancestry clearly enough, were given extra letters. To this we owe, for example, the silent letters in 'd*oubt*' and '*debt*'. The '*b*' was inserted to show their link to '*dubious*', and '*debit*', thereby altering their earlier simpler spellings of '*dout*' and '*det*'. Fortunately this misguided approach had only very limited effect on the printers.

By the end of the 17th century the different printing houses had arrived at almost identical spelling conventions. In the 1625 edition of Shakespeare's plays different type-setters can still be identified by their spelling preferences, one using *doe, goe, here* and another *do, go, heere*. Fifty years later such discrepancies had become rare.

Some words still had more than one spelling as late as the 18th century, and several writers, including Jonathan Swift, pleaded for final standardisation of spelling, as well as word usage. They were worried that if continuous linguistic change and alteration of spelling was not arrested, their writings would become inaccessible to future generations of readers. In 1635 the French had set up an Academy to regulate French spelling and usage. Swift urged that something similar should be done in England. What England ended up with was a single-handed arbiter - in the person of Dr. Samuel Johnson.

Johnson's main aim was to clarify the meaning of English words, as exemplified in the writings of prominent authors. He spent three years reading books, which others readily provided for him once it became known that he had started the project, and marking passages for future reference. These were then copied by his team of six assistants and collated, word by word in alphabetical order. Johnson then studied them carefully before compiling his own definitions. The first pages were printed in 1750 and the whole work published in 1755.

Johnson compiled an outstanding dictionary of the English language, and before long every educated household possessed one, alongside the Bible and the works of Shakespeare. The work was inevitably used as an authority on spelling as well as word usage. Johnson thereby ensured that the spelling conventions established by printers were adopted for private as well as professional use, and virtually set English spelling in tablets of stone.

Johnson's spelling choices have undergone only minor amendments over the past two and half centuries. The main alteration has been to change unstressed *-ick* endings to *-ic* (e.g. *traffic* and *music* for what had earlier been *traffick* and *musick*).

Since Johnson's time, compilers of dictionaries have taken over from printers as the fixers of English spellings, but the relationship between arbitration and usage has remained circular. Dictionaries spell mostly according to how prominent English writers have done before, and new generations of writers consult dictionaries for spelling.

Since printing first began in England in 1476 there has never been a deliberate, serious attempt to make English spelling more systematic. It continued to change for another three centuries, but the alphabetic principle was consistently ignored in favour of common usage. Those who had the most substantial effect on English spelling and were in a position to make it more alphabetic - Mulcaster in the 16th century, Coote in the 17th and Johnson in the 18th - had little regard for the alphabetic principle. Each believed that fixing the most popular spellings of his time was his chief priority.

Coote was fully aware that the spelling conventions of his time made learning to read more difficult. To help beginners, he used simplified spellings in the first part of *The English Schoole-maister* - 'as *templ* without (e) and *plums*, not plummes etc.'. He asked the reader to *'marvaile not why ...I have there put no moe letters (than) are of absolute necessitie'*. But he stresses that in his normal writing and in the rest of his book *'I have followed custome'*.

For Johnson there was *'general and lasting advantage'* in *'constancy and stability'*. The alphabetic principle was not something that he saw of relevance to English , *'Much less ought our written language to comply with the corruptions of oral utterance,…'*. The oral development of the language which had occurred in the course of 1200 years counted for nothing with him.

Many people assume erroneously that **Shakespeare** must have had a great influence on English spelling, but he appears to have had none at all. We shall never know exactly how Shakespeare spelt, because not a single page in his own hand is still in existance. The Shakespeare texts, which we now read, are much amended and edited versions of those printed in the First Folio Edition of his collected works, published in 1623, seven years after his death. These were compiled from surviving theatre copies, not Shakespeare's hand-written manuscripts.

Some of his plays had already been published in the Quarto edition of 1594, soon after he began acting and writing in London, but later editors have generally chosen the Folio version in preference to the one which was printed in his lifetime. ('Quarto' and 'Folio' refers to paper size. The Folio is roughly A4 size, and twice as big as the Quarto. The Quarto and Folio versions of the plays are nearly all slightly different, with some lines occurring in one but not the other. Modern editions often use a mixture of lines from both the Quarto and Folio, and probably make the plays much longer than they were when performed and directed in Shakespeare's time.)

The printing quality of the Quarto is poor in places, but its spelling is probably much closer to Shakespeare's own than in the Folio which was printed posthumously, and long after he had left the London stage. Both editions, however, show us mainly the spelling preferences of his printers who at that time invariably altered the spelling choices of their authors to fit in with their own style.

Looking at just the first few pages of *'Titus Andronicus'*, the first play in the Quarto, reveals that English spelling has changed a great deal since Shakespeare's time. Ten differences are immediately obvious.

1) In Shakespeare's time many spellings were still used interchangeably:
   e.g. *were /ware, bretheren/brethren, cheer/chear, goe/go.*

2) Short words ending in a consonant usually had this consonant doubled,
   and were often decorated with an *-e* as well: e.g. *farre* (far), *gunne*
   (gun), *interre* (inter), *sonne* (son).

3) Hundreds of words were still decorated with a silent *-e*,
   e.g. arm*e*, book*e*, born*e*, peer*e*, pomp*e*, room*e*, tomb*e*.

4) Endings which we spell with *-y* were predominantly spelt *-ie* (as they
   continue to be spelt in German now),
   e.g. fort*ie*, indignit*ie*, integrit*ie*, merc*ie*.
   This ending was also used in beautif*ie* and sk*ie*.

5) Many unstressed half-vowels had different spellings,
   e.g. **in**joy , **in**treat, **dis**paire.

6) A final *l* was always doubled, not just at the end of short words, as now,
   e.g. *capitall / capitoll, eternall, full well / fullwell, quarrell, wrongfull.*

7) The past tense was generally spelt more simply,
   e.g. *begd, traind, resolvd, returnd, markt.*

8) The EE-sound was often spelt more consistently,
   e.g. *bee, mee, hee, shee, thee, wee, beleeve, neere, yeeld, yeere.*

9) Consonant doubling was often more logical,
   e.g. *pittifull, scholler,* (instead of 'pitiful' and 'scholar').

10) Many others spellings were more logical too:
    e.g. *doo, controwle* (controll), *groning* (groaning), *harts* (hearts),
    hawtie (haughty).

   The only surviving documents that show something of the bard's own
hand are the signatures on his will which he changed several times shortly
before he died in 1616. These are highly embarrassing for those who hold
spelling accuracy in high esteem. Shakespeare spelt his name in at least three
different ways (*Shaksper, Shakspere, Shakspeare*). His handwriting was a bit
shaky by then, but not a single one of his surviving six signatures can be
read as *Shakespeare*, with an *e* after the *k*.

Compilers of dictionaries in the 17th and 18th centuries did not merely disregard the spellings which were used in Shakespeare's lifetime; somebody even had the gall to alter the spelling of his own name. This disrespect for Shakespeare's own spelling and the spellings of his contemporaries is a little puzzling. Dr. Johnson drew very heavily on Shakespeare's usage for his definitions of words, but clearly not on the spellings which were in use at that time.

Was this perhaps because Shakespeare was not regarded as sufficiently versed in Greek and Latin? According to the playwright Ben Jonson, who prefaced the Folio edition of 1623, Shakespeare had only *'small Latine, and lesse Greeke'*. Were the spellings of Shakespeare and his contemporaries perhaps too English for the intellectuals of the 17th and 18th centuries who were besotted with Greek and Latin?

The different spellings of Shakespeare's name on his will hint at the (for some even more disturbing) possibility that Shakespeare may have been a very poor speller. This idea would have been most unsettling to those who tried to convince children that only good spellers produced good writing.

Dr. Johnson himself proved that this was not so. He was an excellent speller but not much of a playwright. The only play he wrote was a flop and has not been heard of since. Closer to our own time, the well-known American writer Scott Fitzgerald was reputed to be a lousy speller. The British author and comedian Ben Elton apparently has spelling problems too.

One thing is certain - the spellings which we use now are very different from those which Shakespeare is likely to have used. English spelling has been changed a great deal since Elizabethan and Jacobean times, but unfortunately it has not been made easier to learn. In view of the chaotic history of English spelling, the reasons for most of the changes will remain obscure. Shakespeare's works could undoubtedly have been an authority on English spelling as well as usage, but the traceless disappearance of all his manuscripts has prevented this.

Because nobody of sufficient stature ever attempted to make English spelling more logical, it has remained as difficult to learn and teach as John Hart found it in 1569. Some small improvements have been made, like dropping a redundant final *-e* (e.g. *booke - book*) or a final -e together with a doubled consonant before it (e.g. *drugge - drug*). Yet even this simplification has not been finished properly (e.g. *more, alternative, infinite*).

Many other changes have merely made learning to spell more difficult, because they have introduced greater unpredictability and uncertainty rather than less (cittie - *city*, cf. *ditty*; doo - *do*, cf. *zoo, go*; shee - *she*, cf *see*). Instead of being relaxed about having several spellings for a word (e.g. *ware/were*), we now have different spellings for several hundred identically sounding words which have to be strictly obeyed (e.g. *there/their*), giving nearly everyone endless trouble.

It is beyond a shadow of doubt that ease of learning has hardly ever been given a thought when spelling changes were made. If Mulcaster, for one, had taken this into consideration when he compiled the first list of modern English spellings in 1582, things might have turned out very differently. Children might have ended up spelling by simply learning and applying basic spelling patterns, instead of having to memorise long spelling lists like the one recently produced by Mr. Blunkett which was discussed in the last chapter.

Chapter 9

US spelling changes
and the ITA experiment in the UK

After Mulcaster's listing of his 9000 preferred spellings in 1582, reform of English spelling was not considered seriously again until the United States attained its independence from Britain in 1783. Benjamin Franklin, one of the most enlightened American statesmen of the 18th century, was a supporter of spelling reform. He believed that the soundness of democracy depended on having a well educated citizenry, and that the irregularities of English spelling made a satisfactory general education difficult to achieve.

The main impetus for spelling change in the US, however, came not from a wish to make learning to spell easier, but from the revolutionary spirit of American independence and a desire to make US English different from British English. For this reason most of the changes which have since been adopted in the US have either not helped learners at all or have even made learning to spell more difficult. Only a small number of them have brought any benefit to learners.

The chief instigator of American spelling change was Noah Webster. Initially he thought much like Jefferson and was in favour of making English spelling easier by means of a proper spelling reform. After graduating from Yale in 1778 he was a schoolteacher for a while. This experience made him keenly aware of the difficulties which English spelling imposes on learners. He also realised that spelling reform was unlikely to come about overnight, and that until it materialised pupils needed to continue mastering the existing spelling conventions. Paucity of teaching materials induced him to start work on *The American Spelling-Book* which proved very popular and a huge commercial success.

As the money poured in, Webster increasingly lost his erstwhile enthusiasm for a proper reform of English spelling. The newly attained American Independence played a part too. He believed that making a difference between the English orthography and the American one would have *'vast political consequences'*. Consequently he concentrated his attention on finding inoffensive spelling changes which would make substantial numbers of American spelling different from British ones but raise few objections from opponents. Shrewdly, he focussed almost exclusively on word endings - the parts of words which we barely register when reading a text.

The best known US changes are:

---

1. alterations to the British *-ise*, *-our* and *-re* endings (spelling words like idol*ise*, harb*our* and cent*re* as idol*ize*, harb*or* and cent*er*);

2. cutting redundant final letters from a few words like program*me* and catalog*ue*;

3. abolition of *l*-doubling in words like *travelled* and *marvelled*.

Spelling derived word forms like *commercialize* and *idolize* (from *commercial* and *idol*) with an *-ize* ending in place of the British *-ise*, makes it clear that the writer is American, but this change is of no help to spellers. The change from *-ise* to *-ize* for a specific group of words has merely introduced more variety, and thereby more difficulty, into the spelling of the Z-sound. To make matters easier for learners, at least all *-ise* endings would need to be spelt *-ize*; i.e. words like *wise, rise* and *guise* would need to be changed too.

Shortening 18 common words with spellings like *harbour* and *labour* to *harbor* and *labor* has also brought no benefit to learners. The dominant American and English spelling pattern for words which end in *-r preceded by an unstressed vowel* is *-er* (e.g. moth*er*, fath*er*, work*er*). *Harbor* and *labor* still need to be memorised as exceptions from the dominant pattern, along with at least 75 other words like *actor, doctor* and *error* (see page 220). If anything, having a peculiar little group of exceptions with *-our* endings makes them a bit more distinctive and thereby perhaps easier to remember.

The change from *-re* to *-er* (e.g. cent*re*, theat*re* - cent*er*, *theater*) has been helpful to learners. It has brought *-re* endings into line with the dominant *-er* pattern. Unfortunately, only seven common words are spelt with *-re* in British English (e.g. cent*re*, fib*re*, met*re*, sab*re*, kilomet*re*, og*re*, theat*re*). This change has therefore also done almost nothing to make American spelling easier.

Webster is also responsible for shortening previous spellings like *traffick* and *musick* to *traffic* and *music* . Quite surprisingly, this change has even been adopted in the UK, but it has also been of little help to learners. Whereas previously most words which ended in a K-sound preceded by a vowel were given a *-ck* ending, learners now have to distinguish between one-syllable words and longer ones (e.g. ki*ck* and automati*c*). Only consistent use of *-c* or *-k* for the final K-sound would make life for learners appreciably easier (e.g. ki*c*, atomi*c*, dar*c* or ki*k*, atomi**k**, dar**k**). For the time being the spelling of the K-sound remains very difficult to master (as explained in Chapter 4), both in the US and the UK.

Cutting totally superfluous final letters from words like program*me* and catalog*ue* and the abolition of *l*-doubling in words like *travelled* and *marvelled* are changes which are undoubtedly helpful to learners. It is a pity for British pupils that these are still not embraced in the UK.

Apart from the US changes discussed above, there have also been a few more random ones which run totally against dominant English spelling conventions. For example, the US spellings of *defense, offense* and *vise* contradict the dominant pattern of *balance, bounce, chance, choice, lice, mice, rice, malice, office, etc.*. Reducing the clearly regular doubled *g* in *waggon* to a single *g (wagon)* runs counter the consonant doubling principle as exemplified in *baggy* and *maggot*.

As far as advancing the cause of a proper English spelling reform is concerned, Webster probably hindered it more than he advanced it. Because his changes have been of such minimal help to learners, many English speakers have perhaps ended up believing that no spelling change can make learning to read and write English any easier.

During the 19th century, as growing numbers of people without knowledge of English began to immigrate into the US, many US school teachers became aware of the difficulties which English spelling poses for learners. The inconsistencies of English spelling always become more evident to those who try to teach English to foreigners. Immigration into the US also helped to bring English spelling to the attention of politicians and phoneticians. As a result of this several spelling reform groups were formed in the US during the second half of the 19th century.

In England the difficulties of English spelling began to attract attention in the 19th century too. As increasing numbers of children from lower socio-economic groups were given the benefits of education from 1833 onwards, the difficulties inherent in the English spelling system became more obvious to many British school teachers. Several reform societies sprang up in England as well.

Many prominent individuals in the US and the UK joined the ranks of spelling reformers in the late 19th and early 20th century. Among them were: Mark Twain, Charles Darwin, Sir Isaac Pitman (the inventor of short-hand) and his grandson Sir James, Melvin Dewey and his son Godfrey, Theodore Roosevelt, Lord Tennyson, the industrialists Andrew Carnegie and Sir George Hunter, the phonetician Henry Sweet and the lexicographer James Murray. Many eminent university professors and vast numbers of school teachers supported the cause.

Before long the different reform groups on the two sides of the Atlantic were even co-operating with each other. Sadly, no substantial improvement to English spelling ever materialised, despite the vast amounts of money and effort which were expended by the reformers for many decades. In the US a few more words like d*oughnut, though* and *through* were shorn of surplus letters and shortened to d*onut, tho* and *thru;* a handful more words were brought into line with dominant patterns (e.g. *'plough'* being changed to *'plow'* to fall into line with *'How now brown cow?')*; the difficult UK distinction between the noun *practice* and the verb *to practise* was abolished; but the bulk of words which contain some element of unpredictability have remained the same.

The most significant result of the efforts of supporters of spelling reform during the second half of the 19th and first half of the 20th century has been to prove that the simplification of English spelling would make learning to read and write English much easier than it is now. This was achieved not in the US but in the UK during the school-year of 1963-64.

Ever since Sir Isaac Pitman first started to pour the vast sums of money which he made from his short-hand into promoting spelling reform in the 1840's, the cause has enjoyed waxing and waning support in England. Even now, the Simplified Spelling Society which was founded in London in 1908 is the only reform group which still survives in the English-speaking world, but few people are even aware of its existence nowadays. It attracted much more attention and patronage during the first half of the 20th century.

The movement to reform English spelling for the benefit of learners reached its zenith shortly after the Second World War. For about a decade it enjoyed a considerable amount of popular support, with large numbers signing petitions to Parliament. This eventually resulted in a private member's Spelling Reform Bill which was put before the House of Commons in 1953. The bill was carried by 65 votes to 53 after its Second Reading and was subsequently approved in Committee too, very much against the wishes of the Conservative government of the day.

Without government support the Bill had no chance of being passed by the House of Lords, which would probably have killed it even if the government had sponsored it. The Bill's success in the House of Commons did, however, persuade the Secretary of State for Education at that time, Miss Florence Horsbrugh, that some further action should be taken. She gave her consent for a large-scale investigation to establish whether traditional spelling had adverse effects on children's progress with learning to read and write, when compared with the use of a simplified spelling system.

The prestigious Institute of Education of the University of London and the National Foundation for Educational Research were entrusted with the conduct of the project and designed it with great care. To ensure that the scientific probity of the study was not sullied in any way, no member of the Simplified Spelling Society took part in the design or conduct of the experiment. The Society provided only the simplified spelling system which the study used for comparison with traditional spelling.

The system used in the project was Sir James Pitman's Initial Teaching Alphabet (ITA or ita). This was an adaptation of Fonotypy, a simplified method for spelling English which was first designed by Sir Isaac Pitman and had already been tried out in the US in the 1850's, in 10 schools in Massachusetts. Sir James made only minor changes to his grandfather's augmented Roman alphabet, consisting of 40 symbols, and gave it a new name.

Since participation in the experiment was voluntary, it took several years to persuade enough directors of education and school heads to take part in it. The research was eventually carried out during the academic year 1963 - 64. The study compared 873 children who learned to read and write in the normal way with 873 children who were taught using the Initial Teaching Alphabet.

The results demonstrated very clearly that children can learn to read and write English must faster when using a more consistent spelling system:

1) Children using ITA moved more quickly through the 5 books of the Ladybird reading scheme. For example, the average pupil using ITA was on the fourth book by the beginning of the fifth term, while the average pupil using traditional spelling had not advanced beyond the second book.

2) The ITA children scored more highly in reading tests: reading more fluently, with fewer errors and attaining higher comprehension scores.

3) The writing of children using ITA was also superior. Their compositions were longer and they used a wider vocabulary.

4) Teachers of the ITA groups commented repeatedly on a more favourable attitude to learning among their pupils.

The study proved beyond doubt that traditional spelling impedes the acquisition of literacy in English. Yet hardly anyone is now aware of this, or even that the study ever took place. Those who have heard of ITA and the children who took part in the experiment almost invariably think that it was a failure. A full-page piece about ITA in the Daily Telegraph on 2 June 2001 was entitled *'A cleer case of educashunal lunacie'*. - Why should this be?

Teachers of the classes which used ITA in the research project were bowled over by the rapid progress which their pupils made with reading and writing. They had previously watched so many children struggle and get stuck on their first reading book. They had seen their writing being severely handicapped by the contradictions of English spelling. With ITA, by contrast, the ablest pupils were flying along, but the slower ones were making good progress too, and enjoying their learning into the bargain. There is nothing that gives teachers more satisfaction than seeing their pupils succeed. Understandably, the majority of teachers who had taken part in the experiment wanted to continue using ITA. They also encouraged others to do the same.

Unfortunately ITA transported pupils and teachers into the more idyllic world of reformed spelling which existed only in their own classrooms. The heady success of ITA made the teachers using it ignore the grim reality of traditional spelling which their pupils would have to confront before long. This was easy to do because, in primary schools teachers usually teach just one age group. How those children later coped with traditional spelling would be someone else's problem.

ITA enabled children to grasp easily what reading and writing was all about, but eventually they still had to switch to traditional spelling and start memorising the erratic spellings of 3500 common English words which have some element of unpredictability in them. The ablest pupils coped reasonably. They experienced a brief set-back during transition, but were soon making good progress again. The least able pupils, those who needed help most, suffered the greatest set-backs when they eventually had to switch to normal, unreformed English spelling.

The research project of 1963-64 had proved that if English spelling conventions were simplified, children would be able to continue learning to read and write in the same satisfactory and confident way in which they progressed with ITA. The prolonged use of ITA for more than a decade after the scientific study proved that *a transitional learning system cannot enable learners to cope with the difficulties of the current English spelling system*. My own experiences taught me the same lesson.

By the time I started to learn English I already knew perfectly well how alphabetic systems are meant to operate. I had acquired this insight not from ITA but from learning Lithuanian and Russian. This knowledge proved useful when I next went on to learn German, another language with a fairly alphabetic spelling system. But it was of no help to me when I subsequently came to learn English. Because English spelling so often fails to adhere to the alphabetic principle, the really hard part of becoming literate in English is memorising the thousands of exceptional spellings after the basics of reading and writing have been grasped. Only spelling reform can ameliorate this. A spelling system riddled with contradictions will always take a long time to master, irrespective of the route by which one approaches it. ITA could not enable children to cope with the vagaries of English spelling any more than learning Lithuanian, Russian and German helped me tackle the same learning burden. Only lots of intensive practice with traditional spelling can do that, or a proper reform of English spelling.

Many children who were introduced to the workings of the alphabetic principle with ITA ended up having greater spelling difficulties than those who were exposed only to traditional English spelling. Parents saw this more readily than teachers and helped to bring about the banishment of ITA from most schools by the early 1980's.

The continued use of ITA for more than a decade beyond the research project of 1963-64 helped to ensure that the results of this study, which proved that English spellings conventions undoubtedly impeded the acquisition of literacy, were almost entirely ignored. Educational experts ended up debating whether schools should use ITA or not, instead of considering the benefits of spelling reform and its implementation.

Chapter 10

The costs of English spelling
and how they could be reduced

As stated at the beginning of this book, the difficulties of English spelling mar the life chances of millions of people - around 40 million adults in the US and about 7 million in the UK. On the 13th March 2002 it was reported by the BBC that while the UK's rate of functional illiteracy is estimated to be around 20 %, that of Germany is only 10 % and Sweden's 8 %. Numerous international comparisons have revealed similar results over the years. Adult speakers of English have regularly been found to have poorer reading and writing skills than users of other languages.

British youngsters also lag behind their European counterparts in international studies. At the British festival of science in Glasgow in 2001 Professor Seymour from Dundee University talked about the EU project "Learning disorders as a barrier to human development" which was conducted between 1995-99. This compared *ease of literacy acquisition in 13 languages*. Such comparisons are never completely straightforward because European children start school at different ages: 5 in the UK; 6 in most of Europe; 7 in Austria, Denmark, Finland, Germany, Norway and Sweden.

Nevertheless, the results left Prof. Seymour in no doubt that *'reading acquisition is slower in English than in most other European languages'*. He calculated that from starting school at 5, children learning to read English need between 2 ½ and 3 years to gain the competence which is achieved in less than one year in most other European languages.

Results from three other countries also showed that the spelling system of a language determined how easily children learned to read. Children from Denmark, France and Portugal were much slower than those from the other nine and took nearly as long to master reading as English-speaking children. Danish, French and Portuguese also have highly unpredictable spelling systems.

This study also found that among English-speaking learners there is greater variation between individuals than users of other languages. In their first year at school some children made very good progress, while others made almost none. Interestingly, this was also true of reading Danish, even though formal education in Denmark does not begin until 7.

Several studies have compared the speed with which children learn to read and write English and one other language. Such two-language comparisons with Italian, German, Greek, Japanese and Turkish have all found that learning to read English is more difficult and takes longer.

Exceptionally, an OECD study published in 2001 which compared reading, science and mathematics skills of 15-year-olds in 31 countries found that the best pupils from the UK had reading comprehension skills not far behind those of top-scoring Finland, another country with a regular spelling system. However, very much unlike those from Finland, 13 % of British participants were found to be seriously deficient in the literacy skills which are required for further learning.

English spelling helps to ensure that many learners achieve lower levels of educational attainment than they could with a more predictable system. A study which examined the relationship between *dyslexia and spelling* among English, French and Italian university students, found that the neurological deficits associated with dyslexia occur just as often among Italians as among other nationals. The Italian subjects also performed equally badly on short-term memory tests, another indicator of dyslexia, but their impairment did not reveal itself in reading tests. A learning difficulty like dyslexia has little effect on an individual's life chances when the spelling system is as predictable as Italian. It becomes seriously detrimental only when the spelling is as erratic as English. The incidence of reported dyslexia in Italy is consequently quite rare, whereas in England and France it affects between 10 - 15 % of people.

The chief researcher of this study, *Prof. Eraldo Paulesu* from Milan concluded that, *"English dyslexics would have an easier life if their writing system was more regular"*. Many other learners would undoubtedly also find life much easier if the English spelling system were less chaotic. It has serious disadvantages for all who have some kind of learning difficulty because the minimum levels of brain power and other skills that are required for mastering literacy in English are simply much higher than for many other spelling systems. Wheel-chair bound individuals can get around perfectly well on level surfaces, but they cannot cope with steps or stairs. For large numbers of learners English spelling contains too many equally insurmountable barriers.

There is even some evidence which suggests that having to cope with the contradictions of English spelling may hinder brain development. In the early 60's Sister John, a nun who taught in Liverpool, gave two groups of children aged four and a half a symbol-matching test. There was no difference in performance between the two groups at that age. One group was then taught reading and writing with a common, traditional scheme, the other using the far more logical Initial Teaching Alphabet. When the two groups were given the same test again a year later, the symbol-matching skills of the ITA group showed considerable gains, whilst the children who had been exposed to traditional spelling performed no better than a year earlier.

It is not easy to calculate all the costs of English spelling. What is the price of demotivation and turning large numbers of young children off learning at a young age? Teachers are regularly reminded that when it comes to motivation, *'Nothing succeeds like success'*. English spelling ensures that many children have to become accustomed to failure from a very young age. Presumably the obverse of success is true of failure, and therefore *'nothing fails like spelling failure'?*

The chief problems caused by the irregularities of English spelling are discussed in the first six chapters of this book. The size of the problem can be appreciated by looking through the word lists in Appendix R and Appendix S. Having to memorise around 3700 words with irregular spellings is a tall order. Having just a few hundred of them, as in Italian and Spanish, or even as many as roughly 1000, as in German, is much more manageable. The most serious drawback of English spelling, however, is undoubtedly that it dooms around 20 % of all learners to guaranteed failure. For about 1/5 of all school children it is quite simply too difficult.

When a system is too difficult, large numbers of people inevitably fail to cope with it. We have seen a vast expansion in the use of computers once they became more user-friendly. If one country had decided to stick with the DOS system and forbidden the adoption of windows, the use of computers in that country would almost certainly still be very low. The refusal to modernise English spelling has a similar effect. We insist that English spelling must stay fiendishly difficult, even though it is clearly beyond the intellectual powers of many millions (7 mil. in the UK, 40 mil. in the US.)

Inability to read and write reduces an individual's life and job prospects in many ways. For example, in the summer of 2000 it was reported in the UK that around 25% of British women fail to take up the offer of free breast screening. How much is illiteracy responsible for this? May functional illiteracy also be the reason why millions of people living in poverty regularly fail to claim the benefits which are aimed at alleviating their problems? How many resort to theft and robbery instead because they cannot cope with filling in an application form?

In June 1999 the Los Angeles Times carried a full-page advertisement for voluntary classroom reading assistants. This claimed that some US states project future numbers of prisoners from child illiteracy rates. According to a recent audit by the UK's Youth Justice Board, half of all young men in custody in the UK have a reading age of 11 or below. The US and the UK both jail a relatively high percentage of their populations. The UK's rate is by far the highest in Europe. English spelling may well be at least partly responsible for this difference.

Those of us who can read and write fluently cannot really grasp what life is like without those abilities. Can we imagine how we would cope with not being able to tell whether a newly arrived letter is something important or mere junk mail? Can we appreciate what it is like not being able to express our views in writing when the need arises, or if we just feel like having our say? The seven million people in the UK who cannot find a plumber in the classified telephone directory never write to complain about poor service or unfair treatment, but a written complaint is invariably taken more seriously than just a verbal one.

The illiterate cannot read the small print on contracts before signing them, much to the delight of loan sharks. A book by John Honey claims *'Language is Power'*, but language is far less powerful in the hands of those who cannot read and write. Without those skills even simple things like sending a Christmas card can become impossible or humiliating. In December 2001 Kamal Ahmed reported in The Observer that around two million Britons wrote nothing inside their cards because they were conscious of their inability to spell.

The English spelling system incurs direct monetary costs too. It has been estimated that £7bn of the UK's £20bn education budget is spent on special needs. The most common manifestation of special needs is invariably difficulty with reading and writing. Assessment of them is itself expensive and time-consuming. Highly paid educational psychologists spend most of their time on this, and schools have to employ many additional teachers and classroom assistants, mainly to help pupils cope with difficulties arising from English spelling. This annual expenditure has occurred for years, without making serious inroads on adult illiteracy. One US senator estimated that over the past 35 years about $ 130 billion had been spent on shortening the long tail of educational underachievement in the USA, but without bringing any noticeable improvement.

Over time many countries have ended up with spelling systems which fewer and fewer of their people could cope with. The majority of such systems have since been updated and made easier to learn. Many have been modernised and simplified several times in order to make them more user-friendly.

A good example of the difference that spelling reform can make has been provided by Sweden and Denmark. These neighbours educate their children in almost identical ways. In both countries infants are allowed to learn mainly through play and formal education does not begin until the age of seven. They also have very similar languages, but Swedish and Danish have very different spelling systems. Danish spelling is still very much as Swedish used to be before it was thoroughly reformed in 1907. As a result of this, Swedish spellers always come near the top in all international comparisons of literacy standards. Danish spellers are usually near the bottom, along with those from the UK and the US.

English spelling differs from nearly all other modern spelling systems in that for at least 570 years no serious attempt has been made to make it more user-friendly. English spelling has changed a great deal since 1430, but with little regard to ease of learning.

Reading and writing open the door to further learning. The simplification of English spelling therefore has the potential to bring great benefits. Professor Eraldo Paulesu, the chief researcher in the study which discovered a link between spelling irregularity and dyslexia, concluded that there is an argument for reforming complex writing systems to improve literacy problems in these languages.

Yet even much-overdue reforms invariably arouse opposition. The chairman of the Queen's English Society immediately rejected Professor Paulesu's suggestion and claimed that, "as soon as you start simplifying things, you *increase* confusion".

Having examined English spelling carefully over the past few years, I have come to believe that there is great potential for *reducing* confusion in English spelling by means of a few very simple and inexpensive measures. H.W. Fowler, one of the two brothers who spent most their lives investigating English spelling and usage, observed in his popular book 'English Usage', published in 1926, *'the substitution for our present chaos of a phonetically consistent method that did not sacrifice the many merits of the old spelling would be of incalculable value".*

He also provided some good pointers as to how this might be achieved: "*English had better be treated in the English way, and its spelling not be revolutionised but amended in detail, here a little and there a little as absurdities become intolerable, till a result is attained that shall neither overburden schoolboys nor stultify intelligence nor outrage the scholar".*

The most frequently committed spelling errors indicate fairly clearly what the most *intolerable absurdities* of English spelling are:

> consonant doubling,
> the different spellings for the long EE-sound,
> unpredictable spellings for short and long vowels,
> the various spellings for unstressed half-vowels,
> silent letters.

Ameliorating even just some of these unpredictable elements would make a difference. Substantial improvement could be achieved without interfering with established English spelling conventions in any way. Just bringing divergent spellings into line with dominant patterns could reduce a great deal of confusion. There is no need to introduce any additional letters or transform well-established rules.

A sensible reform would require some careful thought as well as consultation and co-operation, but it need not be either difficult or expensive to implement. All that is required is official permission to spell more English words according to basic English spelling patterns - instead of insisting that they should be spelt in the various peculiar, divergent ways in use now.

It could be something as simple as:

'From now on children need no longer learn to spell the EE-sound in the many unpredictable ways which we have been using for it. Everyone may forthwith spell the EE-sound consistently as *ee* (e.g. *heer, neer, yeer, greef, theef*....).

Just a handful of such *'permissions'*, if well-chosen, would make an enormous difference at minimal expense and very little disturbance to practised users of traditional spelling. Older people would be free to use the simplified spellings if they wanted to, or they could continue to spell as before. They would initially find words with new spellings a bit strange to look at, but would soon get used to them.

We now spell very differently from the way Shakespeare did, but reeding the First Folio of 1625 presents few problems after one has red a page or two. Competent reeders of modern English soon get into their stride and don't eeven notice the differences. If we altered the spellings of just 500 - 1000 words by just one or two letters this would cause no problem to practised reeders whatsoever. For centuries England had a profusion of different spellings for identical words and lived quite happily with them. Texts from the 14th century are a bit hard for us now, not because of changed spellings, but because *the English language has changed a great deel since then.*

Before Johnson's dictionary of 1755 arrested English spelling change, English spelling had continually changed for many centuries. Some of those changes have made using it less cumbersome (i.e. betwee*ne*, word*e*, mean*e*, read*e*, board*e*, weak*e*, atte, back*e*, leg*ge*). Eeven if we did no more than finish the job of deleeting the remaining redundant, decorative *'e'* at the end of words (*giv, hav, liv, siv, definit*) we would make lerning to reed eesier. We could eesily simplify it quite a bit mor and save much swet, menny teers and vast sums of munny into the bargain, while rasing litteracy standards at a stroke.

If it were ever decided to alleviate the current learning burden by means of spelling reform, the biggest difficulty would probably be resisting the temptation to change too much in one go. Because English spelling has been allowed to drift away from the alphabetic principle without correction for a long time, there is now a great deal that cries out for attention. Examining the English spelling system is a bit like surveying a city that has fallen into disrepair as a result of a few disasters and prolonged failure to reconstruct; but there is no need to aim for sudden complete perfection. No European spelling system is totally phonetic. Most are just *substantially less chaotic* than the English one, and this makes them much easier to learn.

Some may perhaps wonder how we can simplify English spelling while so many different varieties of English are spoken around the world. On closer inspection the differences between them turn out to be far fewer than the similarities. We can all understand each other with remarkable ease, and the mass media are making it ever easier. All English speakers are now hearing and reading different varieties of English from across the world. During previous centuries the majority were exposed just to the accents of their particular corner. Now we are all affected by the different varieties of English which we encounter. We are also all contributing to the continuous evolution of the English language.

Most English sounds, like the EE-sound, are remarkably consistent throughout the different English accents and dialects. We could begin by at least spelling such sounds more regularly. Unpredictable spellings do not serve any variety of English well, be it UK, US, Australian, Canadian, NZ, Scottish or South African. They may even be the reason why slightly different pronunciations have developed in different parts of the world.

I have not heard or read a single serious objection to the simplification of English spelling. Many are based on erroneous assumptions about spelling change, like believing that changing English spelling would change the English language. In 1929 Turkey switched from the Arabic alphabet to the Roman one for spelling Turkish, without changing the Turkish language in any way, but the reform made Turkish spelling much easier than it was before. Most arguments against spelling reform amount to no more than a gut-felt unwillingness to change. Some are inclined to think, "I had to put up with it. Why should others be spared the trouble?"

Perhaps the brainpower of children will improve eventually and they will cope with this learning burden more easily. Perhaps someone will yet discover a more effective way of teaching children to learn to read and write than we have so far. (Perhaps the word lists with irregular spellings which I have compiled will help someone to do so.) The prospects for this appear small. Making English spelling easier to learn by means of simplification is more feasible and more guaranteed to bring improvements in literacy acquisition. It would cut a great deal of recurring expenditure, stress and failure. Unfortunately, those who stand to gain most have little say in the matter.

For as long as half of all English words are spelt unpredictably in some way, even able learners will continue to take at least ten years to become reasonably competent spellers, and about five more in advanced and further education to become really proficient. Many pupils will fail to attain even rudimentary competence for as long as we choose not to spell English simply according to a sensible phonic system, as in the words

creep - crept,   feel - felt,   keep - kept,   speed - sped,   sleep - slept and persist in thwarting the efforts of learners with unnecessary and bewildering inconsistencies like:

deal - dealt, dream - dreamt, lean - lent, mean - meant, read - read.

There is no good reason why they should not be spelt far more easily as

deel - delt, dreem - dremt, leen - lent, meen - ment, reed - red.

'Red' would then acquire a second meaning and would initially irritate practised users of traditional spelling a little, but learners would benefit greatly from the demise of 'read'. Having different meanings for a single spelling as in *deal, dealt, lean, lent, mean* and *meant* never cause any trouble to anyone. 'Red' could serve perfectly well for both the current 'red' and 'read', just as it does in speech.

I hope that my book will enable all those who teach English, at whatever level and in whatever capacity, to get a better understanding of the learning burden which stems from the inconsistencies of English spelling and help them to teach more effectively. Should it also encourage them to begin thinking about reducing it, so much the better.

The word lists in the Reading Appendix (pages 123-200) and the Spelling Appendix (pages 201-71) which follow are derived from an analysis of 6800 words in common usage, the kind of vocabulary that the average speaker of English would readily understand. (Chapter 2 explains how the list of 6800 words was obtained.)

APPENDIX R (Ap. R) - READING

The bulk of the Reading Appendix consists of word lists - from phonically easy words to words with highly unpredictable pronunciations. It is divided into seven sections. Each section begins with a discussion of the word lists which follow.

THE EASY PART

1. Decoding 900 simple words with *a, e, i, o* and *u* -   tables R 1 - 5, p. 124 -30

2. 570 phonically more complex words with predictable sounds   R 6 -12, p. 131-6

3. 360 words with *ar, air;   er, ir, ur;   or, oar, ore*   R 13 - 15, p. 137-9

PROBLEMATIC CONSONANTS

4. *c, g, h, q, s* and *w*   R 16 - 26, p. 140-51

5. the digraphs *ch, gh* and *th*   R 27 - 30, p. 152-5

6. *silent letters*   R 31 - 33, p. 156-7

UNPREDICTABLE VOWELS

7. *a, i, o, u, y*   R 34 - 40, p. 158-64

8. *ea, ei, ie;   ou, oo, ui, ue;   ure, ture, are*   R 41 - 56, p. 165-77

9. Vowel length and stress problems   R 57 - 65, p. 178-87

10. Words with different pronunciations
     and pointers to stress patterns   R66 - 69, p. 188-91

11. Assorted odd spellings   R 70, p. 192

Summaries

69 graphemes with one clearly dominant pronunciation   R 71, p. 193
37 graphemes with several pronunciations   R 72, p. 194
2032 common English words which are likely to cause
     reading problems, listed in alphabetical order   p 195 -200

The easy part - decoding phonically spelt words

Most of the 21 letters which are used for spelling English consonants have relatively predictable pronunciations - 13 of them can be taught easily enough in conjunction with the simple vowel patterns which are listed in the next five tables. Their dominant pronunciations are exemplified in the following words:

bib, dad, fun, jam, kit, lid, mum, nun, pop, tot, vet, box, zip.

Yet even 12 of these 13 letters are not totally phonic. Ten of them are occasionally silent (e.g. doubt, Wednesday, marijuana, knee, salmon, mnemonic, autumn, receipt, often, choux). Two others are sometimes used to modify other sounds (e.g. half, halfpenny, Czech - UK pronunciation: [harf], [haypenny], [chek]).

Only *v* can be relied on to spell nothing but the V-sound; but at the end of words, the letter *v* is always followed by *e,* irrespective of whether this serves a phonic function (e.g. gave) or not (e.g. have). Such words are therefore not included in the early reading lists.

Very few English graphemes are totally problem-free, reliable guides to pronunciation. One of them is *sh*, and it occurs in many common English words, e.g. *sh*arp, *sh*ip, *sh*op, *sh*ut. Words with *sh* are therefore listed in the next five tables.

Words with *th* also rarely cause pronunciation problems for native learners. These are therefore also included among the phonically easy words. (Anyone needing guidance about the pronunciation of words with *th* should consult tables R 29 and R 30 on pages 154 and 155.)

The pronunciations of the consonant *c* is governed by slightly more complex rules, but *before a, o* and **u***, and consonants other than h*, the letter *c* is invariably pronounced with a K-sound. Such words are therefore also listed in the phonically easy reading lists.

So are words with the graphemes *ch* and *tch* which are pronounced as in *chat* and *catch*, i.e. the dominant pronunciations for these graphemes. The 47 common words in which the pronunciation for *ch* is unpredictable are listed in table R 27, on page 152.

Y can serve as both a consonant (*y*es) and a vowel (s*y*stem). The pronunciation of *y* is therefore discussed among vowel graphemes with unpredictable pronunciations, and words containing *y* are listed in tables R 38 - 40, on pages 162-4.

English vowels are far more difficult to decode than consonants, even when they occur singly. Even in one-syllable words vowels can have unpredictable pronunciations, e.g.: *scalp - scald*[scauld] , *shall*[shal] - *all*[aul]; *milk - mild*[miled]; *cloth - both*[boath]; *lost - post*[poast]; *gull - full* [fooll], with a short OO-sound as in w*ool*. (Consonants with unpredictable pronunciations are listed in tables R 16 - 33, vowels in tables R 34 - 70.)

The next 15 tables list only words which obey dominant spelling patterns for both vowels and consonants. Tables 1-5 list words with short vowel sounds, tables 6-15 words with long vowels and vowel blends (*see detailed index to the reading lists on page 123.*)

Commonly occurring words that have a divergent pronunciation for a listed grapheme are spelt out more predictably, e.g. for *prove* [proov] and the seven examples above.

A

The first table (table R 1 on the next page) lists words with the dominant pronunciation of the letter *a* in one-syllable words, as in *cat, sat* and *mat*.

There are however also quite a few words in which the pronunciation of *a* varies between different English accents. The words *ask* and *bath*, for example, are pronounced with an **AH/AR**-sound in standard UK English, but in Northern English and American accents they have the standard shorter **A**-sound as in table R 1 (*a, an, and, ant, at, etc.*).

(Table R 34 lists all the words in which *a* is pronounced differently in different varieties of English.)

Table R1. 211 words contain the regular _short **A-sound** for **a**_ , combined _with single consonants, consonant blends_, the graphemes _th, ch, sh_ and _ck_ and words which end with _-le_.

a	drab	lab	sap	valve	flash		black
an	drag	lag	sat	van	gash		hack
and	drank	lamp	scalp		lash		jack
ant		land	scan	wag	mash		lack
at	fact	lap	scant	wax	rash		pack
	fad	lass	scrap		sash		rack
bag	fan		slam	yak	slash		sack
ban	fang	mad	slang	yap	smash		slack
band	fat	man	slap				smack
bang	flag	map	snap	zap			snack
bat	flan	mat	span				stack
blank	flank		spank	than			tack
brag	flap	pact	spat	thank			track
brand	flat	pad	sprang	that			
	frank	pan	sprat	thatch		amble	apple
camp		pants	stab	thrash		ample	baffle
can	gag	pat	stag	maths		angle	battle
cap	gang	plan	stamp			antler	cackle
cat	glad	plank	stand	chat		axle	cattle
	grab	pram	strand	catch		bramble	crackle
clam	gram	prank	strap	hatch		candle	dabble
clamp	gran	prat	swam	latch		dangle	dappled
clan	grand			latch		handle	dazzle
clang		ram	tact	match		jangle	gabble
clank	had	ran	tad	patch		mangle	grapple
clap	ham	rang	tag	scratch		ramble	paddle
	hand	rank	tan	snatch		scramble	prattle
crab	hang	rap	tank			shambles	raffle
cramp	hank	rat	tap	sham		spangle	rattle
crank	has		tax	shrank		strangle	saddle
	hat	sad	tract			tangle	straggle
dab		sag	tram	bash		trample	tackle
dam	jab	sand	tramp	cash		wangle	
damp	jam	sang	trap	clash			
dank		sank	twang	crash			

$\boxed{\text{E}}$

As a single vowel in one-syllable words, the <u>letter *e*</u> presents few pronunciation problems. It spells a different sound in only 6 common words: *be, he, me, she*, <u>*we*</u> and *pretty* - pronounced [bee, hee, mee, shee, wee] and [pritty].

Table R 2. The 147 words below contain a *phonically simple* **E-sound**.
Note the unpredictable spelling of *egg*, cf. *beg* and *leg*.

elf	flex	nest	stress	check	deck
elm	fret	net	swell	chess	neck
end	held	nettle	swept	chest	peck
	hell	never			speck
bed	helm	next	tell	bench	speckled
beg cf. *egg*	help		tempt	clench	
belt	hem	peg	ten	drench	dredge
bend	hen	pelt	tend	sketch	edge
bent	hence	pen	tense	stench	hedge
best		pet	tent	stretch	ledge
bet	jest	press	test	trench	sledge
bled	jet		text		
blend		red	trend	shed	temple
bless	kept	rent		shelf	
bred		rest	vent	shell	kettle
	led		vest	shred	pebble
crept	left	self	vet		peddle
crest	leg	sell	vex	flesh	settle
	lend	send		fresh	
dent	lens	sent	web		
desk	lent	set	weld	*the**	* *'the'* is
dress	less	sex	well	them	occasionally
dwelt	let	slept	went	then	pronounced
		smell	wept		as *'thee'*
fed	melt	sped	west	theft	
fell	men	spell	wet	thresh	
felt	mend	spelt			
fence	mess	spend	yell	depth	
fend	met	spent	yelp	length	
fled		stem	yet	strength	
		step			
			zest		

Table R 3. This lists 250 phonic words with a *short* **I-sound**.
(Table R 35 lists 20 words in which *i* has an unpredictable long pronunciation.)

ill	fling	lid	silk	till	ri*ch*	brick	crinkle
in	flint	lift	sin	tilt	ditch	click	dimple
inn	flip	limp	sing	tin	hitch	flick	dwindle
is	flit	link	sink	tint	itch	kick	jingle
it	frisk	lip	sip	tip	pitch	nick	kindle
its		list	sit	trim	stitch	pick	mingle
	gift	lit	six	trip	switch	prick	nimble
bid	gild		skid	twig	twitch	quick	pimple
big	gills	milk	skill	twin	witch	sick	shingle
bin	gilt	mill	skim	twist		slick	swindle
bit	glint	mink	skin			stick	thimble
blink	grill	mint	skip	will	shift	thick	tingle
brim	grim	miss	slid	win	shin	tick	tinkle
bring	grin	mist	slim	wind	ship	trick	twinkle
brisk	grip	mix	sling	wing	shrill	pickle	winkle
	grit		slink	wink	shrimp	tickle	
cling		picnic	slip	wit	shrink	trickle	
clink	hid	pig	slit				gristle
clip	hill	pills	snip	zinc	dish	cripple	
crib	him	pin	spill	zip	fish	dribble	
crisps	hint		spilt		swish	drizzle	cringe
	hip	pink	spin		wish	fiddle	fridge
did	his	pip	spit			giggle	fringe
dig	hiss	print	split			grizzle	hinge
dim	hit		spring	chip	thin	little	ridge
dip		quill	sprint	finch	thing	middle	singe
disk	jig	quilt	squint	flinch	think	nibble	tinge
drift	jilt	quit	stiff	inch	thrift	quibble	twinge
drink			still	pinch	thrill	riddle	
drip	kid	rib	stilts	winch		ripple	
	kill	rid	sting	chin	fifth	scribble	
fill	kiln	rig	strict	chink	filth	sizzle	
film	kilt	rim	string	chintz	pith	skittle	
fin	kin	ring	strip		width	sniffle	
fist	king	rip	swift		with	tipple	
fit	kink	risk	swim			twiddle	
fix	kiss		swing			wiggle	

128

O

The list of phonically simple words with *o* is relatively short because this letter often has an unpredictable pronunciation (e.g. *month* [munth], *both* [boath]) - see table R 36).

Table R 4. 108 words have a phonic *short* **O-sound** in UK English.
In American English these are pronounced with a sound which is more like the *aw* in 'saw' or the *au* in 'autumn'.

off	from	plot	chop	fondle	block
on		pod			clock
ox	gloss	pond	notch	bottle	cock
	god	pot		cobble	dock
blond	golf	prod		gobble	flock
blot	gong	prop	shock	goggle	lock
bob	got		shod	hobble	mock
bog		rob	shop	nozzle	rock
bomb	hog	rod	shot	throttle	smock
bond	hop	romp		topple	stock
boss	hot	rot		wobble	sock
box			throb		
	job	slog	throng	jostle	dodge
cod	jog	slot			lodge
cop	jot	snob			
cot		sob			
crop	lob	soft			
cross	loft	solve			
	log	song			
dog	loll	spot			
doll	long	stop			
don	lop	strong			
dot	loss				
drop	lot	tongs			
		top			
flog	mob	toss			
flop	mop	tot			
fog	moss	trod			
fond		trot			
fox	nod				
frog	not				

129

The dominant pronunciation for the letter *u* is as in *up* and *cup*, but in several common words it is pronounced with a short OO-sound, as in *good wood,* and *truth* has a long OO-sound (see page 162 for a fuller explanation).

Table R 5. 184 words have the dominant *short* **U-sound** for *u* , 15 words don't.

up	glum	nun	sum	shrub	bumble	struggle
	grub	nut	sun	shrug	bundle	supple
blunt	gruff		sung	shrunk	bungle	tussle
bulb	grunt	plug	sunk	shun	crumble	bustle[busl]
bulk	gulf	plum	swum	shunt	fumble	hustle[husl]
bung	gull	puff	swung	shut	grumble	rustle[rusl]
bunk	gulp	pulp			humble	
but	gun	pump	truck	blush	jumble	bulge
buzz	gust	pus	trunk	brush	jungle	grudge
			truss	crush	mumble	judge
club	hug	rug	trust	flush	rumble	lunge
clump	hum	run	tuck	gush	stumble	nudge
clung	hump	rung	tuft	hush	tumble	smudge
crust	hung	rust	tug	rush	uncle	trudge
cub	hunt		tusk	slush		plunge
cuff		scrub			bubble	
cup	jug	scrum	chug	thrust	cuddle	
cut	jump	scull	chum	thud	guzzle	
	junk	snug	chunk	thug	huddle	
drug	just	sprung		thumb	muddle	
drum	jut	spun	bunch	thump	muffle	
drunk		strum	crunch		muzzle	
dug	lug	strung	hunch	buck	nuzzle	
dull	lull	strut	lunch	cluck	puddle	
dump	lump	stuck	munch	luck	puzzle	
dusk	lungs	stud	punch	pluck	rubble	
dust		stuff		struck	ruffle	
	mud	stump	much	suck	scuffle	
flung	mug	stun	such		scuttle	
fun	mumps	stung		buckle	shuffle	
fund	must	suds	Dutch	chuckle	smuggle	
fuss		sulk	hutch	knuckle	snuggle	

with short OO-sound of *good wood:*
b*u*ll
b*u*llet
b*u*sh
b*u*tcher
c*u*ckoo
c*u*shion
f*u*ll
p*u*dding
p*u*ll
p*u*sh
p*u*ssy
p*u*t
s*u*gar
sh*u*sh

with long OO-sound: tr*u*th[trooth]

130

Table R 6. The graphemes *a-e, ai, -ay* and *eigh* all spell the <u>**AI-sound**</u> (or the open, long **A-sound**). Their pronunciations are predictable; but words with *ai* and *eigh* have to be individually memorised for spelling, as can be seen more clearly in Appendix S, table S 22 on page 214 and table S 29 on page 218.

age	flake	nave	state	aid	sprain	bay	neigh
ale	flame	pace	take	ail	stain	bray	sleigh
ape	frame	page	tale	aim	strain	clay	weigh
ate*	gale	pale	tame	ain't	straits	day	
babe	game	pane	tape	bail	tail	fray	
bake	gape	place	trace	bait	trail	gay	
bale	gate	plane	trade	braid	train	hay	straight
blade	gave	plate	wade	brain	vain	jay	
blame	gaze	quake	wage	chain	wail	lay	
blaze	glade	race	wake	claim	waist	May	
brace	grace	rage	wave	drain		may	
brake	grade	rake		fail		pay	
brave	grape	rate	label	gain	plaice	play	
cage	grate	rave		grain	praise	pray	
cake	grave	safe	<u>also with</u>	hail	raise	ray	
came	hate	sake	<u>AI-sound</u>	jail	raisin	say	
cape	haze	sale	able	laid	tailor	slay	
cave	jade	same	cable	maid	trailer	splay	
crane	lace	save	fable	mail	trainers	spray	
crate	lake	scale	gable	maim	traitor	stay	
crater	lame	scrape	stable	main	waiter	stray	
crave	lane	shade	table	nail		sway	
craze	late	shake		paid		tray	
dale	lathe	shame		pail		way	
dame	laze	shape		pain	exclaim		
date	made	slate		plain	explain		
drake	make	slave		quaint	obtain		<u>Please note:</u>
drape	male	snake		raid	prevail		**have** [hav]
face	mane	space		rail	proclaim		
fade	mate	spade		rain	refrain		**said** [sed]
fake	maze	stage		sail	remain		**plait** [plat]
fame	name	stake		slain	retail		
fate	nape	stale		snail	retain		**says** [sez]

* The pronunciation of *ate* is [et] in some accents and [ate] in others.

Table R 7. The **EE-sound** is spelt in many different ways (e.g. *treat, street, eve, machine, thief, seize, she, key* - tables S 43 - S 48), but only the *ee* grapheme has a fully predictable pronunciation.

The *e-e* grapheme, or *'open e'*, spells the EE-sound in the words shown below, but its pronunciation is not always predictable, e.g. *decent* [de̲e̲cent] - *defend*.

The endings *-y, -ey* and *-i* are predominantly pronounced with an EE-sound too, but an unstressed one. (For spelling, the *-ey* and *-i* endings have to be individually memorised.)

eel	heel	sleek	here	baby, daddy	bikini [bikeeny]
bee	jeep	sleep	mere	mummy	broccoli
fee	jeer	sneer	adhere	..and hundreds	confetti
flee	keel	speech	compete	more like them	corgi
free	keen	speed	complete	abbey	graffiti [grafeety]
glee	keep	steel	decent	alley	kiwi [keewy]
see	knee	steep	demon	attorney	safari
three	kneel	steer	female	barley	salami
tree	leek	street	frequent	bogey	semi [semmy]
beech	meek	sweep	hero	chimney	ski
beef	meet	sweet	meter	cockney	spaghetti
been	need	teem	period	donkey	taxi
beer	peek	teeth	peter	hockey	yeti [yetty]
beet	peel	tweed	recent	holey	exceptions:
bleed	peep	weed	relay	honey	**matinee**
bleep	peer	week	serious	jersey	[mattinay]
breed	preen	weep	sphere	jockey	
cheek	queen	wheel	swede	journey	**there** [thair]
cheer	reed	beetle	tedious	key	**were** [wer]
creek	reef	feeble	theme	kidney	**fete** [fait]
creep	reel	needle	these	medley	
deed	screech	steeple	zero	money	**hi!** [hy]
deep	screen	fleece	eve	monkey	**hi-fi** [hy-fy]
deer	seed	geese	even	parsley	
feed	seek	sleeve	evil	pulley	**grey** [gray]
feel	seem	breeze	fever	storey	**hey** [hay]
feet	seen	cheese	lever (UK)	trolley	**obey** [obay]
fleet	seep	freeze	*with short E:*	turkey	**they** [thay]
greed	sheep	sneeze	**eleven**	valley	**whey** [way]
green	sheer	squeeze	**lever** (US)	volley	**convey** [convay]
greet	sheet	wheeze	**never**	whiskey	**survey** [survay]
			seven	**several**	

Table R 8. The graphemes *i-e* and *igh* can both spell the **IE-sound**;
so can *-y, -ie* and *-ye* as vowel endings of one-syllable words.
In the endings of longer words the *i-e* grapheme spells the EE-
sound (e.g. mar*i*ne, pol*i*ce), as do *-y* and *-ie* in two-syllable
words (e.g. bab*y*, cut*ie*).

bike	nice	stride	fire	blight	by	die
bite	Nile	strike	hire	bright	cry	lie
chime	nine	stripe	spire	fight	dry	pie
cite	pike	swine	tire	flight	fly	tie
crime	pile	swipe	wire	fright	fry	vie
dice	pine	thrive		knight	my	
dike	pipe	tide	bible	light	ply	high
dine	price	tile	idle	might	pry	nigh
diner	pride	time	rifle	night	shy	sigh
dive	prime	tribe	stifle	right	sky	thigh
drive	prize	trite	title	sight	sly	
file	quite	twice	trifle	slight	spy	bye
fine	rice	twine		tight	sty	dye
five	ride	vice			thy	rye
glide	ripe	vile			try	
gripe	rise	vine			why	
guide	rite	while			wry	
hide	shine	whine				
hike	shrine	white			guy	
hive	side	wide				
ice	site	wife				
jive	size	wine				
kite	slice	wipe				
life	slide	wise				
like	slime	wives				
lime	smile	write				
line	smite					
live	snipe					
mice	spike		NB:			
mike	spine		**give** [giv]			
mile	spite		**live***			
mine	stile		*[liv]as verb			
			[live] as adjective			

133

Table R 9. The graphemes *o-e, oa, ol, oll, -o* and *-oe* all spell predominantly the **OE-sound,** but not always, as can be seen in the last column.

					Exceptions
bone	quote	boast	bold	fro	
broke	robe	boat	cold	go	
choke	rode	cloak	fold	no	**come** [cum]
chose	role	coach	gold	pro	**done** [dun]
close	rope	coal	golden	so	**dove** [duv]
code	rose	coast	hold	solo	**glove** [gluv]
cone	rove	coat	old		**love** [luv]
cope	scope	coax	scold	doe	**none** [nun]
cove	slope	croak	sold	floe	**one** [wun]
dole	smoke	float	solder	foe	**shove** [shuv]
dome	sole	foal	soldier	hoe	**some** [sum]
dose	spoke	foam	told	oboe	
dote	stoke	gloat		roe	**gone** [gon]
doze	stole	goat	bolt	sloe	**shone** [shon]
drone	stone	groan	colt	toe	**scone** [scon]
drove	strode	load	dolt	woe	*or [scone]*
elope	stroke	loaf	jolt		
froze	those	loan	revolt		**lose** [looz]
frozen	throne	loathe			**move** [moov]
hole	tone	moan	folk		**prove** [proov]
home	vote	oaf	yolk		**whose** [hooz]
hope	whole	oak			
hose	woke	oath	control		
joke	wove	oats	enrol		**board** [bord]
lone	wrote	poach	patrol		**broad** [braud]
mode	yoke	road			**oasis** [oe-aisis]
mole	zone	roam	poll		
node		roast	roll		**doll** [dol]
nose		shoal	scroll		
note		soak	stroll		**do** [doo]
poke		soap	toll		
pole		throat	troll		
pope		toad			
pose		toast			

134

Table R 10. The *oi* and *oy* graphemes occur in relatively few English words, but their pronunciations are mostly predictable. Only six common words have less predictable pronunciations [spelt out phonically in the last column, in brackets under each, with the stressed vowels underlined].

boil	choice	poison	boy	loyal	Exceptions:
coil	noise	rejoice	buoy [boy]	loyalty	**choir**
coin	voice	soil	joy	royal	[quier]
foil		spoil	toy	oyster	**coincide**
hoist	anoint	thyroid	annoy	voyage	[coe-incide]
join	appoint	toilet	convoy		**heroic**
joint	avoid	turmoil	corduroy		[heroe-ic]
joist	boisterous	turquoise	destroy		**heroine**
moist	cloister		enjoy		[herro-in]
oil	embroider		employ		**reservoir**
soil	exploit		employee		[rezzervuar]
spoil	loiter		employer		**tortoise**
toil	ointment		employment		[tortus]

Table R 11. The *au* grapheme, is also not very common, and in 17 words its pronunciation is not predictable.

auburn	cause	nautical	With different sounds for 'au'	
auction	caution	Paul	**assault**	[asolt]
August	cautious	pause	**aunt**	[ahnt]
author	cosmonaut	Santa-Claus	**Australia**	[Ostralia]
autumn	daub	sauce	**because**	[becoz]
audacious	daughter	saucer	**cauliflower**	[colliflour]
audible	dinosaur	slaughter	**chauffeur**	[shofer]*
auspicious	exhaust	somersault	**draught**	drahft]
authentic	gaudy	staunch	**fault**	[folt]
authorise	haughty	tarpaulin	**gauge**	[gage]
authority	haul	taught	**hydraulic**	[hide-rollic]
automatic	haunt	taunt	**laugh**	[lahf]
autonomy	jaunt	taut	**laureate**	[lorreat]
applaud	launch	vaunt	**laurel**	[lorrel]
applause	launder		**mauve**	[moav]
astronaut	laundry		**restaurant**	[resto-rent]
caught	maul		**sausages**	[sossages]
cauldron	naughty		***vault***	[volt/vault]

* *Chauffeur* is still pronounced the French way by some people, with stress on the last syllable.

Table R 12. The grapheme *-ti-, in conjunction with final -al, -an, -on* and
-ous, is used in the endings of many multi-syllable English
words for spelling the <u>**SH-sound**</u> (e.g. spa*ti*al, Mar*ti*an, sta*ti*on,
ficti*ti*ous). Sometimes *-ci-, -si-* and *-ssi-* serve the same
function, but *-si-* can also spell the **ZH-sound,** when used after
a vowel, in such endings.

The pronunciations of these endings are all relatively predictable, but the
length of the vowel which precedes the endings is not totally predictable
(e.g. *nation* with an AI-sound, but *ration* with a short A-sound - see tables
R 57 - R 70 on pages 178-92 for more about uncertain vowel length). -
Spelling problems which stem from uncertainty about when to use *-ti-* and
when *-ci-* are discussed on page 243.

with long vowel before '-tion'	with short vowels		less predictable vowels - long ones picket out in bold	si = zh
calculation	ration	passion	circumstan*ti*al	conclusion
conversation			confiden*ti*al	confusion
declaration	action	confession	consequen*ti*al	decision
demonstration	construction	depression		division
destination	election	procession	artifi*ci*al	explosion
education	fiction		benefi*ci*al	
explanation	fraction	admission	fa*ci*al	
foundation		emission	finan*ci*al	
generation	consumption	fission		
motivation			Alsa*ti*an	
	dimension	competition	Chris*ti*an	
lotion	expansion	composition	Dalma*ti*an	
promotion		condition		
	conception	expedition	cosmeti*ci*an	
constitution	perception	intuition	electri*ci*an	
distribution	prescription			
solution	reception	discussion	ambi*ti*ous	
			cau*ti*ous	
	conversion		ficti*ti*ous	
	diversion		nutri*ti*ous	
	excursion			
			atro*ci*ous	
			deli*ci*ous	
			fero*ci*ous	
			suspi*ci*ous	

The effect of 'r' on preceding vowels

For foreign learners the pronunciation of words with an *r* can be puzzling because it varies between different English accents. - The pronunciation of this letter is what most clearly differentiates between English accents.

In rhotic accents, like North American, an *r* has much the same pronunciation in different positions of a word. In standard UK English, an *'r' after a vowel* is not pronounced. It merely lengthens the vowel and gives it a throaty quality.

Within different English accents, vowels which are followed by *r* have highly predictable pronunciations.

Table R 13. Below are 81 common words containing **-ar-** and 14 words with **-air-**.

arc	harsh	start	alarm	affair
arch	hart	starve	apart	air
ark	jar	tar	army	chair
arm	larch	tart	artery	dairy
art	lard	yard	bargain	despair
bar	large	yarn	barley	éclair
barb	lark		cargo	fair
barge	mar		carnival	flair
bark	march		carpet	hair
barn	mark		carton	lair
car	mars		charge	pair
card	marsh		depart	prairie
cart	par		farther	repair
carve	parch		garden	stairs
char	park		gargle	
charm	part		garlic	
chart	scar		larder	
dark	scarf		larva	
darn	shark		market	
dart	sharp		parcel	
far	smart		pardon	
farm	snarl		partner	
hard	spark		party	
harm	star		remark	
harp	starch		target	

Table R 14. The stressed <u>ER-sound</u> has three different spellings (*er, **ur*** and ***ir***), but they all sound the same (within a particular English accent).

berth	nervous	blur	absurd	birch
fern	observe	burn	burden	bird
germ	perfect	burst	burglar	birth
her	permanent	church	burly	chirp
herb	permit	churn	disturb	dirt
herd	person	curl	excursion	fir
jerk	pertinent	curt	furnish	firm
nerve	preserve	fur	further	first
perch	reserve	hurl	murder	flirt
serve	reverse	hurt	murmur	girl
stern	sermon	lurch	nursery	mirth
swerve	serpent	lurk	return	shirk
term	terminate	purr	sturdy	shirt
verb	termite	slur	surgery	sir
verge	thermal	spur	surplus	skirt
verse	universe	spurn	Thursday	smirk
	verbal	spurt	topsy-turvy	squirm
alert	verdict	surf	turban	squirt
certain	vermin	turf	turkey	stir
concern	vertical	turn	turmoil	swirl
convert		urn	turnip	third
deserve		yurt	urban	thirst
detergent			urchin	twirl
emerge		surge		whir
eternal		urge		whirl
expert		burgle		
external		gurgle		circle
hermit		hurdle		circus
impertinent		hurtle		skirmish
insert		purple		thirty
internal		turtle		
interpret	exception:			
kernel	**clerk is**	curse		
merchant	pronounced	nurse		
Mercury	[clark] in	purse		
mercy	the UK	curve		

Table R 15. The **OR-sound** has three spellings with predictable pronunciations (*or, ore* and *oar*) which all sound the same.

or	scorch	absorb	ordinary	bore	boar
orb	scorn	afford	ornament	chore	board
born	shorn	border	perform	core	coarse
cord	short	conform	platform	gore	hoard
cork	snort	corgi	popcorn	more	hoarse
corn	sort	corner	portable	ore	oar
corpse	sport	cornet	portion	pore	roar
for	stork	divorce	portrait	score	soar
force	storm	enormous	proportion	shore	
ford	sword	forbid	record	snore	
forge	sworn	forever	recorder	sore	
fork	thorn	forget	reform	store	
form	torch	forgive	report	swore	
fort	torn	forgot	reporter	tore	
forth		forgotten	resort	wore	
gorge		fortress	scorpion		
gorse		fortune	shortly	adore	
horn		forty	storage	before	
horse		forward	story	ignore	
lord		glory	thunderstorm	implore	
nor		important	tortoise		
norm		morning	transform	forecast	*Exception:*
north		normal	transporter	forehand	**forehead**
porch		northern	uniform	foreleg	[forred]
pork		orbit		foreman	- with short 'o'
port		orchard			and silent 'h'
		order			in UK English

The letter *r* is also used in the unstressed endings *-ar, -er, -re, -or,* and *-our* (e.g. burgl*ar*, gambl*er*, cent*re*, visit*or*, harb*our*). Such endings are all pronounced as *-er* in normal speech (although the pronunciation of *r* itself, is different between accents, as explained above).

Learners are often encouraged to adopt an exaggerated spelling pronunciation for these different unstressed endings, in order to help them remember the different spellings, but usually they all sound the same.

Letters with unpredictable pronunciations:

the consonants *c, g, h, q, s, w,*

the digraphs *ch, gh* **and** *th*

and words with *silent letters*

C

The pronunciation of *c* depends on the letters which follow it, and also on its position in a word:

1. The predominant pronunciation for *c* is *k*. This applies

    a) *before* the vowels *a, o* and *u* (e.g. cat, cot, cut) and

    b) before all *consonants, except h* (e.g. cling, cram, act - chop),

    c) *at the end of words* with more than one syllable (e.g. comic, music).

2. Short words which end with a K-sound (after a short vowel) are spelt with *ck* (e.g. brick, lick, stick), i.e. *-ic* and *-ick* endings sound the same.

3. C is also used *to mark a short vowel before k* (e.g. stacked, kicking), i.e. we use *ck* instead of *kk* when the letter *k* needs doubling.

4. *Before* **e, i** and **y,** *c* is usually pronounced with an S-sound (e.g. centre, fence, city, cylinder), but not in <u>cello</u> [*chello*].

5. *After an s,* *c* is usually silent (e.g. scene, science).

6. **Cc** is pronounced **ks** *before e* and *i* (e.g. access, accident
                                     - except <u>soccer</u> [*socker*])
    and as *k* *elsewhere* (e.g. occasion, account).

Table R 16 opposite provides examples of the different pronunciations for *c*.

Table R 16. The letter *c* occurs in 1781 common English words. Below are some examples of the most frequent letter combinations in which it is used, as explained opposite.

c = k		c = s	c = k / c = s	cc = k	sc with silent c
cackle	biscuit	cease	cancel	accompany	abscess
cake	cascade	ceiling	cancer	accomplish	adolescent
came	describe	celery	certificate	accord	ascend
camp	disc	cellar	circle	accordance	ascertain
can	disco	**cello**	circular	accordion	condescend
cap	discover	*[chello]*	circus	account	convalesce
clap	discuss	cement	civic	accrue	crescent
click	escape	cent	concept	accumulate	descend
cling	mollusc	centre	concern	accurate	disciple
clock	muscular	century	concert	accuse	discipline
club	obscure	cereal	confidence	accustom	fascinating
cluck	scurry	certain	convince	broccoli	muscle
cock				hiccough	proboscis
conflict		cider		hiccup	scene
cork		cinema		occasion	scent
cosmic		citizen		occupy	science
crab		city		occur	scissors
crack		civil		piccolo	scythe
crackle				succulent	
crop		face		succumb	
crush		ice			
cry		lace		cc = ks	sc = sh
cup		mice		accelerate	conscience
scalp		price		accent	conscientious
scar		advice		accept	conscious
scoff		brace		access	fascism
scope		device		accident	luscious
scorch		fence		eccentric	
score		hence		success	
scrap		pence			
scrape		force		*except:*	
scratch		prince		**soccer**	
scuttle				*[socker]*	

G

Table R 17. The pronunciation of the letter **g** is not entirely predictable. Before the vowels **e, i** and **y**, g is pronounced *predominantly with a J-sound*, as in the words below; but see also last column in table R 18.

gem	tangent	language	urge	apologise
general	tangerine	large	verge	eligible
generation	vegetarian	lounge	village	engine
generous	vengeance	lozenge	voyage	engineer
genie		manage	wage	fugitive
genius	advantage	marriage		giant
gentle	age	message	ginger	hygiene
gentleman	arrange	orange	gin	ideological
genuine	average	package	ginger	imagination
geography	bandage	page	giraffe	legion
geology	barge	passage		legitimate
geometry	bulge	percentage		magician
geranium	cabbage	postage		marginal
germinate	cage	prestige		meteorologist
gesture	carriage	privilege		origin
	challenge	rage		ornithologist
agency	change	range		palaeontologist
agent	charge	refuge		regime
algebra	college	revenge		region
angel	cottage	rummage		registration
danger	cringe	salvage		strategic
degenerate	emerge	sausage		tangible
detergent	engage	savage		
digest	enlarge	scavenge	gym	archaeology
dungeon	enrage	shortage	gypsy	astrology
emergency	exchange	siege	gyrate	clergy
gorgeous	foliage	singe		dingy
hydrangea	forge	sponge		effigy
hydrogen	fringe	stage		energy
intelligent	garbage	storage		geology
manger	gorge	strange		pathology
oxygen	hinge	surge		psychology
passenger	hostage	syringe		strategy
sergeant	huge	tinge		theology
surgery	image	twinge		

142

Table R 18. A short, stressed vowel *before -ge or -gi* is often marked with *d* (e.g. badger), but not consistently so (e.g. *magic, logic*).

A *gg* is supposed to indicate a *hard G-sound* after a short, stressed vowel *before e, i and y* (e.g. *dagger*), but it fails to do so in *suggest [sujest]* and *exaggerate [exadjerate]*.

In the 32 common words in the last two columns *g* is pronounced with a *hard sound* despite occurring *before e, i and y*. This is normally the case only before *a, o* and *u* (e.g. *garden, got, gum* - see pages 126, 129, 130-1 for more examples).

Short vowels before ge and gi marked with d	unmarked	gg = g	ge / gi / gy with a *hard* G-sound	
badge	agile	baggage	**anger**	**giddy**
badger	agitate	baggy	**bogey**	**gift**
bridge	fragile	digger	**eager**	**giggle**
budget	illegible	jagged	**finger**	**gild**
budgie	imagine	luggage	**fishmonger**	**gills**
dodge	legislate	nugget	**forget**	**gilt**
dodgems	logic	ragged	**gear**	**girder**
dredge	magic	rugged	**geese**	**girdle**
edge	magistrate	scraggy	**get**	**girl**
fridge	original	shaggy	**geyser**	**forgive**
grudge	religion	snigger	**hamburger**	**give, given**
hedge	religious	soggy	**hunger**	**longevity**
hedgehog	rigid	stagger	**linger**	**longitude**
judge	tragic	swagger	**target**	
ledge	regiment	trigger	**tiger**	**gymkhana**
lodge	register		**together**	
midget		*Exceptions:*	**begin**	
nudge	pageant	**suggest**	**corgi**	
podgy	pigeon	[sujest		
ridge	refrigerator	and US sujest]		
sledge	vegetables	**exaggerate**		
smudge		[exadjerate]		
trudge				

H

The letter *h* is frequently **silent** (e.g. *hour* - [our], *rhyme* - [rime], *white* - [wite]), although learners are often taught to pronounce such words with a hint of an *h*, as an aid to help them remember the spellings. In such exaggerated pronunciation, *wh* is often pronounced *hw*.

Table R 19. In normal speech, the following 49 words have a *silent h*.
A few longer words have unpredictable stress as well, i.e. they are not stressed on the first syllable, as the majority of commonly used English words are. Vowels with unusual stress are picked out in bold and underlined [and unexpected pronunciations are spelt out more simply in brackets.]

exhaust	whack	which
exh**i**bit [ex**i**bbit]	whale	whiff
exhib**i**tion	wharf	while
heir [air]	what	whilst [wielst]
honest [onnest]		whimper
honour [onner]	wheat	whine
hour	wheedle	whip
khaki [cahki]	wheel	whir
rheumatism [roomatism]	wheelie	whirl
rhin**o**ceros [rin**o**sseros]	wheeze	whisk
rhododendr**o**n	whelk	whiskers
rhubarb [roobarb]	when	whiskey
rhyme [rime]	where	whisky
rhythm [rithm]	whether	whisper
	whey	whistle [wisl]
		white
	overwh**e**lm	whiz
	shepherd	
		whoosh
		why

144

Q

The letter *q* is almost invariably followed by *u*. (*Iraq* is a rare exception.) The dominant pronunciation of the *qu* grapheme is **kw**, but this is not completely reliable (e.g. *queue* [kue], *conquer* [conker]). The pronunciation of the letter *a* *after* *qu* is also somewhat unpredictable.

Table R 20. 92 common words with *qu* and the different pronunciations of this grapheme.

qu = kw		qu = k	qua = kwo
acquaint	quill	bouquet	quadrangle
acquire	quilt	chequered	qualify
acquit	quince	conquer	quantity
aquarium	quintet	lacquer	quarrel
banquet	quit	liquor	quarry
conquest	quite	liquorice [lickerish]	quarter
consequence	quiver	marquee	quartz
enquire	quiz	mosquito [moskeeto]	squabble
equation	quota	quay [kee]	squad
equator	quote	queue [cue]	squander
equipment	request	quoit	squash
equivalent	require	turquoise	squat
exquisite	sequence		
frequent	sequin	antique [anteek]	
inquire	squall	boutique [booteek]	qua = kwa
liquid	square	cheque	quack
quaint	squawk	mosque	equal
quake	squeak	opaque	adequate
queen	squeal	picturesque	aquatic
queer	squeeze	technique [tecneek]	
quell	squelch	unique [yooneek]	
quench	squint		
query	squirm		
quest	squirrel		
question	squirt		
quibble	squishy		
quick	subsequent		
quiet	ventriloquist		

S

In word endings, the *plural marker s can spell an* <u>*S-sound or Z-sound*</u>. Its pronunciation depends on the letter before it: After *f, k, p, t* and *th*, the letter *s* has an <u>S-sound</u> (e.g. *cliffs, bricks, shops, flats, maths*); but after other letters *s* is pronounced with a <u>Z-sound</u> (e.g. *labs, kids, bags, badges, hills, mums, pins, cars, gloves, mazes, boxes*).

After vowels, final *s* tends to have predominantly an *S-sound* (e.g. *atlas, axis, circus)*, but there a few exceptions.

<u>Table R 21.</u> Examples of words in which a *final s* is pronounced with an S-sound or Z-sound;
also examples of how the sound of plural *-s* is determined by the preceding letter.

s = s			**s = z**	**plural s = z**	**plural s = s**
analysis	hippopotamus	tonsillitis	always	proceeds	aerobatics
apparatus	hypothesis	trellis	as	suds	economics
asparagus	iris	Uranus	does		politics
atlas	its	us	goes	lungs	tropics
axis	minus	Venus	has	findings	
basis	nucleus	walrus	his		chiefs
bronchitis	oasis	yes	is	nails	cliffs
bus	octopus		lens	vegetables	puffs
cactus	pampas		Mars		
campus	pelvis		says	customs	
canvas	perhaps		was	grams	
chaos	platypus				
chorus	plus			jeans	
Christmas	radius			regulations	crisps
chrysalis	rhinoceros		**Silent s**		mumps
circus	species		corps	scissors	
citrus	status		debris	slippers	battlements
crisis	surplus				pants
emphasis	synopsis			clothes	
eucalyptus	synthesis			wives	maths
focus	tennis			gallows	
fungus	tetanus				
gas	this			crutches	
genius	thus			resources	

Table R 22. The pronunciation of *-se endings* is *highly variable.*
After vowels, it is mostly pronounced *with a Z-sound,* but there are 23 common exceptions. After consonants, it is pronounced with an *S-sound,* with the exception of *cleanse* which ends with a *Z-sound.*

se = z				se = s		
				after vowels	*after consonants*	
praise	despise	noise	arouse	base	else	coarse
raise	devise	turquoise	blouse	case	impulse	course
mayonnaise	disguise		house*1	chase	pulse	curse
	emphasise	arose	rouse	purchase	dense	gorse
erase	enterprise	chose	browse	cease	expanse	hoarse
phase	exercise	close*1	drowse	crease	expense	horse
phrase	fertilise	compose		grease	immense	nurse
vase	hypnotise	dispose	choose	increase	intense	purse
[UK: vahz]	idolise	enclose	bruise	release	license	rehearse
	memorise	expose	cruise	geese	nonsense	reverse
please	merchandise	hose	abuse*1	these	response	universe
tease	organise	impose	accuse	practise*2	rinse	verse
disease	recognise	nose	confuse	precise	sense	worse
ease	revise	oppose	excuse*1	premise	suspense	
cheese	rise	pose	use*1	promise	tense	
Chinese	sterilise	primrose		tortoise		
Japanese	surprise	propose	applause	dose	collapse	
	synchronise	rose	cause	goose	copse	
advise	tantalise	suppose	pause	loose	corpse	
agonise*3	wise	those		noose	eclipse	
apologise				purpose	elapse	
arise	analyse	lose		douse	glimpse	
authorise	breathalyse	[looz]		mouse	lapse	
baptise	paralyse	whose				
compromise		[hooz]			se = z	*cleanse*

* 1) The words *abuse, close, excuse, house* and *use* are pronounced with a final *Z-sound* when used as *verbs,* but with an *S-sound* when used as *nouns or adjectives* (e.g. *use* = [to *uze*] and [it has no *uce*]).

* 2) In the US, *practice* has just one spelling; but in the UK, the verb is spelt *practise* and the noun *practice* - in complete contrast to the five words above which have just one spelling for two different pronunciations.

* 3) In US English, some British *-ise* endings are spelt *-ize* (e.g. agon*ize* for UK agon*ise*).

W

The letter *w* serves several different functions, as can be seen in the tables on this and the next three pages.

1) It can be a *consonant* (e.g. *win, sweep*).

2) As an initial letter, before other consonants, *w* is often *silent* (e.g. *who*).

3) *W* is also used to *modify vowels*.

   a) Sometimes it modifies the vowel *after it*
      (e.g. w<u>a</u>nt = [w<u>o</u>nt], w<u>or</u>k = [w<u>e</u>rk]).

   b) Sometimes it modifies the vowel *before it* (e.g. *blew* [bloo],
      how [hou], *low* [lo]. - The pronunciation of the *ow* grapheme is
      highly unpredictable, as can be seen in table R 24 opposite.

Table R 23. 31 common words have a *silent w*, i.e. the *w* is not pronounced.
[Words with other unpredictable elements in them are spelt out more simply in brackets.]

who	wrangle	wriggle	answer
[hoo]	wrap	wring	sword
whom	wrath	wrinkle	two
[hoom]	[roth]	wrist	[too]
whose	wreak	writ	knowledge
[hooz]	[reek]	write	[nollege]
whooping	wreath	writhe	
whole	[reeth]	written	
	wreck	wrong	
	wren	wrote	
	wrench	wrung	
	wrestle	wry	
	wretch		

Table R 24. This shows the different pronunciations for *ow*.

* In the words ***bow, row*** and ***sow***, -*ow* has different pronunciations for different meanings:
 bow - [bou] your head, but tie a [bo];
 row - [ro] a boat and sit in a [ro], but hear a [rou];
 sow - [so] seeds, but feed a [sou].

At the end of longer words, *ow* is predominantly pronounced with an OE-sound (e.g. *borrow* = borro, *follow* = follo), apart from *allow* and *miaow /meow* with a final sound of *ou*.

ow=ou			ow= oe			
brown	browse	*bow**	blow	blown	arrow	shadow
brownie	coward	brow	flow	flown	barrow	shallow
clown	crowd	cow	grow	grown	bellow	sorrow
crown	drowse	how		growth	below	sparrow
down	flower	now	know	known	billow	swallow
drown	powder	*row**	mow	mown	borrow	tomorrow
frown	power	*sow**		own	bungalow	wallow
gown	rowdy	vow	show	shown	burrow	widow
town	shower	wow		sown	elbow	willow
	towel		throw	thrown	fellow	window
growl	tower	allow			follow	yellow
howl	vowel	miaow	crow	bowl	gallows	
owl			glow		hollow	
prowl			low	owe	marrow	
scowl			slow	rowan	meadow	
			snow		narrow	
			stow		pillow	
			tow			

149

Table R 25. The effect of *w on the vowel after it* is not reliable, (e.g. *swan*=swon, *swag*=swag).

vowels with the expected sound after w	wa=wo	war=wor	wor=wer
	swallow	dwarf	word
	swamp	war	work
swag	swan	warble	world
swagger	swap	ward	worm
swam	waddle	wardrobe	worse
twang	waft	warm	worship
wag	walk	warn	worst
wangle	wall	warp	worth
wax	wallaby	wart	
sway	wallet	award	
wade	wallop	reward	
wage	wallow	toward	
wail	walnut		
waist	walrus	warrant	
wait	waltz	warren	
waiter	wan	warrior	
wake	wand		
wares	wander	**unstressed**	
wary [wairy]	want	**war=wer**	
waste	wanton	awkward	
wave	was	coward	
waver	wash	forward	
way	wasp	steward	
wobble	watch	upward	
wont	watt		
	wattle		
oddities:	wagon [waggon]	**wo=wu**	**wo=wi**
		won	women
		wonder	
	water [wauter]	worry	
			wor/e=wor
		wo=woo	wore
		wolf	worn
		woman	swore
		womb	sworn

150

Table R 26. This shows *the effect of **w** on a preceding a and e.*
The pronunciation of the grapheme *ew* is mainly *oo* or *ue*
(except for *sew* which is pronounced [so]).

The sound of *ew* is partly determined by the consonant which precedes it
(e.g. *grew* = [groo], but *new* = [nue]); but this is less certain with *lew* (e.g.
blew =[bloo], *curlew* = [curl'yoo]).

ew= oo	ew = ue/yoo	ew=oe	aw = au		aw= a-w
blew	curlew	sew	awe	prawn	await
brew	lewd	[so]	awful	raw	awake
slew	askew	sewn	awkward	saw	awaken
crew	chew	[sone]	awning	sawn	award
drew	curfew		bawl	scrawl	aware
flew	dew		brawl	seesaw	away
grew	ewe		brawn	shawl	
screw	few		claw	spawn	
shrew	interview		crawl	sprawl	
shrewd	Jew		dawdle	squawk	
strew	jewel		dawn	straw	
threw	knew		draw	strawberry	
cashew	mildew		drawl	thaw	
	nephew		drawn	trawler	
	new		fawn	yawn	
	newt		flaw		
	pew		gnaw		
	pewter		hawk		
	review		jaw		
	sewage		jigsaw		
	skewer		law		
	spew		lawn		
	stew		lawyer		
	steward		Macaw		
	view		paw		
	yew		pawn		

CH

The dominant pronunciation for **ch** is as in *chat, chip, chop* and *much*. The tables with phonically simple spellings, at the beginning of this appendix, contain many words with *ch* which have the expected pronunciation for this grapheme. But at least 46 words have a different pronunciation for this letter combination, as can be seen in the table below.

.

Table R 27. Words with *unpredictable pronunciations for ch*.

ch = k		ch = sh
ache	mechanical	chalet
anchor	mechanism	champagne
archaeology	monarch	chandelier
architect	psychology	charade
architecture	orchestra	chauffeur
chameleon	orchid	chef
bronchial	schedule*	crochet
bronchitis	scheme	microfiche
chameleon	scholar	moustache
chaos	school	chivalrous
character	schooner	machine
chasm	stomach	choux
chemical	synchronise	chute
chemistry		parachute
cholesterol		
chorus		**lichen**
echo		[litchen or liken]
		choir
		[quier]

* *Schedule* is sometimes pronounced [sheddule] in US English.

A short, stressed vowel is predominantly followed by **tch** (e.g. ca*tch*, fe*tch*, despa*tch*), rather than just *ch*, but not in atta*ch*, deta*ch*, mu*ch*, ri*ch*, su*ch*, tou*ch* or whi*ch*.

GH

The pronunciation of **gh** is often unpredictable. The grapheme itself is predominantly silent, but it modifies the sound of the preceding vowel (e.g. high = hie/hy).

The **igh** grapheme is pronounced consistently with an IE-sound (see table R 8). Other letter combinations with *gh* have less predictable pronunciations (e.g. b*ough*t = [baut], dr*ough*t = [drout]).

In 3 words the *h* after *g* merely indicates a hard sound for *g* - *gherkin, dinghy, spaghetti*. Readers have to learn the pronunciations of most words with *gh* as whole words.

Table R 28. 44 words with *unpredictable gh* have their pronunciations spelt out more simply [in brackets] next to each word.

neigh	[nay]	rough	[ruf]	caught	[caut]
neighbour	[naber]	tough	[tuf]	daughter	[dauter]
sleigh	[slay]	slough*	[sluf]	haughty	[hauty]
weigh	[way]		or slou]	naughty	[nauty]
eight	[ate]			slaughter	[slauter]
freight	[frate]	cough	[cof]	taught	[taut]
weight	[wate]	trough	[trof]		US / UK:
				draught	[draft/drahft]
height	[hite]	dough	[doe]*	laugh	[laf / larf]
sleight	[slite]	though	[tho]		
		bough	[bou]	**With hard G-sound**	
straight	[strate]	plough	[plou]	aghast	[agast] (US)
					[agarst] (UK)
bought	[baut]	through	[throo]	ghastly	[gastly] (US)
brought	[braut]				[garstly] (UK)
fought	[faut]	enough	[inuff]	ghost	[goast]
nought	[naut]			ghoulish	[goolish]
ought	[aut]	hiccough	[hickup]	yoghurt	[yogurt]
sought	[saut]				
thought	[thaut]	thorough	[thrurru]		
drought	[drout]				

* The pronunciation of *dough* has been spelt out as [doe] rather than [do] in order to avoid confusion with the word *do* which is pronounced [doo].

The pronunciation of *th* is problematic for non-native learners of English, since the sound of *th* can be *sharp* (e.g. *th*is) or *soft* (e.g. *th*ink). At the end of words *th* is usually soft, with the exception of *with*. Occasionally *th* is pronounced *t* (e.g. *th*yme).

Table R 29. This shows the different pronunciations for ***th***.

th with a *soft* sound			*th* with a *sharp* sound		
thank	aesthetic	bath	than		
thatched	Arthur	birth	that		
theatre	athletic	both [boath]	the		
theme	authentic	breath	their		
theology	author	broth	them		
theory	authorised	cloth	then		
therapy	authority	death	there		
thermal	cathedral	depth	these		
thick	catholic	earth	they		
thin	enthusiasm	fourth	this		
thing	enthusiastic	froth	those		
think	ethical	growth	though		
third	ethics	health	thus		
thirty	hypothesis	length			
thistle	mathematics	month	bathe	slither	
thorough	method	mouth	bother	smother	
thought	orthodox	myth	breathe	together	
thousand	pathology	ninth	brother	weather	
thread	sympathy	north	clothes	whether	
threat	sympathy	path	either	writhe	
threaten	synthesis	sloth	farther		
three		smooth	father		
threw		south	feather		
throat		strength	further		
through		teeth	gather		
throughout		tooth	heather		
throw		truth	leather		
thrown		warmth	mother		
thrust		wealth	neither		
thumb		worth	other	**th = t**	
thunder		youth	rather	Anthony	
		with	rhythm	thyme	

Compounds and derivatives from words containing *th* usually keep the same sound as the word from which they derive, as can be seen in the examples below.

Table R 30. Compounds and derivatives with *th*.

with soft *th*	with sharp *th*
anything	although
mathematical	altogether
sympathetic	another
theological	grandfather
theorem	grandmother
theoretical	nevertheless
therapist	otherwise
thermometer	that's
theoretical	themselves
	thereafter
bathroom	thereby
birthday	therefore
earthquake	thereof
	there's
health - healthy	they'd
length- lengthen	they'll
strength - strengthen	they're

A few words which are derivatives from root words ending with a soft *th* acquire a sharp pronunciation. Some undergo vowel changes as well.

cloth - clothing [cloathing]
      clothes [cloathes]
North - northern
South - southern [suthern]
worth - worthy

In addition to words with *silent gh, h* and *w* (listed in tables 19, 23 and 28 above), another 119 words have assorted silent consonants, as can be seen in tables R31, R32 and R33.

Words with silent consonants as well as other unpredictable elements in their pronunciation (e.g. *climb* = [clime]) are spelled out in brackets, using more usual English graphemes.

Table R 31. Words with *silent b, c, d, g, k, l, m* and *p.*

silent b:	silent g	silent k
dumb	gnome	know [no]
debt	gnu [noo]	knew
climb [clime]	foreign [forren]	known [noan]*
comb [coam]*	phlegm [flem]	knowledge [nollege]
tomb [toom]	diaphragm [diafram]	knuckle
womb [woom]	cognac [coniac]	
	poignant [poiniant]	silent l:
silent c:	sovereign [sovren]	could [coo/ud]*
acquaint	campaign [campane]	should [shoo/ud]*
acquire	champagne [shampane]	would [woo/ud]*
acquit	reign [rane]	folk [foke]
lacquer[lacker]	feign [fane]	half [UK harf]
exceed	align [aline]	salmon [sammen]
excel	benign [benine]	talk [tauk]
except	consign [consine]	
excess	design [dezine]	silent m:
excite	resign [rezine]	mnemonic
		[nemonnic]
silent d:	silent k:	
adjacent	knack	silent p:
adjoin	knacker	psalm
adjust	knave	pneumatic
handkerchief	knead [need]	pseudonym [sudonim]
handsome	knee	pterodactyl [terradactil]
Wednesday	knickers	empty
	knife	receipt
silent g:	knight [nite]	sapphire
gnarled	knit	cupboard [cubberd]
gnash	knob	raspberry
gnat	knock	corps
gnaw	knot	coup [coo]

* For explanations see top on next page.

156

* Two explanations concerning phonic respelling in table 31:

1) If *comb* and *known* were respelt using basic English phonics, they would have to be spelt [*come*] and [*none*]; but this could be misleading because *come* and *none* are words in current use and have the unpredictable pronunciations of [cum] and [nun].

2) The short OO/U-sound is the only English sound which has no clearly identifiable spelling for it. It occurs in *good*, *put* and *should*, but these graphemes are more commonly pronounced as in the words *food*, *but* and *shoulder*.

Table R 32. Words with *silent s* and *t.*

silent s:	silent t:	depot [deppo]	mortgage [morgaj]
aisle [ile]	apostle [aposl]	fasten [UK farsn]	nestle [nesl]
isle [ile]	bristle [brisl]	glisten [glisn]	often [ofn/oftn]
island [iland]	bustle [busl]	gristle [grisl]	rustle [rusl]
	castle [UK carsl]	hasten [hacen]	thistle [thisl]
	chasten [chacen]	hustle [husl]	trestle [tresl]
	christen [crisn]	jostle [josl]	whistle [wisl]
	Christmas [crismas]	listen [lisn]	wrestle [resl]

Table R 33. Some English words still retain their original ***French spellings and pronunciations.***

beret [berray]	crochet [croshay]	chamois [shammua]
ballet [ballay]	croquet [crokay]	debris[debree]
bouquet [bookay]	parquet [parkay]	choux [shoo]
buffet [buffay]	richochet [rickoshay]	prix [pree]
cabaret [cabbaray]	valet [vallay]	
chalet [shallay]		

4. Pronunciation problems caused by:

a, i, o, u, y,

ea, ei, ie, ou, oo, ui,

'magic e' and *'open vowels'*

English vowels present many challenges for learners. Even single vowels in short words can have unexpected pronunciations (e.g. *kin - kind* [kined]). Longer words provide even more scope for uncertainty. The patterns of *mile* and *miller,* for example, are not much help with the pronunciation of *militant* [millitent] if you have not met the word before.

Getting the vowel length and stress right is a problem with all English vowel letters. This difficulty is therefore discussed as a separate topic on pages 178-91. Different pronunciations for *al* as in <u>al</u>*titude* [**al**titude] and *al<u>though</u>* [**au**ltho] are also [**au**lso] discussed there (page 187).

The letter **a** has four kinds of unexpected pronunciations, in addition to its dominant sound in words like *as, at, cat* and *mat.*

1) *Any* and *many* are pronounced as [*enny*] and [*menny*].

2) The words a*ble, cable, fable, gable, stable* and *table* rhyme with the phonically spelt *label.* They still retain their French spellings, but not their French pronunciations.

3) The word *bass* is pronounced [bace] when it means low voice, but [bas] when it means fish.

4) In standard UK English speech, the letter *a* often has an unpredictable pronunciation as [ah/ar]. In standard BBC English, the word *pant* has the same vowel sound as *and,* but *plant* is pronounced like *plahnt* or *plarnt.* (*Ah* and *ar* have the same sound in UK English.)

158

Table R 34. The words below have an **AH/AR**-sound for *a* in
   standard UK English.

Only in the graphemes *aft* and *ance* is the UK AH-sound predictable.
(Although *-ance* has a different sound when used as an unstressed ending -
e.g. dist*ance*.) In all the other words below, *the long AH-sound is
unpredictable*. In many similar looking words *a* has the *dominant A-sound*:
Africa, balcony, ass, aspect, asthma, drastic, gather.

(Nearly all the multi-syllable words in the last column have more than one
a. The stressed long *a* is underlined.)

after	chance	almond	ask	task	bra	advance
daft	dance	calm	bask	vast	la	avalanche
craft	enhance	calf	blast	contrast	ma	armada
draft	glance	gala	cask	disaster	pa	banana
graft	lance	half	cast	ghastly	spa	bastard
raft	prance	halve	caste	raspberry		drama
shaft	stance	palm	castle	vase[vahz]	ah	example
	trance		clasp		hurrah	flabbergast
			fast	brass	shah	mama
staff	branch		flask	glass		panorama
giraffe	chant		gasp	class	bath	papa
graph	piano		grasp	grass	lather	promenade
	plant		last	mass*	father	rascal
	slant		mask	pass	path	salami
	soprano		mast		rather	strata
			past			

* When *'mass'* means *'quantity'* it is pronounced with the usual A-sound;
when it means *'a church service'* it has an AH-sound in standard UK
English, although this distinction is gradually disappearing in the UK too.

The lengthening of the A-sound first occurred in refined, upper-class speech
in England long after the first British settlers emigrated to America. So while
this vowel change became standard in educated British speech during the
19th century, it was never adopted in American English, where these words
have kept their earlier pronunciation.

E

The letter *e has a relatively predictable pro*nunciation, at least when used in one-syllable words. The only exceptions are *be, he, me, she* and *we*, as already mentioned earlier.

I

The letter *i* is pronounced *with an IE-sound* in 19 common words.

Table R 35. In brackets, next to each word is the spelling that would be used, if these words were spelt using the dominant English spelling pattern for the **IE**-sound, as in *life, filed* or *lined*.

rifle [rifel]	behind [behined]	ninth [nineth]
stifle [stifel]	bind [bined]	pint [pinet]
trifle [trifel]	blind [blined]	
	find [fined]	sign [sine]
child [chiled]	grind [grined]	
mild [miled]	kind [kined]	climb [clime]
whilst [wilest]	mind [mined]	
wild [wiled]	rind [rined]	

wind [wind or wined] - *wind* has two pronunciations

160

O

The letter _o is particularly apt to be misread_. In many words _o_ is pronounced with the same sound as the _u_ in _but_ (e.g. _other_ [uther]) and the _open vowel /magic e_ principle often has to be disregarded as well.

Table R 36. In all the 60 words below, normal pronunciation patterns do not quite apply. [They are spelt phonically, in brackets next to each word.]

o / o-e / open o = u (as in 'but')				oddments	
above	[abuv]	none	[nun]	both	[boath]
among	[amung]	nothing	[nuthing]	gross	[groce]
brother	[bruther]	once	[wunce]	host	[hoast]
colour	[culler]	one	[wun]	most	[moast]
come	[cum]	onion	[unnien]	only	[onely]
comfort	[cumfert]	other	[uther]	post	[poast]
compass	[cumpas]	oven	[uvn]	poster	[poaster]
cover	[cuvver]	shove	[shuv]		
does	[duz]	shovel	[shuvl]		
done	[dun]	slovenly	[sluvvenly]	womb	[woom]
dove	[duv]	smother	[smuther]	wolf	[wu/oolf]
dozen	[duzzen]	some	[sum]		
front	[frunt]	son	[sun]	woman	[wu/oomman]
glove	[gluv]	sponge	[spunge]	today	[tu/ooday]
honey	[hunny]	stomach	[stummac]	tomorrow	[tu/oomorro]
love	[luv]	thorough	[thurra]		
Monday	[Munday]	ton	[tun]	women	[wimmen]
money	[munnyl]	tongue	[tung]		
monger	[munguer]	won	[wun]	comb	[coam]
mongrel	[mungrel]	wonder	[wunder]		
monk	[munk]	worry	[wurry]		
monkey	[munky]			_to_ *	
month	[munth]			*the _o_ in _to_ can be	
mother	[muther]			_a short oo_, as in 'to go',	
				or a long oo, as in 'to town'	

U

Fourteen common words with **u** do *not* have *the dominant pronunciation of 'but, cut'* and *'nut'*. They have the *short OO-sound of 'good'*; and *'truth'* has a long OO-sound.

Table R 37. Words with *unusual pronunciation for the letter **u***.

bull full	bush put	cuckoo	pussy *	**truth** [trooth]
bullet pull	push pudding	cushion		
	shush butcher	sugar [shoogger]		

* *pussy* has two different pronunciations:
1) with the *short oo* when meaning *'cat'*,
2) with the more common *U-sound of 'but'* when referring to *the liquid produced by infected tissue*.

In Northern English and Scottish English all the words above are pronounced with a longer OO-sound, almost identical to the long OO-sound of *'food'* and *'moon'*. Moreover, in those accents the standard UK long OO-sound is a little shorter. The two UK short and long OO-sounds are pronounced more or less identically there.

Y

The letter **y** is challenging for beginning readers, because it serves many different purposes and because the pronunciation of words with **y** is frequently unpredictable.

1) **At the beginning of words,** **y-** is used as a consonant, including the very frequently used word *you* which does not follow the more usual pattern of *unit* and *use*.

Table R 38. This shows 27 common *words beginning with **y**;*
14 contain some kind of unpredictable element in them.
[Their pronunciations are spelt more predictably in brackets.]

yacht [yot]	yawn	yell	yeti [yetty]	yoke
yahoo	yeah [yeh]	yellow	yew	yolk [yoke]
yak	yearn [yern]	yelp	yield [yeeld]	you [u]
yap	yeast [yeest]	yes [yess]	yodel	young [yung]
yard		yet	yoga	your [yor]
yarn			yoghurt [yogurt]	youth [yooth]

162

2) **In word endings**, *-y* has *two main pronunciations*: an **EE**-sound and an **IE**-sound:

a) In hundreds of multi-syllable words *-y* spells an unstressed **EE**-sound (e.g. bab*y*, oddit*y*, slowl*y*),

but

b) in one-syllable words *-y* is pronounced with an **IE**-sound (e.g. b*y*, fl*y*, sk*y*); and

c) also in and about 50 longer verbs which end with the suffix '-*fy*' (e.g. glori*fy*, horri*fy*, justi*fy*, simpli*fy*);

Table R 39. 12 multi-syllable words which end in *-y* (*but not the suffix -fy*) also have a *stressed -y ending* which is pronounced *with an IE-sound*, unlike the dominant pattern of *daddy, mummy* or *thirty*.

ally	defy	imply	occupy	reply	July
apply	deny	multiply	rely	supply	pigsty

3) The *biggest reading difficulty* is caused by **y** as a *vowel inside words*, where **y** is a **replacement for i** and serves to indicate that the word is of foreign (predominantly Greek) origin.

In many words the pronunciation of medial *y* is predictable.
a) It has a *short I-sound* when it is followed by two consonants, as in the following 28 words:
> *abyss, bicycle, crypt, crystal, cyclical, cygnet, cymbals, cyst, eucalyptus, gym, hymn, hypnotise, hysteric, lynch, lynx, mysterious, myth, nymph, Olympics, rhythm, synchronise, syllable, symbol, symptom, syndicate, syndrome, synthesis, system.*

b) When followed by a single consonant and another vowel, or just a vowel as in *'hyena'*, *y* is pronounced with an *IE-sound*, as in the following 23 words:
> *analyse, asylum, breathalyse, dyke, dynamic, dynamite, dynamo, gyrate, hyena, hygiene, hypothesis, nylon, paralyse, pylon, python, rhyme, scythe, style, thyroid, type, typhoon, tyrant, tyre.*

But 29 words disobey the *'open'* and *'closed'* vowel rules (see next page).

163

In 21 words the *y* looks *open*, but is pronounced as if it were *closed*, i.e. with a *short i*; and 8 words have a *long IE-sound*, despite being followed by two consonants, i.e. *despite looking as if they are closed* - as if they should be pronounced with a short I-sound.

Table R 40. Words with *irregular pronunciations for y*.

y = stressed or unstressed short I-sound				long IE-sound
analysis	[anallisis]	physiology	[fiziollogy]	
analytic	[analittic]	platypus	[plattipus]	cycle*
anonymous	[anonnimous]	pyjamas	[pijahmas]	cyclone*
asphyxiate	[asfixiate]	pyramid	[pirramid]	cypress
chrysalis	[crissalis]	synagogue	[sinnagog]	hydrangea
cylinder	[sillinder]	synonym	[sinnonim]	hydraulic
cynical	[sinnical]	synopsis	[sinopsis]	hydrogen
lyric	[lirric]	syringe	[siringe]	hygrometer
oxygen	[oxigen]	syrup	[sirrup]	psychology
physical	[fizzical]	typical	[tippical]	
physics	[fizzics]			

* cf. *cyclical* which has a short I-sound.

164

EA, EI, IE, OU, OO and UI

The most numerous pronunciation problems for readers are presented by the spellings used for long vowel sounds and vowel blends (or 'diphthongs'). The digraphs *ea, ei, ie, ou, oo* and *ui* are especially difficult because they can never be reliably decoded. They are all used to spell several different sounds.

The main groups of sounds which *ea, ei, ie, ou, oo* and *ui* can spell are:

ea = **ee** / **e** / **a-e**, e.g. l*ea*p, l*ea*pt, st*ea*k - [leep, lept, stake];

ei = **ee** / **a-e** / **i-e** / **e**, e.g. s*ei*ze, v*ei*n, *ei*der, h*ei*fer - [seez, vane, ider, heffer];

ie = **ee** / **e** / **ie**, e.g. f*ie*ld, fr*ie*nd, d*ie* - [feeld, frend, dy/die];

ou = **ou** / **u** / **oo**, e.g. c*ou*nt, c*ou*ntry, gr*ou*p - [count, cuntry, groop];

oo = **u** / **o** / **long or short oo**; e.g. bl*oo*d, door [blud, dor];
pool - wool [*pool* with *long oo*, *wool* with *short*];

ui = **oo** / **i** / **ooi**, e.g. fr*ui*t, b*ui*ld, fl*ui*d - [froot, bild, flooid].

EA

Ea is particularly hard for learners, because it has no standard pronunciation but is used in 229 common English words. In the 154 words in table R 41 it spells the *EE-sound*, but in another 75 words (table R 42) it spells *different sounds* (e.g. *threat* [thret], *break* [brake], *hearth* [harth]), and none of the pronunciations are predictable. Words with *ea* therefore always have to be read as complete items. Only by looking at them as wholes, can readers pronounce them correctly.

Three words with *ea* - *read, lead* and *tear* - cannot even be read accurately as whole words when looked at in isolation. Their pronunciation can only be determined in the context of a whole phrase or sentence:
  1) You may like to *read* [reed] every day, but perhaps you *read* [red] nothing yesterday.
  2) We know that the metal *lead* [led] can harm our health, but not until governments gave a *lead* [leed], did oil companies begin to reduce *lead* [led] in petrol.
  3) A child might burst into *tears* [teers] if a dog *tears* [tairs] one of its toys to pieces.

Table R 41. In 150 common English words *ea* spells the EE-sound, but in 75 other words *ea* spells several more sounds, as can be seen in the table on the next page.

beach	fear	peace	streak	Easter
bead	feast	peach	stream	feature
beak	feat	peak	tea	heathen
beam	flea	peal	teach	increase
beard	freak	peat	teak	league [leeg]
bean	gear	plea	team	meagre
beast	gleam	plead	tease	measles
beat	glean	please	treat	ordeal
bleach	grease	pleat	veal	peanut
bleak	heal	preach	weak	queasy
bleat	heap	reach	wean	really
breathe	hear	real	weave	reason
cease	heat	reap	wheat	release
cheap	heath	rear	wreak	repeat
cheat	heave	sea	wreath	retreat
clean	jeans	seal	year	reveal
clear	knead	seam	yeast	season
creak	leach	sear	zeal	squeamish
cream	leaf	scream		treacle
crease	leak	seat	appeal	treason
deal	lean	sheaf	appear	treaty
dean	leap	shear	beacon	weary
dear	lease	sheath	beaver	weasel
dream	leash	smear	beneath	
each	least	smear	colleague	
eager	leave	sneak	conceal	
eagle	meal	speak	congeal	
ear	mean	spear	creature	
ease	meat	squeak	decrease	
east	near	squeal	defeat	
eat	neat	steal	disease	
eaves	pea	steam	dreary	

Table R 42. In 58 words *ea* spells the *short E-sound*. In 14 words *ea* has *5 other pronunciations,* and the words *lead, read* and *tear* have two different pronunciations, depending on the context in which they are used, as explained on page 165.

ea spells short E-sound				*ea* spells neither EE- or E-sound
bread	leapt	already	ready	break [brake]
breadth	learn	breakfast	rehearse	great [grate]
breast	meant	cleanliness	steady	steak [stake]
breath	pearl	early	stealthy	
cleanse	realm	earnest	treacherous	bear [bair]
dead	search	endeavour	treadmill	pear [pair]
deaf	spread	feather	treasure	swear [swair]
dealt	sweat	heather	weapon	wear [wair]
death	thread	heaven	weather	
dread	threat	heavy	zealous	heart [hart]
dreamt	wealth	instead		hearth [harth]
earl	yearn	jealous		
earn		leather		*e* and *a* as separate vowels
earth		meadow		create [cree-ate]
head		measure		linear [linne-ar]
health		peasant		nuclear [nukecle-ar]
heard		pheasant		reality [re-allity]
leant		pleasant		theatre [thee-atter]
words with two pronunciations:				
lead [leed / led]		**read** [reed / red]		**tear** [teer / tair]

Learning to read words with *ea* requires far more complex skills than mere decoding of simple phonic spellings, positional spellings or words with other complications. They represent the height of phonic unpredictability.

The *ea* grapheme is particularly difficult for children who start learning to read when their vocabulary is still very limited. Words like *dream* [dreem] and *dreamt* [dremt] or *heal* [heel] and *health* [helth] cannot be decoded as easily as *sleep* and *slept* which have predictable pronunciations. For foreign learners of English words with *ea* are always extremely difficult to read.

The 229 common English words with *ea* were probably also chiefly responsible for persuading some teachers in the 1960's that the teaching of phonics was of only limited use in English, and that learning to read whole words might be more economical in the long run.

EI

The *ei* grapheme is pronounced in several different ways, but it occurs in only a relatively small number of words.

Table R 43. This shows 41 common words with the grapheme *ei* and their pronunciations.

ei = ee	ei = a-e/ay		ei = i-e	
ceiling	deign	[dane]	eider-down	[ider-doun]
conceit	eight	[ate]	Fahrenheit	[Farrenite]
conceive	feign	[fane]	height	[hite]
deceit	freight	[frate]	kaleidoscope	[calidoscope]
deceive	neigh	[nay]	sleight	[slite]
protein	neighbour	[naber]	either, neither*	[UK: ither, nither
receipt	reign	[rane]		US: eether, neether]
receive	reindeer	[ranedeer]		
	reins	[ranes]	**assorted sounds for ei**	
seize	skein	[skane]	their	[thair]
sheikh	sleigh	[slay]	heir	[air]
weir	veil	[vale]		
weird	vein	[vane]	heifer	[heffer]
	weigh	[way]	leisure*	[UK: lezher
	weight	[wate]		US: leezher]
			foreign	[forren]
			forfeit	[forfit]
			sovereign	[sovren]
			reinforce	[ree-inforce]

* Perhaps lack of a definite pronunciation for the *ei* grapheme has helped to produce the US/UK pronunciation differences for *either* and *neither.*

The situation is not helped by the *ie* grapheme which also has several different pronunciations, some of which are identical to those of *ei*. In *heifer* and *friend,* for example, they both spell the short E-sound.

168

IE

Table R 44. In 44 words, including 11 endings, *ie* spells the **EE-sound**.

achieve	fiend	medieval	relieve	thieve	brownie	budgie
belief	fierce	niece	series	tier	caddie	pixie
believe	glockenspiel	piece	shield	wield	collie	prairie
brief	grief	pier	shriek	yield	cookie	wheelie
chief	grieve	pierce	siege		eerie	
diesel	handkerchief	priest	species		genie	
field	hygiene	relief	thief		movie	

Table R 45. In another 45 words, *ie* spells several different sounds. One of the difficulties in reading *ie* is knowing when it spells a single vowel, as in table R 44, or two vowels as in the word *'diet'* [dy-yet] and many others below.

* Please note the variable pronunciation of *-ier* endings.

ie = y - ye		ie = short i - ye	ie - ye
anxiety	[ang-zy-yety]	alien	convenient [conveen-yent]
client	[cly-yent]	[ai-li-yen]	ingredient [ingreed-yent]
diet	[dy-yet]	experience	lenient [leen-yent]
proprietor	[propry-yeter]	[expeeri-yence]	obedient [obeed-yent]
quiet	[kwy-yet]	oriental	serviette [serv-yet]
science	[sy-yence]	[ori-yental]	soviet [sove-yet]
society	[so-sy-yety]	twentieth	spaniel [span-yel]
variety	[va-ry-yety]	[twenti-yeth]	pannier* [pan-yer]
			premier* [prem-yer]
amplifier*	[amplify-yer]	barrier* [barri-yer]	**ie = ee**
crier*	[cry-yer]	carrier *[carri-yer]	cavalier* [cavaleer]
pliers*	[ply-yers]	courier* [coori- yer]	chandelier* [shandeleer]
		glacier*[glassi- yer]	frontier* [frunteer]
ie = y		**oddities**	**ie = e**
die	[dy]	friend [frend]	ancient [ane-shent]
lie	[ly]	lieutenant [leftennant]	conscience [con-shence]
pie	[py]	mischief [mischif]	efficient [efi-shent]
tie	[ty]	sieve [siv]	patient [pay-shent]
vie	[vy]	soldier [sole-jer]	sufficient [sufi-shent]

OU

The pronunciation of *ou* is highly unpredictable. It has a predictable unstressed OS-sound in the ending *-ous* (e.g. curi*ous*, dubi*ous*, glamor*ous*) and an ER-sound in the ending *-our* (e.g. glam*our*, harb*our*).

In the stem of words, it is pronounced predominantly as in *count* (as in all the words in table R 46 below); but in 75 words the *ou* grapheme has different pronunciations, e.g. *group* [gr<u>oo</u>p], *country* [c<u>u</u>ntry], *court* [c<u>o</u>rt], *journey* [j<u>er</u>ny], *soul* [s<u>ole</u>] - (as in table R 47 opposite).

Table R 46. In 78 common words the grapheme ***ou*** *has the expected pronunciation.*

abound	counter	mound	scoundrel
about	county	mount	scout
account	crouch	mountain	shout
aloud	doubt	mouse	slouch
amount	douse	mouth	snout
announce	drought	ounce	sound
around	encounter	our	sour
arouse	flounder	out	south
astound	flour	outer	spout
blouse	foul	plough	sprout
bough	found	pouch	stout
bounced	foundation	pounce	surround
bound	fountain	pound	thou
boundary	ground	pout	thousand
cloud	hound	profound	trousers
compound	hour	pronounce	trout
couch	house	proud	voucher
council	loud	rebound	without
counsel	lounge	round	
count	lout	rouse	

170

Table R 47. In 75 words the sound of *ou is unpredictable*.

ou = long oo		ou= u		ou = o	
acoustic	[acoostic]	country	[cuntry]	course	[corce]
bivouac	[bivooac]	couple	[cupl]	court	[cort]
bouquet	[bookay]	courage	[currage]	four	[for]
boutique	[booteek]	cousin	[cuzzen]	fourth	[forth]
choux	[shoo]	double	[dubl]	mourn	[morn]
coupon	[coopon]	encourage	[encurrage]	pour	[por]
ghoulish	[goolish]	enough	[inuff]	resource	[resorce]
group	[groop]	hiccough	[hickup]	savoury	[savory]
route	[root]	moustache	[mustash]	source	[sorce]
routine	[rooteen]	nourish	[nurrish]	tour	[tor]
soup	[soop]	rough	[ruf]	tour-	[tor-
souvenir	[sooveneer]	slough*	[sluf/slou]	nament	nament]
toucan	[toocan]	southern	[suthern]	your	[yor]
tourist	[toorist]	touch	[tuch]	poultry	[poltry]
wounded*	[woonded]	tough	[tuf]	cough	[cof]
you	[u]	trouble	[trubl]	trough	[trof]
through	[throo]	young	[yung]		
		thorough	[thurra]	**ou= au**	
				bought	[baut]
				brought	[braut]
ou=short oo		**ou = oe/oa**		fought	[faut]
could	[cood]	boulder	[bolder]	nought	[naut]
courier	[coorrier]	mould	[moald]	ought	[aut]
should	[shood]	moult	[moalt]	sought	[saut]
would	[wood]	shoulder	[sholder]	thought	[thaut]
camouflage	[cammooflage]	smoulder	[smolder]		
silhouette	[silooet]	soul	[sole]	**ou = e**	
tambourine	[tambooreen]			courtesy	[kertecy]
		dough	[doe]	journal	[jernal]
		though	[tho]	journey	[jerny]

* *Wound* as in 'wound down' has the dominant sound for *ou*, but 'a wound' that bleeds is pronounced [woond];
* *slough* is pronounced [sluf] when it means 'to shed', but [slou] when it means 'a muddy place' or 'a mire'.

OO

The grapheme *oo* has a predictable pronunciation in word endings (e.g. boo, bamboo). In 68 other words it also has the expected long OO-sound, but 25 words have an unpredictable pronunciation for *oo*.

Table R 48. Pronunciation of the *oo* grapheme in 110 common words.

long OO-sound				short OO-sound*
bamboo	baboon	loose	soothe	book
boo	balloon	loot	spook	brook
cockatoo	bloom	macaroon	spool	cook
coo	boom	maroon	spoon	cookie
cuckoo	boot	mood	stool	foot
goo	brooding	moon	stoop	good
hullabaloo	broom	mushroom	swoon	hood
igloo	cartoon	noodle	swoop	hook
kangaroo	choose	noon	tool	look
loo	cocoon	noose	tooth	rook
moo	cool	pontoon	troop	shook
shampoo	doom	poodle	typhoon	stood
shoo	droop	pooh	whoop	took
tattoo	food	pool	zoom	whoosh
too	fool	proof		wood
voodoo	gloom	roof		wooden
woo	goose	room		wool
yahoo	groom	root		woollen
zoo	groove	saloon		**assorted sounds**
	harpoon	school		door [dor]
	hoof	schooner		floor [flor]
	hooligan	scoop		moor [mor]
	hoop	scooter		poor [por]
	hoot	shoot		
	lagoon	smooth		blood [blud]
	loom	snooker		flood [flud]
	loop	soon		
				brooch [broach]

* As already mentioned, the short OO-sound has no clearly identifiable grapheme in English. It is spelt in several different ways, with letters which can all spell other sounds too (e.g. g*oo*d, c*oul*d, p*u*t) - cf. f*oo*d [long *oo*], m*oul*d [oul = ole], c*u*t, h*u*t, n*u*t [with the dominant sound for *u*]).

UI

The pronunciation of the diagraph *ui* which is sometimes also used to spell the long OO-sound (e.g. fr*ui*t) is problematic too.

1) *After g,* the letter *u* is often used to keep the sound of *g* hard (e.g. g*ui*de, g*ui*lt) - but not always: e.g. *anguish* [angwish], *distinguish* [distingwish] and *penguin* [pengwin].

2) *U* also combines with *q* in the grapheme **qu** and spells the KW-sound. A following *i* then usually has the normal short I-sound (e.g. qu*i*nce, qu*i*t), but not in the word *mosquito* which is pronounced [mos*kee*to].

3) In 21 other words *ui* spells the **sounds** of short I, OO, OO-I , YOO, YOO-I or WEE . These need to be learned word by word.

Table R 49. This shows the different sounds which the digraph *ui* can spell. Sometimes *ui* is not a digraph which spells a single sound but two separate vowels (e.g. *genuine* = gen-yoo-in, *fluid* = floo-id).

ui = i	*ui* = oo	*u* marks **hard g**
bisc*ui*t [biskit]	br*ui*se [brooz]	dis*gui*se
b*ui*ld [bild]	cr*ui*se [crooz]	*gui*de, *gui*dance
b*ui*lt [bilt]	fr*ui*t [froot]	*gui*llotine [gilloteen]
circ*ui*t [cerkit]	j*ui*ce [jooce]	*gui*lt
	recr*ui*t [recroot]	*gui*nea-pig [ginny-pig]
	sl*ui*ce [slooce]	*gui*t*ar* [stressed on *ar*]
ui = yoo/ew	*ui* = oo-i	*gui* = gwi
n*ui*sance [newsence]	fl*ui*d [floo-id]	an*gui*sh
purs*ui*t	r*ui*n [roo-in]	distin*gui*sh
s*ui*cide		pen*gui*n
s*ui*t	*ui* = yoo-i	
s*ui*table	gen*ui*ne [gen-yoo-in]*	
	t*ui*tion [tyoo-ition]	
	int*ui*tion [intyoo-ition]	

* In US English the *-ine* ending of *genuine* tends to be pronounced with an IE-sound - as the spelling suggests [gen-yoo-ine].

U- E

The graphemes *u-e* and *ue* are also used for spelling the *OO-sound*, but the *predominant pronunciation* for *u-e* and *ue* is *yoo*, as in t*u*n*e* and d*ue*. There are five main exceptions to this rule:

1) *After r*, *u-e* and *ue* are pronounced with a *long OO-sound*, as in r*u*d*e* [r*oo*d] and tr*ue* [tr*oo*] - see table R 51 opposite.

2) After *l*, the *ue / u-e* graphemes are also pronounced predominantly with a *long OO-sound* (gl*ue*-[gl*oo*]), but not always (val*ue*-[val-*yoo*]) - table R 52.

3) At the end of words, -*ue* can be silent (catalog*ue*), or serve various other functions (see table R 53).

4) In *American English* some accents now use the OO-sound even for several words which have a YOO-sound in standard UK English (e.g. *tuna*-[toona]).

5) A few words do not fit into any of the above patterns and have to be learned individually - see bottom of next page.

Table R 50. The 73 words below have the dominant *yoo* pronunciation for an **open *u*** and **ue**.

with stressed open *u* and *ue*					stressed on
uniform	cube	accuse	funeral	student	**1st syllable**
union	cure	amuse	immune	super	*ar*gue
unique	fume	assume	introduce	supervise	*a*venue
unite	fuse	bureau	juvenile	supervisor	*iss*ue [ishue]
universe	huge	commute	manure	tuna	rescue
universal	June	commuter	mature		revenue
university	mule	compute	museum	cue	statue
uranium	nude	computer	numeral	due	tissue [tishue]
Uranus	pure	confuse	obscure	sue	venue
usual	tube	consume	procure	imbue	virtue
utensil	tuber	consumer	reduce	pursue	**stressed on**
utility	tune	dispute	resume	queue [cue]	**2ⁿᵈ syllable**
utopia		endure	secure	subdue	con*ti*nue

174

Table R 51. *After the letter r the graphemes **ue** and **u-e** are pronounced with a long OO-sound.*

accrue	construe	cruel	gruesome	prune	rue	rural	truce
brutal	crucial	crusade	intrude	ruby	rule	truant	true
brute	crude	frugal	intrude	rude	rumour	truce	truly

Table R 52. The pronunciation of an *open **u** after l* is also mainly with a *long OO-sound*, but in some words an *open u* after *l* is pronounced *yoo*.

u-e / ue = oo					u-e/ue = yoo	
blue	absolutely	include	illuminate	lukewarm	deluge	salute
clue	aluminium	seclude	illusion	luminous	dilute	solution
flue	aluminum	fluent	influence	lunar	lure	value
glue	conclude	fluke	lubricate	lunatic	resolution	volume
flu	exclude	flute	ludo		revolution	

Table R 53. Words which end in *-gue* and *-que* have neither a final YOO-sound or OO-sound (unlike *cue* or *blue*).

A *-ue ending **after g*** is sometimes used to indicate a long vowel sound before a final hard *g*, as in *rogue*.

In five words which use *q* to spell a final **K**-sound, and the *-ue* ending indicates a preceding long vowel, but in another 8 words the *-ue* ending serves no purpose.

-ue ending indicates a preceding long vowel			-ue ending is redundant		
fatigue [fateeg]	opaque	[opake]	catalogue	[cattalog]	mosque
plague [plaig]	antique	[anteek]	colleague	[colleeg]	[mosc]
rogue [roag]	boutique	[booteek]	dialogue	[dialog]	picturesque
	technique	[tecneek]	epilogue	[eppilog]	[picturesc]
	unique	[yooneek]	league	[leeg]	
			meringue	[merang]	

Oddments:

' Minute' has two different pronunciations: *[minnit]* as a unite of time (i.e. *60 minutes = 1hour*), or as a verb, meaning *'to record'*; but it has the expected pronunciation for *u-e [i.e. mine-yoot]* when it means *'very small'*.

'Upon' does not follow the usual pattern for an open *u* either. It is a merger of the two words *'up'* and *'on'*.

In the following four words the *open u* is also pronounced with an OO-sound, although it follows neither the letter *r* or *l* .

duvet [doovay],   *chute* [shoot],   *sure* [shoor] (also *assure, insure*), *zulu* [zooloo].

-URE

Words which end in *-ure* can present reading problems, because this ending can be:

     a) *stressed* and pronounced *-yoor* (e.g. sec*ure*) or

     b) *unstressed* and pronounced *-er (e.g.* in*j*ure - with stress on 1st syllable).

Table R 54. This shows the two different stress patterns for words ending with *-ure* and their pronunciations.

stress on 1st syllable		stress on 2nd syllable	
conjure	[conjer]	assure	[ash<u>oo</u>r]
failure	[failyer]	endure	[end-<u>yoor</u>]
figure	[figger]	insure	[insh<u>oo</u>r]
fissure	[fisher]	manure	[man-<u>yoor</u>]
injure	[injer]	obscure	[obsc-<u>yoor</u>]
leisure	[lezher]	procure	[proc-<u>yoor</u>]
measure	[mezher]	secure	[sek-<u>yoor</u>]
pleasure	[plezher]	exposure	[exp<u>oa</u>zher]
pressure	[presher]	procedure	[proc<u>ee</u>jer]
treasure	[trezher]		

-TURE

Table R 55. Words which end in *-ture* are nearly always stressed on the first syllable, and the *-ture* ending is pronounced as *-cher* (e.g. culture [culcher]).

     Mature [mat-yoor], and a few other words with stress on the second or third syllable, are exceptions to this rule.

1st syllable stressed				stress on 2nd syllable
agriculture	fr<u>a</u>cture	m<u>i</u>niature	str<u>u</u>cture	adv<u>e</u>nture
<u>a</u>rchitecture	f<u>u</u>rniture	m<u>i</u>xture	t<u>e</u>mperature	dep<u>a</u>rture
c<u>a</u>pture	f<u>u</u>ture	n<u>a</u>ture	t<u>o</u>rture	exp<u>e</u>nditure
c<u>a</u>ricature	g<u>e</u>sture	p<u>i</u>cture	v<u>e</u>nture	mat<u>u</u>re [mat-yoor]
cr<u>ea</u>ture	l<u>e</u>cture	p<u>u</u>ncture	v<u>u</u>lture	**sress on 3rd syllable**
c<u>u</u>lture	legisl<u>a</u>ture	scr<u>i</u>pture		manuf<u>a</u>cture
f<u>ea</u>ture	l<u>i</u>terature	s<u>i</u>gnature		

ARE

The *are* grapheme is mainly just one of the three unpredictable ways of spelling the **AIR**-sound (e.g. c*are*, b*ear*, h*air*). It occurs only in a small number of words, and is used predominantly in word endings, as can be seen in table R56.

Unfortunately, *are* by itself is also one of the most frequently used English words, but with a different sound [*ar*]. This can undermine learner confidence about the pronunciation of the grapheme *are* in other words.

In the middle of words, the letter chain *are* must be read as *ar* + *e* (e.g. *are*na [*ar-ee*na] - apart from the word *parent* [*pair*ent].

Table R 56. 25 words in which *are* spells *air*, and some with a different
            sound.

are = air					are = ar + e	
bare	flare	rare	square	compare	apparent	[aparrent]
blare	glare	scare	stare	declare	arena	[areena]
care*	hare	share	wares	prepare	cabaret	[cabbaray]
dare	mare	snare	area		transparent	[transparrent]
fare*	pare	spare	aware		cigarette	[si*gg*aret or sigar*ett*]
*also derivatives: caress, warfare, welfare					dungarees	
					career	
Exceptions:						
the word **are** is pronounce [**ar**]				**parent**	[pairent]	

Difficulties with identifying vowel length
and locating stress

Many reading problems for learners of English stem from the loose application of the *open* and *closed* vowel spelling method in multi-syllable words. Vowels which look open often require a short, stressed pronunciation (e.g. *cabaret* = [cabbaray]), while vowels before a doubled consonant, which look as if they should be stressed, are unstressed (e.g. *apparent* = [aparrent]). Such spellings always offer scope for mispronunciation.

Words which end with an *-e* which does not keep the vowel before the preceding consonant open (i.e. words in which an *-e* is not 'magic' but redundant) are also a problem. Students must learn to ignore the final *-e* in them. They must, for example, not be misled into pronouncing *'indefinite'* with the same long IE-sound before *'t'* as in *'finite'*.

Table R 57. In the 19 words below, which end in *-ine, -ite* and *-one,* the final *-e* has no phonic function. The words are pronounced as if they have no *-e* endings, as indicated [in brackets].

determine	[determin]	composite	[compozit]	gone	[gon]
discipline	[dissiplin]	definite	[deffinit]	scone*	[scon]
famine	[fammin]	exquisite	[exquizzit]	shone	[shon]
feminine	[femminin]	favourite	[favorit]		
genuine *	[genn-yooin]	granite	[grannit]		
heroine	[herroin]	infinite	[infinit]		
imagine	[imadgin]	opposite	[oppozit]		
masculine	[masculin]				
medicine	[meddicin]				

* In American English, *'genuine'* is often pronounced with a long vowel in the *'-ine'* ending, i.e. it is pronounced as the spelling suggests it should be. Some people pronounce *'scone'* with a long vowel too, i.e. rhyming with *'stone'*.

The length of vowels before 'v'

Before the letter *v*, *a vowel can be long or short*, but this is almost never decodable from the spelling (e.g. *drive - give*). Only the *-ive* ending of multisyllable words can be relied on to have the pronunciation *-iv* (e.g. nega*tive*).

Learning to read words with *v* in them is difficult because the rules for spelling the V-sound break several other English spelling rules:

1) A *final V-sound* is always spelt *-ve* irrespective of vowel length (e.g. sha*ve*, ha*ve* [hav] – cf. pa*ne*, pa*n*).

2) The letter *v* is generally *not doubled*, except in few modernisms like 'na*vv*y' and 'ski*vv*y' – i.e. a short, stressed vowel before *v* is usually not followed by *vv* (e.g. ca*v*ern, li*v*er – cf. pa*tt*ern, thi*nn*er).

3) Substantial numbers of words with *v* also spell the preceding vowel in unpredictable ways (e.g. lo*v*e [luv], mo*v*e [moov] – compare these with *but* and *moon*).

Table R 58. In the stem of words, 43 words with *v* have the expected long vowel sound, but another 43 words have short vowels or completely unexpected long vowels.

with long vowel before v			with short vowels		with different unpredictable vowels	
behave	wave	lively	have	driven	above	[abuv]
brave	waver	revive	cavern	given	covenant	[cuvvenent]
cave	eve	survive	gravel	quiver	cover	[cuvver]
crave	even	thrive	javelin	river	covet	[cuvvet]
engrave	fever	wives	travel	rivet	covey	[cuvvy]
gave	lever	cove	clever	shiver	dove	[duv]
grave	alive	drove	crevice	shrivel	glove	[gluv]
knave	arrive	rove	ever	snivel	govern	[guvvern]
nave	derive	stove	level	swivel	love	[luv]
pave	dive	wove	never	grovel	oven	[uvven]
rave	divert	alcove	seven	hover	shovel	[shuvvel]
raven	drive	clover	several	novel	slovenly	[sluvvenly]
save	five	over	give	poverty	move	[moov]
shave	hive		live*		improve	[improov]
slave	jive		drivel		prove	[proov]

* *'Live'* has a short vowel when the word is a verb, e.g. 'I *[liv]* in England', but a long sound when the word is an adjective, e.g. 'I like *live* music'.

179

'Missing' and 'surplus' doubled consonants

Uncertainly about *vowel length* and *vowel stress* is a recurring reading problem for learners of English. The causes of this difficulty are *'missing'* and *'surplus'* *doubled consonants*.

When doubled consonants are used as they are meant to be, they are very helpful to readers. They can indicate both vowel length and stress, as in *latter, bitter, utter* and *distress,* which are clearly distinct from *later, biter, uterus* and *atlas*.

When a short, stressed vowel is *not followed by a doubled consonant*, pronunciation is far less predictable (e.g. *lateral, medal, obituary, robin*). If the English consonant doubling rule was used consistently, these should really be spelt *[latteral, meddal, obittuary, robbin]*. As with other spellings which are not a reliable guide to pronunciation, readers have to know what the words sound like before they can 'read' them correctly.

This is equally true of words which have doubled consonants which do not follow a short stressed vowel and appear to be *'surplus'*. The word *apply,* for example, is not stressed on the first syllable but the last. The *pp* is apt to mislead, by anlogy with *apple.*

Learners often try to read by analogy with other words they have come across. For example, they pronounce *fugitive* as [fuggativ] after learning to read *negative* [neggativ].

Words with *c* instead of *ss* after a short vowel (e.g. *acid* - [assid]) or *s* instead of *zz* (e.g. *chisel* - [chizzle]) are also difficult to read; so are those which spell a short, stressed vowel unpredictably and fail to double the consonant after it (e.g. *any, busy, meadow*)- which are pronounced [enny, bizzy, meddow].

With some consonants English indicates a short, stressed vowel not by doubling the consonant but by inserting another letter (e.g. *checking, badger, despatch*). When this does not happen, pronunciation is also less certain (e.g. *speculate, legislate, attached*).

The following 4 tables (R 59 - 62) list 366 multi-syllable words in which a short, stressed vowel is not indicated. Tables R 63 and R 64 list words with doubled consonants which do not follow a short, stressed vowel. The 7th shows the different pronunciations of vowels before *ll*.

Table R 59. In 119 common 2-syllable words *a short, stressed vowel is not followed by a doubled consonant*. - These words have to be pronounced *as if the consonants picked out in bold were doubled.*

Arab	edible	metal	salon
arable	edit	miracle	satin
arid	enamel	model	second
atom	epic	modern	semi
balance	famished	modest	solemn
banish	finish	moral	solid
baron	flagon	olive	spinach
baton	florist	orange	spirit
beret [berray]	forest	palace	study
bilious	frigate	palate	talent
body	garage*	palette	talon
British	habit	panel	tepid
cabin	hazard	panic	timid
café [caffay]	herald	parish	tonic
camel	heron	pedal	topic
carol	image	peril	tragic [tradgic]
chalet [shallay]	legend [ledgend]	perish	tribute
chapel	lemon	petal	tropics
cherish	leper	pigeon [pidgen]	valiant
city	limit	pity	valid
column	lizard	profit	value
comet	logic	promise	vanish
comic	lozenge	proper	very
copy	magic [madgic]	radish	video
coral	manage	rapid	volume
credit	manor	refuge	vomit
damage	medal	relic	wizard
decade	melon	rigid	wizened
deluge	menace	robin	yeti
dragon	merit	salad	

* *'Garage'* sometimes still has the original French pronunciation of *[garahge]* instead of the more common English *[garrage]*.

Table R 60. Like the 119 two-syllable words in the last table, 172 words of three or more syllables also have *unmarked short vowels*, i.e. *followed by a single consonant*.

ability	caricature	develop	italic	opinion	sinister
abolish	catalogue	document	laminate	organic	skeleton
abominable	catapult	dominate	lateral	parasol	somersault
academy	category	domino	latitude	pedigree	spaniel
adequate	celery	dynamic	legislate	pelican	sterilise
agony	cemetery	economic	liberal	penetrate	strategy
aluminium	ceremony	economy	liberty	platinum	supersonic
amateur	chariot	educate	lieutenant	platypus	tapestry
America	charity	electronic	linear	policy	telescope
analysis	chemical	element	literally	politics	tetanus
animal	cinema	eligible	magnetic	polythene	therapist
anorak	citizen	eliminate	magnificent	popular	tolerate
asparagus	clarity	emerald	majority	priority	transparent
astonish	clinical	empirical	manual	probable	vacuum
athletic	colony	enemy	medical	prominent	valentine
authority	comparison	energy	melody	property	vegetable
banister	compatible	epidemic	memory	radical	venison
battalion	competitive	executive	military	reality	ventriloquist
benefit	conifer	fabulous	minimal	recognise	veteran
botany	conspiracy	hexagonal	minister	regiment	vinegar
cabaret	continue	federal	minority	register	vitality
cabinet	criminal	feminine	monarch	relevant	voluntary
calendar	critical	galaxy	monastery	religion	
camera	crocodile	helicopter	monument	religion	
canopy	dedicated	heritage	morality	remedy	
capita	delegate	heroine	nebula	salary	
capital	delicacy	hideous	negative	secular	
capitol	democrat	historic	obliterate	separate	
caramel	demolish	holiday	opera	significant	
caravan	derelict	horoscope	operate	sincerity	

Table R 61. In this table 17 words have a *single c* after a short, stressed vowel where one would expect *ss* (e.g. acid [assid] - cf. ma*ss*ive, a*c*e);

16 others have a *single s* where one would expect *zz* (e.g. miserable [mizzerable] - cf. di*zz*y, mi*s*er).

Read as if **c = ss**			Read as if **s = zz**		
acid	municipal	simplicity	chisel	hesitate	resident
capacity	pacifist	solicitor	closet	miserable	risen
decimal	participate	specify	deposit	positive	visible
electricity	precipice	specimen	desert	present	visit
explicit	publicity	velocity	designate	president	
glacier	recipe		desolate	prison	

Table R 62. The 42 words below have *unpredictably spelt short vowels and* *'missing' doubled consonants*.

Some of the words contain even further unpredictable elements. Their pronunciations are all spelt out more predictably [in adjacent brackets].

already	[aulreddy]	jeopardy	[jepperdy]	quarantine	[quorranteen]
any	[enny]	laurel	[lorrel]	ready	[reddy]
bury	[berry]	leopard	[lepperd]	sausage	[sossage]
busy	[bizzy]	lyric	[lirric]	steady	[steddy]
chrysalis	[crissalis]	many	[menny]	stomach	[stummac]
colour	[culler]	meadow	[meddo]	synagogue	[sinnagog]
courage	[currage]	money	[munny]	synonym	[sinnonim]
cousin	[cuzzen]	nourish	[nurrish]	syrup	[sirrup]
cylinder	[sillinder]	onion	[unnien]	thorough	[thurra]
cynical	[sinnical]	peasant	[pezzent]	typical	[tippical]
dozen	[duzzen]	pheasant	[fezzent]	tyranny	[tirrany]
heifer	[heffer]	physics	[fizzics]	weapon	[weppen]
honey	[hunny]	pleasant	[plezzent]	women	[wimmen]
jealous	[jellos]	quality	[quollity]	zealous	[zellos]

Table R 63. The 139 words below all contain *doubled consonants, but not after a short, stressed vowel.*
(The stressed vowel in each word is underlined).

accompany	assail	commuter	mayonnaise
accomplish	assault	connect	midday
accord	assemble	constellation	necessary
accordion	assert	correct	occasion
account	assign	correlation	occupation
accumulate	assist	correspond	offend
accuse	associate	curriculum	official
accustom	assort	dessert	omelette
affair	assume	differential	opportunity
affect	attach	diffusion	oppose
affection	attach	effect	palette
afford	attain	efficient	paraffin
ammunition	attempt	embassy	parallel
anniversary	attend	erratic	pastille
announce	attention	essential	personnel
annoy	attorney	excellent	possibility
appal	attract	hello	programme
apparatus	attributed	hippopotamus	questionnaire
apparent	barricade	hurrah	recommend
appeal	battalion	illegible	satellite
appear	caterpillar	illiterate	serrated
appendix	collage	illuminate	settee
applaud	collapse	illusion	succumb
apply	collect	illustration	sufficient
appoint	collide	immediate	suggest
appreciate	command	immense	supply
apprentice	commemorate	immortal	support
approach	commence	immune	suppose
appropriate	commercial	interrupt	surrender
approve	commit	irregular	surround
approximate	commodities	irrigation	tattoo
arrange	commotion	jewellery	terrific
array	communication	llama	tonsillitis
arrest	communion	lasso [lasoo]	torrential
arrive	community	marvellous	

184

Table R 64. A few words contain *two sets of doubled consonants*. Since no English words contains two stressed syllables, at least one of them is redundant. In *accommodation* both sets of doubled consonants are surplus.

accommodate	aggressive	cassette	occurrence
accommodation	assassin	committee	possess
address	assessment	mattress	

All seemingly *'surplus'* doubled consonants - those which do not mark a short, stressed vowel, but serve to indicate a word's origin (e.g. *apply*) - or are used for grammatical rather than phonic reasons (e.g. *surround*) – are unhelpful to readers. They have to teach themselves not to be misled by them.

Surplus letters make words longer, and young learners especially, tend to find long words more intimidating than short ones. Many students take quite a while to become accustomed even to words like *nettle* and *nibble* which contain more letters than are phonically strictly necessary (cf. *treble, triple, tramp, trend*). Many pupils even find the longer spelling for the final K-sound, as in *stick* (when compared to *comic*), bewildering.

Unfamiliar words in which a doubled consonant suggests the wrong stress (e.g. *commit, erratic*) are particularly confusing for young learners. Such words have to be read without reference to the more reliable English patterns which occur in *common* and *error*, or *Tommy* and *terror*.

Erratic consonant doubling makes native learners of English from not very literate backgrounds wary of using longer words in their speech, because they are aware that these contain pronunciation pitfalls. *'Missing'* and *'surplus'* doubled consonants often also cause foreign speakers to stress English words incorrectly or to misjudge vowel length, thereby making them more difficult to understand than they could be.

185

The purpose of *doubling an l after an a* is phonically particularly baffling:

a) The letter *l* is *frequently not doubled* where one would expect it to be
    (e.g. *salad* - cf. *gallon*).

b) The grapheme **all** is pronounced *aul* in some words (**galling**) and *al*
    in others (**gallant**).

c) The grapheme *al* also has such two different pronunciations. It has the
    expected pronunciation in **album** and **algebra**, but has to be read as *aul*
    in *alter* [aulter]) and **al**ways [aulways].

d) In UK English there is a further complication:
    verbs which end in *-l*, double this letter before suffixes which begin with a
    vowel (e.g. *marvel - marvelled, marvelling, marvellous*), even when the
    final vowel is not stressed.

Other final consonants are doubled only when the final vowel is stressed (e.g.
commit -committed, but profit - profited). - In American English a final *-l* is
treated like other final consonants before suffixes (e.g. *travel - traveled,
traveling*).

The table opposite sets out the different pronunciations for words with *al*
and *all*.

186

Table R 65. Expected and unexpected pronunciations for *al* and *all*.

al and all with expected pronunciation		With unpredictable pronunciations		
		single *l* after short *a*	**al = aul**	**unstressed, open al = al** (i.e. unlike *'ale'*)
ale	alley	balance	almost	alarm
alien	ally	calendar	already	alert
Australia	alligator	chalet	also	alight
bale	ballast	devalue	altar	alike
dale	ballet	galaxy	alter	alive
gale	ballot	italic	alternate	alone
halo	challenge	palace	alternative	along
inhale	gallant	palate	altogether	aloud
male	gallery	palette	always	aluminium
pale	gallon	reality		aluminum
sale	gallop	salad	bald	
saline	gallows	salary	chalk	**all = al**
scale	mallet	salon	falter	alliance
stale	rally	talent	halt	allocation
tale	shallow	talon	instalment	allotment
albino	stallion	valentine	paltry	allow
album	valley	valiant	salt	ballistic
alcohol		valid	scald	balloon
alcove	**final all=aul**	value	stalk	installation
algebra	all	analysis	talk	parallel
alphabet	ball			
Alsatian	call			**oddities:**
altitude	fall			
balcony	(fallen)			appal [apaul]
calculation	gall			
cymbals	hall			gala [gahla]
Dalmatian	install			
emerald	pall			halfpenny [haypenny]
herald	recall			
	small			salmon [sammon]
	squall			
	stall			qualify [kwollify]
	tall			
	wall			
	except: **shall** [shal]			

187

Words with different pronunciations

Most English reading problems are caused by graphemes within words, be they single letters or letter strings, which have to be pronounced differently (e.g. b*o*th - cl*o*th, tr*ea*t - thr*ea*t). Readers have to register such words as wholes before they can decode the ambiguous graphemes in them.

The biggest challenge of all is presented by *identically looking whole words* which have to be pronounced differently in different contexts. Sixteen frequently occurring words with dual pronunciation have already been mentioned:

> *lead, read, tear; bow, row, sow; abuse, excuse, use, close, house; live; minute; slough; wind, wound.*

A further 83 words also have dual, or even triple, pronunciations. Among them are: *buffet, mouth, pasty* and *second*. These are pronounced as follows:

buffet: as a *verb*, with normal pronunciation - to beat or toss about;
as a *noun* - [buffay] - a place where food is served.

mouth: with a *soft* final *'th'* as a *noun*;
as a *verb* to [mouthe] - to move your lips silently, with a *sharp 'th'*;

pasty: with phonic pronunciation when used as a *noun* meaning *'meat pie'*;
but [pacety] as the *adjective* from *'paste'*;

second: [seckond] when it means 2nd; or a unit of time (*1/60 of a minute*);
as a *verb*, with stress on the second syllable, to [sec*o*nd]- meaning *'to support'* or *'approve'*.

Shifting stress to which the spelling of a word provides no clue, as in *'a sec*o*nd'* and *'to sec*o*nd'* is a pronunciation difficulty in 78 other words. This is bewildering for most learners, but especially for students of English as a foreign language and learners who get little help with learning to read at home.

Table R 66. Below are 50 words which are *stressed on the **first syllable***
when used **as *nouns***, but on the ***second syllable*** when used **as
*verbs*** (e.g. *rebel* - [a r*e*bbel - to reb*e*ll];
defect - [a *dee*fect - to def*ect*]).
The nouns *content* and *invalid* are stressed on the second
syllable when used as *adjectives* [cont*e*nt, inv*a*llid]; and the
adjectives frequent and *perfect* when used as *verbs* [frequ*e*nt,
perf*ect*].

attribute	construct	entrance	present	refund	content
commune	contest	escort	produce	refuse	invalid
compact	contract	export	progress	reject	
compound	contrast	extract	project	relay	frequent
concert	converse	fragment	prospect	subject	perfect
conduct	convert	impact	protest	survey	
conflict	convict	incense	rebel	suspect	
conscript	defect	insert	rebound	torment	
console	digest	object	recall	transfer	
consort	discharge	permit	record	transport	

Several of the above words have very different meanings, as well as different
stresses, when used as different parts of speech (e.g. *console* can mean *a
control panel*, or *to comfort*; *defect* can mean *a fault*, or *to run away*;
subject can be *a topic*, or it can mean *to submit to force*).

Twenty nine words which end with *-ate* have changing vowel length, as
well as changing stress, when used as different parts of speech. For example,
in the sentence, 'He *advocates* the use of alternative remedies', the *'-ates'*
ending is pronounced as one would expect it to be [*-aits*]; but in 'He is *an
advocate* of alternative remedies' the *'-ate'* ending is pronounced [*-at*].

Table R 67. The 29 words below are pronounced with an *-ait* ending when
used as *verbs*, but with an *-at* ending when used as *nouns or
adjectives*.

advocate	associate	designate	estimate	separate
alternate	co-ordinate	desolate	graduate	subordinate
appropriate	degenerate	dictate	intimate	syndicate
approximate	delegate	duplicate	laminate	triplicate
articulate	deliberate	elaborate	moderate	

It is common for closely related English words to have very different
stresses (e.g. *reside, resident; volunteer, voluntary, voluntarily*). Since
these changes cannot be decoded from their spelling, they nearly all present

189

reading problems (e.g. *confer – conference, finite – infinite, prefer – preference, refer – reference).*

Fortunately, such shifts of stress occur predominantly in more sophisticated vocabulary. They are therefore a problem mainly for more advanced readers rather than beginners.

A few word endings are of help in locating stress in an English word. But since making use of this aid involves registering longer letter sequences, or even *whole words at a glance*, these clues are of help predominantly to practised readers rather than beginners.

The are five types of clues to stress which word endings provide:

1) *The vowel which precedes* the ending **-tion** is always *stressed.*

2) The endings **-ation, -otion** and **-ution** have nearly always *a long,* stressed vowel before *-tion* [-aishn, -oashn, -yooshn], as in n*a*tion, prom*o*tion, sol*u*tion. - One exception is the word *'ration'*, which has a short A-sound, like in *'passion'* or *'fashion'.*

3) The *i* in **-ition** is invariably *stressed and short* (e.g. ign*i*tion, part*i*tion); so are *vowels which precede* the ending **'-ssion'** (e.g. conf*e*ssion, m*i*ssion, perc*u*ssion).

4) The *vowel before* **-ity** is *always stressed*, and *predominantly short* (e.g. curi*o*sity [curi*o*ssity]); but sometimes also long (e.g. pr*o*bity).

5) Words with the endings **-ial, -ian** and **-ical** also have *reliable stress* patterns, but the preceding *vowel may be long* (e.g. palatial, comedian, musical) or *short* (e.g. *fanatical, special, judicial).*
    They may have the same vowel length as the stem word from which they are derived (e.g. m*u*sic - m*u*sical, with a long vowel), but not reliably so (e.g. p*a*lace with a short vowel [pallace] - *palatial* with a long vowel).

The tables opposite may help to give a clearer picture of how word endings can help with identifying stress and vowel length in some English words.

190

Table R 68. This shows examples of *regular stress patterns* and *predictable vowel length* in word endings.

with long, stressed vowels in endings	with short, stressed vowels		
sta*tion*	cal*am*ity	ambi*tion*	mi*ssion*
delega*tion*	popul*ar*ity	igni*tion* ·	admi*ssion*
	pos*ition*	transm*i*s*sion*
mo*tion*	ab*il*ity	tui*tion*	
devo*tion*	electr*i*city		se*ssion*
			profe*ssion*
instit*u*tion	auth*or*ity		
revol*u*tion	curi*os*ity		
f*u*sion			
conf*u*sion			

Table R 69. Many words have *predictably stressed* endings, but with *unpredictable vowel length*, e.g. *'crucial'* with a long vowel [crooshal] is derived form *'crux'* with a short one.

with long vowels		with short vowels	
com*e*dian	cr*u*cial	artif*i*cial	anal*y*tical
Dalm*a*tian	gla*cial	benef*i*cial	ch*e*mical
	so*cial*	jud*i*cial	fan*a*tical
mat*e*rial		offi*cial*	pol*e*mical
mem*o*rial		in*i*tial	pol*i*tical
m*u*sical	pal*a*tial	civ*i*lian	
	hist*o*rian		
	Gr*e*cian	electr*i*cian	
		sp*e*cial	

Most of the graphemes which have been discussed and listed in the different tables in Appendix R apply to substantial numbers of words. These spellings are all summarised in tables R 71 and R 72.

There are also a few dozen English words with graphemes that are unique, or used in just a handful of words. Occasionally, some commonly used graphemes have very unexpected pronunciations. Fifty two such words are listed below.

Table R 70. Words with *idiosyncratic spellings* or *unexpected pronunciations*. [In brackets next to them, their pronunciations are spelt out more predictably, using dominant English spelling patterns.]

bible	[bibel]	beauty	[buty]	canoe	[canoo]
debris	[debree]	eucalyptus	[ucaliptus]		
indict	[indite]	feud	[fude]	colonel	[kernel]
island	[iland]	feudal	[fudal]		
kiosk	[keeosk]	neutral	[nuteral]	lettuce	[lettis]
kiwi	[keewy]	nuclear	[nukelear]		
parliament	[parlament]	pneumatic	[numattic]	pretty	[pritty]
souvenir	[sooveneer]	pseudo	[sudo]		
trio	[treeo]	rheumatism	[roomatism]	patrol	[patrole]
triple	[tripl]				
vineyard	[vinyard]	anxious	[ankcious]	pharaoh	[fairo]
		conscious	[concious]		
area	[airia]	luscious	[lucious]	quay	[kee]
April	[aperil]				
apron	[aperon]	fascist	[fashist]	queue	[cue]
dahlia	[dalia]				
halfpenny	[haypenny]			subtle	[suttle]
pageant	[padgent]	bye	[by]		
pastry	[pacetry]	dye	[dy]		
		rye	[ry]		
		buy	[by]		
jeopardy	[jepperdy]				
leopard	[lepperd]	anemone	[anemmony]		
leotard	[le-otard]	karate	[carahty]		
people	[peeple]	simile	[simmily]		
truncheon	[trunchen]				

192

Table R 71. **69 graphemes with one clearly predominant pronunciation.**

a-e	make	*h*	hat	*p*	pop
ai	paid				
air	hair	*i-e*	time	*qu*	queen
ar	car	*-ie*	die		
au	author	*--ie*	cutie	*r*	run
aw	awful	*-igh*	high		
-ay	day	*ir*	sir	*sh*	shop
				-sion	vision
b	bib	*j*	jam	*-ssion*	session
ca	cat	*k*	keep	*t*	tot
co	cot	*kn*	knee	*-tch*	catch
cu	cup			*-tion**	station
ce	centre	*l*	lick		
ci	city	*-le*	handle	*ur*	turn
-ce	fence	*-al*	musical		
-cial*1	social			*v*	vain
-c	music			*-ive*	negative
-ck	kick	*m*	mum		
		n	nan	*we*	went
d	dad			*wi*	with
-dge	edge	*-o*	so		
		oa	foam	*x*	mix
e	end	*-oe*	toe		
ee	see	*oi*	coin	*y*	yard
er	her	*-oy*	toy	*-y*	my
		ol	old	*--y*	mummy
f	fun	*or*	normal	*z*	zip
		-ore	more		
ga	gap	*-our*	armour		
go	got	*-ous*	famous	*-ccle**2	nibble, middle
gu	gulp				apple, little

*1) *-ci-* and *-ti-* also spell the SH-sound in 5 other endings (e.g. musi*ci*an, suspi*ci*on, pre*ci*ous, gen*ti*an, cau*ti*ous), as they do in *-cial* and *-tion*, but they are used in only a small number of words.

* 2) Endings in which *a doubled consonant is followed by -le* are always preceded by a short vowel.

193

GRAPHEMES WITH SEVERAL PRONUNCIATIONS

(The 69 English graphemes which have one clearly predominant pronunciation are listed on the previous page.)

Table R 72. The 37 graphemes below have *at least two common pronunciations*, as can be seen in the examples next to them. [Less common or unpredictable pronunciations are shown in brackets.]

a	and, plant [plahnt]	*oll*	pollen, polling[poling]
are	care [cair], **are** [ar]	*o*	cloth, both[boath]
ch	chat, character, chalet	*o-e*	dome, one[wun]
	[carracter, shallay]	*oo**	food, wood[would/wud]*
ea	heath, heather [heet, hether]	*ou*	count, country, group
ear	ear, earn, bear [eer, ern, bair]		[cuntry, groop]
e-e	here, there [heer, thair]	*-our*	flour, four [for]
ei	ceiling, eight, heifer, eider	*-ow*	how, low [lo]
	[seeling, ate, heffer, ider]	*-s*	makes, tries, bus, as,
-ew	chew, grew [chue, groo]		[tryz, buss, az]
-ey	convey, monkey	*-se*	phase, chase [faze, chace]
	[convay, munkee]	*th*	this, thing [sharp/soft th]
ge-	get, gem [ghet, jem]	*u*	pun, push [poosh]*
gi-	give, ginger [ghiv, jinger]	*-ue*	cue, rue[roo]
gh	cough, through [cof, throo]	*u-e*	tube, rude[rood]
gy-	gym, gymkhana	*ui*	build, bruise, fluid
	[jim, ghimkahna]		[bild, brooz, flooid]
i	it, kind [kined]	*wa-*	wag, want[wont]
ie	chief, friend, diet	*wh-*	what, who [wot, hoo]
	[cheef, frend, dyet]	*wo-*	worn, work[werk]
-i-e	define, police, engine	*-y-*	cycle, cyclic
	[poleece, enjin]		[sikel, siclic]
al	algebra, always [aulways]	*-y*	gently, comply
all	gallant, fallen [faulen]		[gentlee, compl*ie* - as in t*ie*]

* English has no grapheme which is used chiefly for the short OO/U-sound of *wood, would* and *put* - cf. *mood, mould, cut.*

A list of all 2031 common words which contain the unpredictable graphemes shown above can be found on pages 195 - 200.

2032 words with unpredictable pronunciations for vowels, consonants, unpredictable stress, unpredictable vowel length or silent letters

(* Words with two possible pronunciations are marked with an asterisk.)

abdomen ability able abolish abominable abound about above absolutely abuse* academy accommodate accommodation accompany accomplish accord accordion account accrue accumulate accuse accustom ache achieve acid acoustic acquaint acquire acquit address adequate adjacent adjoin adjust advance adventure advertisement advertising advocate* affair affect affection afford after aggressive aghast agony ah aisle alarm alcove alert alien alight align alike alive all alliance allocation allotment allow ally almond almost alone along aloud already also altar alter alternate* alternative altogether aluminium aluminum always amateur America ammunition among amount amplifier anaesthetic analysis analytic anchor ancient anemone anger animal anniversary announce annoy anonymous anorak answer antique anxiety anxious any apostle appal apparatus apparent appeal appear appendix applaud apply appoint appreciate apprentice approach appropriate* approve approximate* April apron aquatic Arab arable archaeology architect architecture are area arena arid armada around arouse arrange array arrest arrive articulate* as ask asparagus asphyxiate assail assassin assault assemble assert assessment assign assist associate* assorted assume assure astonish astound athletic atom attach attain attempt attend attention attorney attract attributed aunt Australia authority avalanche avenue average aviary await awake awaken award aware away awe awful awkward awning

balance bald ball ballet ballistic balloon banana banish banister baron barricade barrier base bask bastard bath baton battalion beach beacon bead beak beam bean bear beard beast beat beauty beaver because begin behave behind belief believe beneath benefit benign beret bible bilious bind biscuit bivouac blast bleach bleak bleat blew blind blood blouse blow blown blue board body bogey book botany both bough bought boulder bounced bound boundary bouquet boutique bow* bowl bra branch brass brave bread breadth break breakfast breast breath breathe brew brief bristle British broad bronchial bronchitis brooch brook brother brought brow brown brownie browse bruise buffet build built bull bullet bury bush bustle busy butcher buy bye

cabaret cabin cabinet cable cadet cafe* calendar calf call calm camel camera camouflage campaign canal canoe canopy capacity capita capital capitol caramel caravan career caricature carol carrier case cask cassette cast caste castle catalogue catapult category caterpillar caught cauliflower cavalier cave cavern cease ceiling celery cello cemetery ceremony

chalet chalk chameleon chamois champagne chance chandelier chant chaos chapel character charade chariot charity chase chasm chasten chauffeur* cheap cheat chef chemical chemistry cheque chequered cherish chief child chisel chivalrous choir cholesterol chorus choux christen Christmas chrysalis chute

cigarette cinema circuit citizen city clarity clasp class clean cleanliness cleanse clear clerk clever client climb clinical close* closet cloud clover clown clue coarse cognac coincide collage collapse colleague collect collide colonel colony colour column comb come comet comfort comic

command commemorate commence commercial commit committee commodities commotion communication communion community commuter

comparison compass compatible competitive composite compound conceal conceit conceive concert* conclude conduct* conflict* congeal conifer conjure connect conquer conscience conscious conscript* consign consort* conspiracy constellation content* contest* continue contract* contrast* convenient converse* convert* convey convict* cook cookie co-ordinate* copse copy coral corgi corps correct correlation correspond couch cough could council counsel count counter country county coup couple coupon courage courier course court courtesy cousin cove covenant cover covet covey cow coward craft crave creak cream crease create creature credit crevice crier criminal critical crochet crocodile croquet crouch crow crowd crown cruise crusade cuckoo cupboard curlew curriculum cushion cycle cyclical cyclone cylinder cynical cypress

daft dahlia damage dance daughter dead deaf deal dealt dean dear death debris debt decade deceit deceive decimal decrease dedicated defeat definite defy degenerate* deign delegate* deliberate* delicacy deluge democrat demolish dense deny departure deposit depot derelict derive desert design designate desolate* dessert determine devalue develop dialogue diaphragm die diesel diet differential diffusion digest* dilute disaster discipline disease dive divert documents doe does doll dominate domino done door dose double doubt dough douse dove down dozen draft dragon drama draught dread dream dreamt dreary drive drivel driven drought drove drown drowse dumb dungarees duplicate* duvet dwarf dye dynamic

each eager eagle ear earl early earn earnest earth ease east Easter eat eaves echo eclipse economic economy edible edit educate effect efficient eider-down eight either elaborate* elapse electricity electronic element eligible eliminate else embassy emerald empirical empty emu enamel encounter encourage endeavour endure enemy energy engrave enhance enough epic epidemic epilogue equal erratic essential estimate* eucalyptus eve even ever exaggerate example exceed excel excellent except excess excite exclude excuse* executive exhaust exhibit exhibition expanse expenditure expense explicit exposure exquisite eye

fable fabulous Fahrenheit failure fall fallen falter famine famished fascist fast fasten father fatigue fault favourite fear feast feat feather feature federal feign feminine fete fever field fiend fierce figure find finger finish fishmonger fissure five flabbergast flagon flask flea flood floor florist flounder flour flow flower flown flu flue fluent fluid fluke flute folk foot foreign forest forfeit forget forgive forward fought foul found foundation fountain four fourth freak freight frequent friend frigate front frontier frown fruit full

gable gala galaxy gall garage* gasp gauge gave gear geese genuine* get geyser ghastly ghost ghoulish giddy gift giggle gild gills gilt giraffe girder girdle girl give given glacier glance glass gleam glean glimpse glisten glockenspiel glove glow glue gnarled gnash gnat gnaw gnome gnu goes gone good goose gorse govern gown graduate* graft granite graph grasp grass grave gravel grease great grey grief grieve grind gristle gross ground group grovel grow growl grown growth gruesome guarantee guard

habit half halfpenny hall halt halve hamburger handkerchief handsome has hasten haughty have hazard head heal health heap hear heard heart hearth heat heath heathen heather heave heaven heavy heifer height heir helicopter hello herald heritage heroic heroine heron hesitate hexagonal hey hi! hiccough hideous hi-fi hippopotamus his historic hive hoarse holiday honest honey honour hood hook horoscope horse host hound hour house* hover how howl hunger hurrah hustle hydrangea hydraulic hydrogen hygiene hygrometer

illegible illiterate illuminate illusion illustration image imagine immediate immense immortal immune imply improve impulse include increase indict infinite influence ingredient injure install installation instalment instead insure intense interrupt interview intimate* intuition irregular irrigation island isle italic

javelin jealous jeans jeopardy jewellery jive jostle journal journey juice July

kaleidoscope karate khaki kind kiosk kiwi knack knacker knave knead knee knew knickers knife knight knit knob knock knot know knowledge known knuckle la lacquer laminate* lance lapse lasso last lateral lather latitude laugh laureate laurel leach lead* leaf league leak lean leant leap leapt learn lease leash least leather leave legend legislate leisure* lemon lenient lens leopard leotard leper lettuce level lever lewd liberal liberty license lichen lie lieutenant limit linear linger liquor liquorice listen literally live* lively lizard llama logic longevity longitude look loose loud lounge lout love low lozenge lubricate ludo lukewarm luminous lunar lunatic lure luscious lyric

ma machine magic magnetic magnificent majority mama manage manor manual manufacture manure many marquee Mars marvellous masculine mask mass* mast matinee mattress mature mauve mayonnaise meadow meagre meal mean meant measles measure meat mechanical mechanism medal medical medicine medieval melody melon memory menace meringue merit metal miaow microfiche midday mild military mind minimal minister minority minute* miracle mischief miserable mnemonic model moderate* modern modest monarch monastery Monday money monger mongrel monk monkey month monument moral morality mortgage mosque mosquito most mother mould moult mound mount mountain mourn mouse mousse moustache mouth move movie mow mown multiply municipal

naughty nave near neat nebula necessary negative neigh neighbour neither* nestle never niece ninth none noose nothing nought nourish novel now nuclear nuisance nurse

oasis obedient obey object obliterate obscure occasion occupation occupy occurrence offend official often olive omelette* once one onion only opaque opera operate opinion opportunity oppose opposite orange orchestra orchid ordeal organic oriental other ought ounce our out outer oven over overwhelm owe owl own oxygen

pa pacifist pageant palace palate palette pall palm paltry panel panic pannier panorama papa parachute paraffin parallel parasol parish parliament parquet participate pass past pastille pastry path patient patrol pavement peace peach peak peal peanut pear pearl peas peasant peat pedal pedigree pelican penetrate people peril perish personnel petal pharaoh pheasant phlegm physical physics physiology piano picturesque pie piece pier pierce pigeon pigsty pint pity plague plait plant platinum platypus plea plead pleasant please pleasure pleat pliers plough plumage plural Pluto pneumatic poignant policy politics polythene popular positive possess possibility post poster pouch poultry pounce pound pour pout poverty powder power practise prance preach precipice precise premier premise present president pressure priest priority prison prix probable probe procedure procure produce* profit profound programme promenade prominent promise pronounce proper property proprietor protein proud prove prowl psalm pseudonym psychology pterodactyl publicity pudding pull purchase purpose pursuit push puss* put pyjamas pyramid

quack quadrangle qualify quality quantity quarantine quarrel quarry quarter quartz quay queasy questionnaire queue quiet quiver quoit

radical radish raft rapid rascal raspberry rather rave raven ravenous reach read* ready real reality really realm reap rear reason rebound recall receipt receive recipe recognise recommend record recruit refuge refuse regiment register rehearse reign reindeer reinforce reins reject release relevant relic relief relieve religion rely remedy repeat reply reservoir resident resign resolution resource response restaurant retreat reveal reverse review revive revolution reward

rheumatism rhinoceros rhododendron rhubarb rhyme rhythm

ricochet rifle rigid rind rinse risen river rivet robin rogue rook rough round rouse route routine row* rowan rowdy ruin rustle rye

said salad salami salary salmon salon salt salute sapphire satellite satin sausage save savour says scald schedule scheme scholar school schooner science scone scoundrel scout scowl scream sea seal seam sear search season seat seclude second* secular secure seize semi separate* series serrated serviette settee seven several sew sewn shaft shah shall shave sheaf shear sheath sheikh shepherd shield shiver shone shook should shoulder shout shove shovel show shower shown shriek shrivel shush siege sieve sign significant silhouette simile simplicity sincerity sinister skein skeleton slant slaughter slave sleigh sleight slew slouch slough* slovenly slow sluice small smear smother smoulder sneak snivel snout snow soccer society soldier solemn solicitor solid solution some somersault son soprano sough* sought soul sound soup sour source south southern souvenir sovereign soviet sow* sown spa spaniel speak spear species specify specimen spinach spirit sponge spout spread sprout squabble squad squall squander squash squat squeak squeal squeamish stable staff stalk stall stance steady steak steal stealthy steam sterilise steward stifle stomach stood stout stove stow straight strata strategy streak stream study subtle succumb sufficient sugar suggest suicide suit suitable suite supersonic supply support suppose sure surrender surround survey survive suspect suspense swag swagger swallow swam swamp swan swap swear sweat swivel sword swore sworn synagogue syndicate* synonym synopsis syringe syrup

table talent talk tall talon tambourine tapestry target task tattoo taught tea teach teak team tear* tease technique telescope tense tepid terrific tetanus theatre their therapist there these they thief thieve thistle thorough thou though thought thousand thread threat thrive through throw thrown

tie tier tiger timid to* today together tolerate tomb tomorrow ton tongue tonic tonsillitis took topic torrential tortoise toucan touch tough tour tourist tournament tow toward towel tower town tragic trance transparent travel treacherous treacle treadmill treason treasure treat treaty trestle tribute trifle trio triple tropics trouble trough trousers trout truncheon truth tuition turquoise twang twentieth two type typical tyranny tyrant

unique universe upon upward use*

vacuum valentine valet valiant valid value vanish variety vast vault veal vegetable veil vein velocity venison ventriloquist verse very veteran video vie view vinegar vineyard visible visit vitality volume voluntary vomit voucher vow vowel

waddle waft wag wagon walk wall wallaby wallet wallop wallow walnut walrus waltz wan wand wander wangle want wanton war warble ward warm warn warp warrant warren warrior wart was wash wasp watch water watt wattle wave waver wax

weak wealth wean weapon wear weary weasel weather weave Wednesday weigh weight weir weird were

whack whale wharf what wheat wheedle wheel wheelie wheeze whelk when where whether whey which whiff while whilst whimper whine whip whir whirl whisk whiskers whiskey whisky whisper whistle white whiz who whole whom whooping whoosh whose why

wield wild wind* wives wizard wizened wolf woman womb women won wonder wood wooden wool woollen word wore work world worm worn worry worse worship worst worth would wound* wove wow

wrangle wrap wrath wreak wreath wreck wren wrench wrestle wretch wriggle wring wrinkle wrist writ write writhe written wrong wrote wrung wry

yacht yak year yearn yeast yes yeti yield yoghurt you young your

zeal zealous zulu

200

APPENDIX S - SPELLING PROBLEMS - tables S 1 - 87

These tables list only words which contain *elements which cannot be taught systematically* - they have to be memorised individually for each word. Words with *teachable,* dominant *spelling patterns* can be found in tables *R 1 - 6, R 8 - 13 and R 15.*

The unpredictable spellings are listed in the following order:

1. **Consonant spellings** *which diverge from* the *dominant patterns* as exemplified in the words below:

film (S 1), gag (S 2), agent (S 3) p. 202-3	ship, ocean, station (S 12) p. 208
K-sound (S 4) p. 204	top, separate (S 15) p. 209
mum (S 5), net (S 6), rat (S 7) p. 205	willow (S 16), p. 209
send, ancestor, case, fence (S 8-11) p. 206-7	Z-sound as in 'wise' (S 17) p. 210

2. **Vowel spellings** *diverging from* the following *dominant patterns*:

Vowels in the stem of words	Vowels in endings
cat, pet, bit, pot, but - p. 211-13	play, daddy, go (S 29, 30, 31) p. 218
(S 18, 19, 20, 21)	pertinent, evidence (S 32, 33) p. 219
cake, bite, stole, tune - p. 214-15	better (S 34, 35, 36) p. 220-21
(S 22, 23, 24, 25)	fatal, amble, adorable (S37-39)p.222-3
out (S 26), p. 215	**Vowels in prefixes**
cart, for (S 27, 28) p. 216-17	decide, induce (S 40, 41) p. 224

3. *Weak* **spelling patterns** - as explained in chapter 4:

Vowels *in the stem* of words	-TIAL /-cial, -CIOUS /-tious p.243
EE / ea, ei, ie, etc. (S43-8) p. 228-31	
OO - short and long (S49,50) p. 232-3	**Doubled consonants**
AIR / are, ear, etc. (S 51) p. 234	Doubled consonants *obeying*
AU / aw, augh, etc. (S 52) p. 235	*the doubling rule* (S 63-7)
ER / ur, ir, ear, etc. (S 53, 54) p. 236-7	p. 244 - 7
	'Missing' doubled
Vowels *in stressed endings*	consonants (68-75)
-Y / -ie, - igh, -ye, etc. (S 55) p. 238	p. 248 - 53
-OO / -ew, -o, -u, etc. (S 56) "	*Unpredictably* doubled
-UE / -ew, -u (S 57) "	consonants (S76-9)
	p. 254 - 7
Vowels *in unstressed endings*	
-ARY / -ery, -ory, -ury (S 58) p. 239	*Predictable* doubled consonants
-EN / -on, -an, -in, -ain (S 59, 60) p. 240-1	*in word endings* (80-6)
-ESS / -ace, -ice, -as, -is (S 61) p. 242	p. 258 - 61

4. *Numerically small* patterns - (table S 42) p. 225-7

3695 unpredictably spelt words listed in alphabetic order   pages 262-70

DIVERGENT CONSONANT SPELLINGS

Table S 1. The **F-sound** is spelt unpredictably in 35 words.

alphabet	elephant	pamphlet	phone	siphon
amphibian	emphasise	phantom	photograph	sophisticated
asphyxiate	graph	pharaoh	phrase	sphere
catastrophe	Joseph	phase	physics	symphony
cellophane	nephew	pheasant	physiological	triumph
decipher	nymph	phenomenon	prophet	trophy
dolphin	orphan	philosophy	sapphire	typhoon

Table S 2. 16 words mark a hard **G-sound** *before e, i* and *y* with *h* or *u* (e.g. gherkin, guess), in order to differentiate them from words with a J-sound, like *gem* and *general*, but 35 do not; and 15 words *have redundant hard g marking before a, o, u* or redundant *final hard g* markings. (Before *a, o* and *u* and at the end of words *g* is normally hard, e.g. *ga*rden, *go*t, *gu*n, big, bang).

marked hard g before e, i and	*unmarked* hard g before e, i and y		*redundant* markings of hard g
dinghy	anger	begin	ghastly
gherkin	eager	corgi	ghost
spaghetti	finger	giddy	ghoulish
disguise	fishmonger	giggle	yoghurt
guerrillas	forget	gild	
guess	gear	gills	guarantee
guest	geese	gilt	guard
guide	get	girder	catalogue
guillotine	geyser	girdle	colleague
guilt	hamburger	girl	dialogue
guinea-pig	hunger	give	epilogue
guitar	linger	longitude	fatigue
guy	target		league
plague* [plaig]	tiger	gymkhana	meringue
rogue* [roag]	together		synagogue
vague* [vaig]			tongue

* The *ue* endings here serve to indicate a *long vowel before g*, as well as indicating a *hard g*.

Table S 3. *At the beginning of words*, *before* **a,** **o,** or **u,** the **J-sound** is spelt **j** (e.g. **ja**b, **jo**b, **ju**g); but *before* **e, i** or **y** the spelling of an initial J-sound is <u>*unpredictable*</u>. It is spelt with **g** in 20 words, in 19 with **j**.

At the end and in the middle of words, the J-sound is spelt almost invariably as **ge**, or **gi** (in at least 286 words e.g. *cage, agent, engine*), but there are 10 exceptions.

JE = *ge*	JI = *gi / gy*	JE = *je*	JI = *ji*	10 exceptions
gem	giant	jealous	jiffy	**to medial and**
general	gin	jeans	jig	**final** ***ge***
generation	ginger	jeep	jigsaw	adjective
generous	gipsy/ gypsy	jeer	jilt	inject
genie	giraffe	jelly	jingle	majestic
genius		jerk	jive	object
gentle	gym	jersey		objection
genuine	gyp	jest		project
geography		jet		reject
geranium	gyroscope	jettison		subject
germ		jetty		
gesture		Jew		spinach
		jewel		sandwich

Table S 4. The spelling of the **K-sound** is governed by 10 different sub-rules (see Chapter 4.1). They all have some **exceptions** - *at least 104 between them.*

1.) 8 words do *not* use *k* for the *K-sound* before *e* or *i* (like *keep, kept, kid*): ache, architect, bronchial, chemical, orchestra, orchid; quay, scheme.

2.) 18 words do *not* use *c* before *a, o* and *u* (as *cat, cod, cup,* and 1022 other words, do): anchor, chameleon chaos, character, chasm, cholesterol, chorus, mechanical, psychological, school; kaleidoscope, kangaroo, karate, kayak; bouquet, queue, quoit, turquoise.

3.) 6 words do *not* use *ck* after a short vowel, at the end of a short word, as 62 others do (e.g. *deck, duck*): mac, sac, rec, trek, yak, cheque.

4.) 5 words do *not* use *k* after a long vowel, as in *'leak'* or *'peek'*: antique, boutique, technique, unique, opaque.

5.) 8 words do *not* spell the final *K-sound* with *c* at the end of multi-syllable words, (e.g. comi*c*, mania*c*): attack, barrack, ransack, rucksack, shuttlecock, kayak, anorak, stomach.

6.) 10 words do *not* use *just c before a consonant*, (e.g. *clip, crane, cactus*): chlorine[cloreen], chocolate [choclat], Christmas, chrome, chrysalis[crissalis], chrysanthemum, technical, cockney, cocktail, mackerel [macrel].

7.) 10 words do *not* use *k after a consonant*, (e.g. *ankle, dark, dusk*): disc, mollusc, circle, uncle, monarch, conquer, marquee, mosquito, mosque, picturesque.

8.) 21 words do *not* use *ck* after a short, stressed medial vowel (e.g. *racket, cricket, rocket, bucket*): crocodile, decade, documents, executive, recognise, record, second, secular, vacuum; accurate, occupy, piccolo, soccer, succulent, tobacco; echo, mechanism, chequered, liquor, lacquer.

9.) 4 words do *not* spell the KW-sound with *qu* as in *queen*: acquaint, acquire, acquit, choir.

10.) 14 words do *not* spell the KS-sound simply with *x* (e.g. *exit, tax, taxi*). accelerate, accent, accept, access, eccentric, succeed, accident, succeed exceed, excellent, except, excess, excite exhibition.

Table S 5. The **M-sound** has 17 unpredictable spellings (in contrast to 1128 regular ones, as in *drum, from, mum*).

bomb	crumb	dumb	lamb	limb	numb
plumber	succumb	thumb	tomb [toom]	womb [woom]	
autumn	column	condemn	damn	hymn	solemn

Table S 6. The **N-sound** has 34 unpredictable spellings (and 2312 regular *n*, as in *no, not, nun, fun*).

knack	knob	gnash	determine	gone
knave	knobbly	gnat	discipline	scone
knead	knock	gnaw	famine	shone
knee	knot	gnome	feminine	
kneel	know		genuine *	
knew		foreign	heroine	
knife	knuckle	sovereign	imagine	
knight			masculine	
knit		pneumonia	medicine	

*   In some accents *'genuine'* is pronounced with a long IE-sound, i.e. the final *-e* is not merely decorative (as in the other words in the fourth column) but serves the 'magic' function.

Moreover, the words *famine,   feminine, genuine, heroine, imagine* and *medicine* also have a short, stressed vowel which is followed by a single consonant. They should really be spelt   [*fammin, femminin, jennuin, herroin, imadgin, meddicin*].

Table S 7. The **R-sound** has 26 unpredictable spellings (and 1670 regular *r*, as in *rat, ring, rope*).

wrangle	wreck	wriggle	wrong	rheumatism	rhyme
wrap	wren	wring	wrote	rhinoceros	rhythm
wrath	wrench	wrinkle		rhododendron	
	wrestle	wrist	wrung		
wreath	wretch	write		rhubarb	
		writhe	wry		
		written			

S-sound

Table S 8. *At the beginning of words,* before *e* or *i*, the **S-sound** has 47 unpredictable spellings (and 138 regular ones, e.g. *send, set, sing, sit*).

cease	central	cider	cistern	scene
cedar	centre	cigar	cite	scenery
ceiling	century	cigarette	citizen	scent
celebrate	cereal	cinder	citrus	science
celery	ceremony	cinema	city	scissors
cell	certain	circle	civic	scythe
cellar	certificate	circuit	civil	
cellophane		circular	civilian	
cement		circulate	civilisation	
cemetery		circumference	civilise	
cent		circumstances		
centigrade		circus		

Table S 9. The **medial S-sound** before *e or i* is spelt mostly with *c* (e.g. *ancestor, decide, perceive* - in at least 62 words); but 29 words spell the medial S-sound with *s* instead.

absent	insect	analysis	insist
advertisement	insert	basic	oasis
arsenic	morsel	basin	persistent
consent	persevere	capsize	prehensile
consequence	prosecute	consider	responsible
conservative		consist	tonsil
counsel		crisis	university
		emphasis	utensil
		hypothesis	

The spelling of the S-sound is even *more unpredictable in word endings,* as can be seen in the next two tables.

Table S 10. *As an ending,* ***after a long vowel***, *the* **S-sound** *is spelt -ce in 41 words (e.g. ace, face, nice, fleece, niece), but 20 words spell the same sound in that position with* *-se.*

base	cease	geese	precise	goose	dose	close*
case	crease			loose		house*
chase	grease	these		noose	mouse	excuse*
	increase					use*
	release					

> * The last four words are pronounced with a
> final Z-sound (like *cloze*) when used as verbs.

Table S 11. *In endings,* ***after a consonant***, *96 words spell the* **final S-sound** *with -ce (e.g. fence, force), but 35 words spell it with -se instead.*

coarse	rehearse	dense	rinse	collapse	else
course	reverse	expanse	sense	copse	pulse
curse	universe	expense	suspense	corpse	impulse
gorse	verse	immense	tense	eclipse	
hoarse	worse	intense		elapse	
horse		license		glimpse	
nurse		nonsense		lapse	
purse		response			

In word endings *after an unstressed vowel* the final S-sound is also spelt very unpredictably, but so is the unstressed vowel before it (e.g. prac*tice*, prom*ise*, sol*ace*, wit*ness*). The 50 common words with such endings are therefore listed under weak vowel patterns in table S 61, on page 242.

Table S 12. The **<u>SH-sound</u>** is spelt *sh* at the ***beginning*** and ***end*** of words in 162 common words (e.g. *shape, shop, fish, push*), but 12 words spell the *SH-sound* in those positions differently.

chalet	**chef**	**avalanche**	sugar
champagne	**chivalrous**	**microfiche**	sure
chandelier	**chute**	**moustache**	also: insure
charade			insurance

Table S 13. The spelling of the *Sh-sound in the **middle*** of words is *highly unpredictable*, as can be seen in the 22 words below.

bishop	ancient	pressure	crochet
cashew	appreciate	assure	machine
marshal	associated	issue	parachute
mushroom	efficient	tissue	
usher	ocean		
	species	conscience	patient
	sufficient	fascism	

Table S 14. The **SHN-blend** ***at the end*** of words is spelt *-tion* in at least 580 common words (e.g. *station, ignition, promotion, action, mention*), but *34 words have a different spelling*.

aspersion	comprehension	admission*	fashion
conversion	condescension	commission*	passion
dispersion	dimension	emission*	
diversion	expansion	mission	cushion
excursion	extension	permission*	
immersion	mansion	transmission*	suspicion
incursion	pension	fission	
inversion	suspension		coercion
subversion	tension	discussion	
version		percussion	ocean

* The spellings of *'admission'*, *'permission'* and *'transmission'* are especially puzzling since they derive from *'admit'*, *'permit'* and *'transmit'*, and the most common way of spelling similar words is as in *'edition'*, *'ignition'*, *'repetition'*.

The **T-sound** is spelt *t* in at least 1398 common words (e.g. *tap, tot, out, terminal, permanent*). When the *T-sound* occurs **at the end of a longer word, and is preceded by an unstressed vowel**, that ending is spelt predominantly as *-ate* (e.g. *delicate, deliberate, separate* - in 56 words), but 11 words have different endings. (For pronunciation problems of words with *-ate* see table R 67, page 189.)

Table S 15. There are just 16 common words which *disobey* the main
            patterns for spelling the T-sound.

de**bt**	compos**ite**	omele**tte***	comba**t**
dou**bt**	defin**ite**	pale**tte***	democra**t**
sub**tle**	exquis**ite**		
	favour**ite**		
two	gran**ite**		
	infin**ite**		
pterodactyl	oppos**ite**		

* The *-ette* ending normally indicates a stressed *e* before the final T-sound, as in   *casse**tte**, courge**tte**, gaze**tte**, kitchene**tte**, rose**tte** and roule**tte***, but *omelette* and *palette* are stressed on the first syllable.

Table S 16. The **W-sound,** *as a consonant*, occurs at the
            beginning of words and after *d, s, th* and *t* (e.g. *wet, dwindle, swag, thwart, twitch*), and in compounds like *afterwards*.
            The consonant *w* has *33 unpredictable spellings*.

what	**wh**ack	**wh**eat	**wh**iff	**wh**irl	**wh**isky
when	**wh**ale	**wh**eedle	**wh**ile	**wh**irring	**wh**isper
where	**wh**arf	**wh**eel	**wh**ilst	**wh**isk	**wh**istle
whether		**wh**eeze	**wh**imper	**wh**iskers	**wh**ite
which	**wh**elk		**wh**ine	**wh**iskey	**wh**iz
why	over**wh**elm	**wh**ey	**wh**ip		**wh**oosh

The letter *w* is often also used to modify vowels (e.g. *raw, blew, how*). In 42 words with the ending *-ow* the *w* is surplus (e.g. *blow, grow, slow* - cf. *no, so, piano*)- see table S 31 on page 218.

(For pronunciation problems of *-ow* see table R 24, page 149.)

At the beginning of words the **Z-sound** is spelt *z* (apart from *xylophone*), but only 15 common words begin with a Z-sound (zany, zap, zeal, zebra, zenith, zero, zest, zigzag, zinc, zip, zodiac, zone, zoo, zoom, Zulu).

The Z-sound occurs chiefly at the *end* or *in the middle of words*, where it is **spelt mainly** *-se*, or *s* *followed by another vowel*, (e.g. *erase, phase, cheese, please, rise, wise, pose, rose, absorb, desire*).

This dominant spelling pattern has been slightly diluted by the expanded use of *-ize* **in America**. In US English, words which gain the UK *-ise* ending as a *suffix* now use the *-ize* spelling instead (e.g. the verb formed from *'idol'* is *'idolise'* in the UK, but *'idolize'* in the US*.*)

Table S 17. This shows *exceptional spellings for the Z-sound* in
                 word endings and in medial position.

Final and medial Z-sound spelt **z** rather than with the more usual **s**			gz = x	With *-ize* in the US:	These should really be spelt with *zz* (cf. *buzzard*):
amaze	gaze	bazaar	anxiety	advertise	
blaze	graze	brazen	exact	agonise	
(blazer)	haze	chimpanzee	exaggerate	apologise	dozen
breeze	laze	citizen	examine	authorise	hazard
bronze	(lazy)	gazelle	example	baptise	lizard
bulldoze	maze	hazel	exasperate	emphasise	lozenge
capsize	prize	horizon	exert	fertilise	wizard
craze	seize	magazine	exist	hypnotise	wizened
(crazy)	size	razor		idolise	
doze	sneeze	tweezers	exhaust	memorise	
freeze	squeeze		[egzaust]	merchandise	sterilise
froze	trapeze			organise	synchronise
(frozen)	wheeze			recognise	tantalise

The Z-sound can also occur as a verb ending for the 3rd person in the present tense (e.g. drive*s*, play*s*, run*s*) or as an ending for plural nouns (e.g. bed*s*, hou*s*e*s*, tile*s*). In such cases the *-s* ending serves as a grammatical marker and is always spelt *-s*.

The sound of such an *-s* ending is determined by the sound of the letter which precedes it: bi*ts*, pie*ces,* pro*ps,* sto*cks* - be*ds* [bedz], bi*ns* [binz], ya*ms* [yamz]. It wood take a great deal more care and effort to pronounce words like *beds* and *runs* with a final S-sound. To spell such grammatical markers phonetically (e.g. bed*z*, run*z*) would also be tedious.

VOWEL SPELLINGS WHICH DIVERGE FROM DOMINANT PATTERNS

Unpredictably spelt short vowels

When a short, stressed vowel occurs before a consonant, followed by another vowel, the normal English convention is to double the consonant after the short vowel to prevent it becoming long as in *later* (e.g. *latter, letter, litter, lottery, utter)*. This dominant spelling for short vowels is never applied when a vowel is spelt with two letters, as in *ready* [reddy] where it would clearly help readers (cf. *reading* [reeding]).

* In the following tables words which use an unpredictable spelling for a short vowel, *and fail to double the following consonant as well*, will be marked with an asterisk (e.g. *jealous*, many** - if these words obeyed dominant English spelling rules, they would be spelt [jellous, menny]).

Only 3 words do *not* use *a* for the **A-sound**, as in *cat, mat* and *sat* (and many more in table R 1, on page 126): salmon, meringue, plait.

Table S 18. The short **E-sound** of *get, set* and *pet* (and the words in table R 2, on page 127) is *not* spelt with just *e* in 64 words.

bread	heather	treacherous	any*	against
breadth	heaven	treadmill	many*	answer
breakfast	heavy	treasure	jealous*	every
breast	instead	wealth	meadow*	friend
breath	lead	weather	peasant*	leisure +
cleanliness	leant		pheasant*	lieutenant +
cleanse	leapt		pleasant*	said
dead	leather		ready*	says
deaf	meant		steady*	Wednesday
dealt	measure		weapon*	
death	read		zealous*	
dread	realm		already*	
dreamt	spread		jeopardy*	
endeavour	stealthy		leopard*	
feather	sweat			
head	thread		heifer*	
health	threat		bury*	

+ *'Lieutenant'* is pronounced [leftennant] in the UK and [lutenant] in the US, and *'leisure'* is often pronounced [leesure] in the US.

211

Table S 19.

Table S 19. The **short I-Sound** of *bit, hit* and *sit* is spelt with *i* in 421 words (including those in table R3, on page 128) but 53 words spell it differently (*45 of them use y*).

				with unstressed short i (the stressed letter is under underlined)
abyss	myth	chrysalis*	build	
crypt	Olympics	cylinder*	built	
crystal	rhythm	cynical*	busy*	
cyclical	syllable	lyric*	English	
cygnet	symbol	physics*	pretty	
cymbals	symmetry	synagogue*	sieve	analysis
cyst	sympathy	synonym*	vineyard	bicycle
eucalyptus	symptom	syrup*	women*	chrysanthemum
gym	synchronise	typical*		hysterical
hymn	syndicate	tyranny*		pyjamas
hypnotise	syndrome			platypus
lynch	synthesis			synopsis
lynx	system			syringe
mystery				

Table S 20.

Table S 20. The **short O-sound** of *hot, not* and *pot* is spelt *o* in 375 words (including those in table R4, on page 129) but not in these:

swallow	wander	wash	quadrangle	squabble	cough
swamp	want	wasp	quality*	squad	trough
swan	wanton	watch	quantity	squander	gone
swap	warrant	watt	quarantine*	squash	shone
waft	warren	wattle	quarry	squat	laurel*
wan	warrior	what			sausage*
wand	was				

The pronunciation of the O-sound has gradually become quite different in US English. It is mostly longer than in the UK, often almost like the UK pronunciation of *ar* in words like *cart* and *part.*

This difference may have come about as a result of spelling the short O-sound after a W-sound (also after a KW-sound) predominantly as *a*, as in the 30 words above. Before the days of television and radio millions of immigrants to the US learned their English from books. Their 'mispronunciations' may have gradually helped to establish a new 'normal' pronunciation.

Table S 21. The **short U-sound** of *but, cut* and *nut* is spelt *u* in 308 words (including those in table R5, on page 130) but 68 words spell it differently.

above	govern	shove	colour*	couple*
among	love	shovel	dozen*	courage*
brother	Monday	slovenly	honey*	cousin*
come	monger	smother	money*	double*
comfort	mongrel	some	onion*	nourish*
company	monk	son	stomach*	trouble*
compass	monkey	sponge	thorough*	
covenant	month	ton		country
cover	mother	tongue		enough
covet	none	won	blood	hiccough
covey	nothing	wonder	flood	rough
does	once	worry		slough
done	one			touch
dove	other			southern
front	oven			tough
glove	pommel			young

In 51 of the 68 words above *o* is used instead of *u*. Of those, 49 are next to, or even between, *n, m* or *v* (which used to be spelt *u* until quite recently).

The use of *o* for *u*, next to or between *m, n* and *v*, was introduced by medieval scribes as a means of avoiding too many downward strokes in succession. That is also why we have *mother* for *muther,* although the word is clearly linked to the German word *Mutter.*

The look of words mattered more to scribes of the early modern English period than consistent representation of sounds. This has been causing many reading problems for learners ever since.

213

Exceptions from the patterns of c<u>a</u>k<u>e</u>, l<u>i</u>n<u>e</u>, n<u>o</u>t<u>e</u>, t<u>u</u>n<u>e</u> and l<u>ou</u>d

The vowel sounds **AY, IE, OE** and **UE** are *spelt predominantly with 'magic e'* (e.g. *cane, file, pole, cute*) - or by the *open vowel method* (e.g. *station, pilot , local, future*) - as listed on pages 131-6 and 174.

<u>**Table S 22**</u>. The **a-e** pattern (as in table R6) is **disobeyed** by at least 107 words.

aid	maid	snail	raisin	detail	deign	**This group can**
ail	mail	sprain	tailor	detain	eight	**perhaps be seen**
aim	maim	stain	trailer	entertain	feign	**as a predictable**
bail	main	strain	trainer	exclaim	freight	**small subpattern:**
bait	nail	straits	traitor	explain	neighbour	acqua<u>in</u>t
braid	paid	tail	waiter	obtain	reign	a<u>in</u>'t
brain	pail	trail		prevail	reindeer	da<u>in</u>ty
chain	pain	train	abstain	proclaim	reins	fa<u>in</u>t
claim	plaice	vain	afraid	refrain	skein	ma<u>in</u>tain
drain	plain	wail	ascertain	remain	veil	pa<u>in</u>t
fail	praise	waist	assail	retail	vein	qua<u>in</u>t
faith	raid	wait	attain	retain	weight	sa<u>in</u>t
gain	rail		available	sustain	campaign	
grain	rain	daily	chilblain		champagne	straight
hail	raise	daisy	cocktail		dahlia	break
jail	sail	gaily	complain		fete	great
laid	slain		contain		halfpenny	steak

<u>**Table S 23**</u>. The *pattern of bite, bike and icon* (as in table R 8) is *disobeyed* by 79 words.

asylum	rhyme	alight	right	behind	bible	either *
dyke	style	blight	sigh	bind	bridle	neither*
dynamic	thyroid	bright	sight	blind	disciple	eider-down
dynamite	type	delight	slight	find	idle	kaleidoscope
dynamo	tyrant	fight	tight	grind	stifle	Fahrenheit
eye	tyre	flight	height	hind	trifle	
hyacinth	cycle	frighten	sleight	kind		indict
hyena	cypress	knight		mind	resign	
hypothesis	hydrangea	light	child	ninth	sign	island
nylon	hydrogen	lightning	mild	pint		
paralyse	hygrometer	might	wild	rind	climb	choir
psychology	python	mighty	whilst	winding		
pylon	scythe	night				
			* 'either' and 'neither' have an EE-sound in the US			

Table S 24. The pattern of *bone, dome and coma* (as in table R 9) is *not followed* by 96 words.

afloat	oaf	knoll	bold	blown	sewn
boast	oak	poll	cold	bowl	
boat	oath	roll	fold	grown	both
cloak	oats	scroll	gold	growth	sloth
coach	poach	stroll	hold	known	
coal	road	toll	old	mown	brooch
coast	roam	swollen	scold	own	
coat	roast	troll	sold	rowan	goes
coax	shoal	wholly	solder	shown	
croak	soak		soldier	sown	mauve
foal	soap	control	told	thrown	
foam	stoat	enrol			only
gloat	throat	patrol	bolt	gross	
goat	toad		colt		
groan	toast	soul	dolt	host	
load		mould	jolt	most	
loaf	approach	moult	revolt	post	
loan	cockroach	shoulder		poster	
loathe		smoulder	folk		
moan			yolk	holster	

Table S 25. In 23 words the pattern of *tune* and *music* (as in table R 50) is *not followed*.

beauty	pneumatic	jewel	juice	nuclear
eucalyptus	pseudo	lewd	nuisance	
feud	rheumatism	newt	suicide	Tuesday
feudal		pewter	suitable	
neutral		sewage	suitcase	
		steward		

Table S 26. The pattern of *out* and *sound* (as in table R 46) is *not used* in 22 words.

brown	drown	growl	scowl	flower	browse	coward
clown	frown	howl		power	drowse	crowd
crown	gown	owl	towel	shower		powder
down	town	prowl		tower		

Departures from the patterns of *ar* and *or*

The **AR-sound** is spelt predominantly, as in *arm, art* and *car* (see table R 13), and in *US English* this spelling has just 4 exceptions: *are, heart, hearth* and *sergeant.*

In standard *UK English* another 88 words are pronounced with the same sound as *arm*, although they do not contain the *ar* grapheme. In standard UK English there is no difference between the vowel sounds in *arm, art* and *car* and those spelt with just *a* in the words below.

Table S 27. For learners with a standard UK accent these words are all spelt unpredictably:

ask	task	advance	after	bath	armada
bask	vast	avalanche	craft	father	drama
blast		banana	daft	lather	example
cask	brass	branch	draft	path	fuselage
cast	class	chance	giraffe	rather	panorama
caste	glass	dance	graft		promenade+
clasp	grass	chant	raft	bra	salami
contrast	pass	enhance	shaft	la	strata
fast	mass*	glance	staff	ma	vase+
flabbergast		lance		pa	
flask		piano	almond	spa	graph
gasp		plant	calf	baa	draught
ghastly		prance	calm		laugh
grasp		slant	gala	**ah**	
last		soprano	half	hurrah	clerk
mask		stance	halve	shah	
mast		trance	palm		
past					
rascal		**aunt**			

* Some English speakers rhyme 'a holy *mass*' with '*glass*', but 'a *mass* of something' rhymes with '*lass*'.

+ The words '*promenade*' and '*vase*' tend to be pronounced with an AY-sound in the US, as the spelling suggests - (cf. '*lemonade*' and '*phase*'). In UK English '*promenade*' has an AY-sound only when used as a verb, but an AR/AH-sound when used as a noun.

In US English most of the words in table S 27 are pronounced with the same sound as the *a* of *cat, hat* and *mat*. This was also the case in UK English, until roughly two centuries ago. Several UK dialects today still pronounce the *a* in words like *bath* and *fast* identically to that in *hat* and *mat*. The lengthening of that sound which became establish in *refined UK speech* in the 18th century was never adopted in the US. Hence the difference in pronunciation.

The main difference between standard UK English and standard American is that *in standard UK English an* **r** *which is preceded by a vowel is normally not pronounced*, whereas in American English it is. In UK English the *r* in **arm, darn** and **smart** lengthens and changes the sound of *a* to **ah**.

Similarly, the endings of *lore* and *sore* become identical to those of **law** and *saw*. In US English the letter *r* lengthens a preceding vowel too, but the *r* itself is pronounced as well.

Table S 28. In UK English, the 62 spellings below all *diverge from the* usual **or** pattern (*for, nor, norm* - more examples can be seen table R 15 on page 139) - as do all the 103 weak spellings for the AU-sound listed in table S 52).

adore	score	four	boar	awe	war
before	shore	pour	oar	claw	warm
bore	snore	tour	roar	draw	warn
carnivore	sore	your	soar	flaw	wart
chore	store	course	board	gnaw	
core	swore	court	coarse	jaw	quarter
folklore	tore	mourn	hoard	saw	
fore	wore	resources	hoarse	straw	corps
gore		source		thaw	
ignore		tournament	door	law	
implore			floor	paw	
ore		also: **fourth**		raw	
more		and *fourteen*			
pore		but *forty*			

Divergent vowel spellings in _endings_ and _prefixes_

The majority of endings are unstressed, because most English words are stressed on the first syllable (f*a*ther, m*o*ther, d*a*ddy, m*u*mmy, p*e*rmanent).

<u>**Table S 29**</u>. The _stressed_ ending _-ay_, as in _day, play_ and _say_, is used in 35 common words, but _19 words spell it differently_.

convey	obey	whey	neigh	ballet	buffet	duvet	café
grey	survey		sleigh	beret	chalet		
hey	they		weigh	bouquet	crochet		matinee

<u>**Table S 30**</u>. The _stressed_ **EE-sound** is spelt as unpredictably in endings (e.g. _tea, tree, key_) as inside words (see tables S 43 - 48).
As an _unstressed_ ending, the _EE-sound_ is spelt mainly _-y_ (_mummy, funny, badly, surely, tasty_), but 51 words do **_not_** spell this ending _with -y_.

abbey	holey	parsley	bikini	spaghetti	brownie	anemone
alley	honey	pulley	broccoli	taxi	budgie	karate
attorney	jersey	storey	confetti	yeti	collie	simile
barley	jockey	trolley	corgi		cookie	
bogey	journey	turkey	graffiti		movie	
chimney	kidney	valley	kiwi		pixie	coffee
cockney	medley	volley	safari		prairie	committee
donkey	money	whiskey	salami		wheelie	
hockey	monkey		semi			

<u>**Table S 31**</u>. The ending _-o_ can be _stressed_ or _unstressed_ (n*o*, g*o* - pot*a*t*o*). The number of 106 common words ending in _-o_ is growing with such modern shortenings as _panto_ for _pantomime_ and _info_ for _information_, but 59 words have a _different spelling_ for the _final_ **OE-sound** .

arrow	follow	sorrow	blow	show	doe	sew
barrow	gallows	sparrow	_bow *_	slow	floe	cocoa
bellow	hollow	tomorrow	crow	snow	foe	depot
below	marrow	wallow	flow	sow*	hoe	**dough**
billow	narrow	widow	glow	stow	oboe	**oh**
bungalow	pillow	willow	grow	throw	roe	**owe**
burrow	shadow	window	know	tow	sloe	**pharaoh**
elbow	shallow	yellow	low		toe	**though**
fellow	swallow		mow		woe	

* _'Bow'_ and _'sow'_ have two different pronunciations - (see table R 24).

218

A few words ending in *-o* gain an unpredictable *e* in their plural form, e.g. *potato - potatoes*, also: *buffaloes, dingoes, dominoes, echoes, heroes* and *tomatoes;* but *armadillos* and *avocados* just add an *-s*, as do *pianos, banjos* and *solos*. It is a mystery why some words were deemed to need the extra *e*.

Many words end with an unstressed ***-ent*** or ***-ence*** (e.g. contin*ent*, insist*ence*), and they are spelt *-ent* and *-ence* in 137 and 39 common words each; but many endings with exactly the same sound are spelt *-ant* or *-ance* instead.

Table S 32. Adjectives and nouns ending with *-ant*.

applicant	elephant	infant	pheasant	sextant
assistant	extravagant	instant	pleasant	significant
brilliant	fragrant	jubilant	protestant	truant
covenant	gallant	lieutenant	relevant	tyrant
defiant	giant	merchant	remnant	vacant
descant	ignorant	pageant	restaurant	valiant
distant	important	peasant	sergeant	warrant
dominant	indignant	pennant	servant	

Many nouns ending in *-ance* can be seen to be related to, or to be derived from, an adjective ending in *-ant* (e.g. *brilliant - brilliance, defiant - defiance, distant - distance*.) In such cases, knowing with certainty how to spell one of the two can help with the spelling of the other.

Unfortunately, often only one half of such pairs is in common usage (e.g. *ambulance - ambulant*), or there is no adjective or noun to which they can be seen to be related (e.g. elephant, balance).

Table S 33. 14 common nouns have *-ance* endings although there is no adjective with an *-ant* ending in common usage.

accordance	appearance	balance	guidance	nuisance
alliance	appliance	endurance	insurance	performance
allowance	assurance	finance	maintenance	

The **-er ending,** *with an unstressed E-sound,* is used in at least 340 common English words (e.g. *better, brother, sister*). Many more can be created when using comparative adjectives (e.g. *big - bigger, fast - faster*), but in 136 words this ending is spelt differently.

Table S 34. The main divergent spellings for **-er** are **-or, -ar, -our** and **-re**.

				In US English
actor	elevator	minor	sensors	*these 18 have*
advisor	emperor	mirror	solicitor	*-or endings too:*
alligator	equator	monitor	spectator	armour
ambassador	error	motor	sponsor	behaviour
ancestors	escalator	navigator	successor	colour
anchor	factor	operator	superior	favour
assessor	gladiator	orator	supervisor	flavour
author	governor	prior	surveyor	glamour
boaconstrictor	indicator	professor	survivor	harbour
calculator	interior	proprietor	tailor	honour
castor	inventor	radiator	tenor	humour
conductor	investors	razor	terror	labour
conveyor	junior	rector	tractor	neighbour
corridor	juror	refrigerator	traitor	odour
decorator	legislator	respirator	tutor	parlour
demonstrator	liquor	rotor	victor	rumour
director	major	scissors	visitor	saviour
doctor	manor	senator	warrior	savour
editor	mayor	senior		splendour
				tumour
angular	linear	radar	*Oddities:*	*and these have*
burglar	lunar	regular		*'-er' endings:*
caterpillar	muscular	scholar	chauffeur	centre
cellar	nectar	secular		fibre
circular	nuclear	similar	jodhpurs	metre
collar	particular	sitar		sabre
dollar	peculiar	solar	martyr	theatre
familiar	pillar	spectacular		ogre
grammar	polar	sugar		kilometre
jaguar	poplar	vicar		
liar	popular	vulgar		

When words have identically sounding endings which are spelt differently, we usually exaggerate the pronunciation of the different spellings during the learning stage, to help us remember them. It is easy to end up thinking that we really can hear different vowel sounds in them.

Some people try hard to make the endings of words like *actor, director* and *doctor* sound different from those of *farmer, lawyer* and *potter*, but in ordinary speech they all sound like the hundreds of other words which spell the ending with *-er*.

A few words which end in *-ar* have a semi-stressed ending, rather than an unstressed one (e.g. *radar, sitar*). - They are not stressed on just one syllable, like most English words. In such cases the *-ar* ending can be heard a little more clearly.

Table 35. 30 words have endings which sound like those of *catcher* or *butcher*, but are spelt *-ture*, with *tu* for the **CH**-sound and *re* for the final **ER**-sound; 9 words have endings which sound *-jer*, as in dan*ger*. They spell the final ER-sound with *-ure*.

adventure	culture	future	miniature	signature
agriculture	departure	gesture	mixture	structure
architecture	expenditure	lecture	nature	temperature
capture	feature	legislature	picture	torture
caricature	fracture	literature	puncture	venture
creature	furniture	manufacture	scripture	vulture
exposure	leisure	pleasure	conjure	procedure
fissure	measure	treasure	injure	

Table 36. 45 words with an *-a* ending also sound very much as if they end with *an unstressed -er*, although these are perhaps marginally different from the other words with divergent spellings for the *-er* ending.

algebra	cobra	gorilla	piazza	replica	utopia
area	data*	idea	piranha	spectra*	veranda
armada	dilemma	lava	pizza	stigma	via
Asia	drama	llama	pneumonia	strata*	yoga
banana	era	militia	propaganda	tarantula	zebra
camera	extra	nebula	phenomena*	tiara	
capita	formula	orchestra	pupa	tundra	
china	gondola	panda	quota	umbrella	

* Sometimes an *-a* ending indicates a Latin plural form (e.g. *data*).

Words which *end with an* **L-sound,** *preceded by an unstressed vowel* tend to be *pronounced with just the L-sound* (e.g. *classical, fatal, liberal, numeral*). In normal speech the unstressed vowel is barely audible.

The dominant spelling for this ending is *-al, especially* where the unstressed vowel is *preceded by a single consonant (and a vowel before that)* as in the examples above. In words like *mental* and *fundamental* the *-al* ending does perhaps contain more of a vowel sound.

Table S 37. The *-al* ending occurs in 195 common words. Many more adjectives can be formed on the pattern of *comic - comical* and *music - musical*, but 33 words do *not* use the *-al* spelling.

caramel	drivel	hazel	spaniel	daffodil	alcohol	parasol
cockerel	duel	hostel	towel	civil	capitol	petrol
colonel	easel	jewel	vowel	devil	carol	pistol
cruel	fuel	label	weasel	evil	cholesterol	symbol
diesel	gravel	novel		pupil	idol	

As with all unstressed vowels, spellers can only learn the *-el, -il* and *-ol* endings by exaggerating their pronunciation during the learning stage. Proficient spellers consequently often end up convinced that they can hear slightly different sounds for the different spellings, but in ordinary speech *local, gravel, civil* and *pistol* all have much the same ending. If they were all spelt with *-al* [*local, graval, cival, pistal*] we would pronounce them all just as we do now. Some of the 9 words ending in *-ol* are perhaps slightly different from the rest.

Table S 38. When the **final L-sound** *is preceded by* **two consonants** the spelling for the ending is usually *-le*. At least 98 words follow this pattern (e.g. *apple, little, whistle, amble, handle*) but 21 words diverge from this pattern.

barrel	mongrel		anvil
channel	pommel	counsel*	council*
flannel	pummel	morsel	fossil
funnel	quarrel	parcel	nostril
kennel	satchel		pencil
kernel	scoundrel		stencil
kestrel	squirrel		tonsil
mackerel [macrl]	tunnel		utensil

* In words with an S-sound before -el or -il the spelling for the S-sound is also unpredictable (e.g. stencil - untensil).

222

Table S 39. **The suffixes** *-able* and *-ible* have a predictable *-le* ending, but the spelling of the *unstressed vowel before b* is *unpredictable*: 33 words use *-able*, as in *doable*, *loveable* and *indubitable*, but 17 words use *-ible* instead.

aud**ible**	feas**ible**	incred**ible**	poss**ible**	terr**ible**	elig**ible**
compat**ible**	flex**ible**	invis**ible**	respons**ible**	vis**ible**	illeg**ible**
ed**ible**	horr**ible**	permiss**ible**	sens**ible**		tang**ible**

The only spelling pattern for endings with unstressed vowels which has **no exceptions** among 6800 common English words is the unstressed *-ard* ending, as in *blizzard, buzzard, forward* or *hazard.* - (If we disregard the compound *'shepherd'*.)

2 F. Prefixes with Unstressed Vowels: de-/di-, in-/en-

Table S 40. 57 common words have the prefix *de-* (e.g. *decide, decline, deprive, derive*), but 28 words use *di-* instead.

dictate	discharge	dismantle	distribute
diffusion	disciple	dismay	disturb
dilapidated	discover	displace	divide
diploma	discuss	display	divine
diplomatic	disease	dispose	division
disappear	disguise	dispute	divorce
disaster	disgust	distinct	dilemma*

* *dilemm a* is sometimes pronounced with an IE-sound in the prefix.

Table S 41. 73 words use the prefix *in-* (e.g. *inform, induce, intrude*), but 28 words use *en-* instead.

enable	encourage	engrave	enrol
enamel	encrusted	engulf	entangle
encamp	endanger	enjoy	entertain
enchant	endeavour	enlarge	enthusiastic
encircle	endure	enlist	entire
enclose	engage	enquire	entitled
encounter	enforce	enrage	environment

We can only learn to spell the prefixes *de- / di-* and *in- / en-* accurately by exaggerating their pronunciation during the learning stage (as we have to with most unstressed vowels). With some of the words we get in the habit of preserving this more emphatic pronunciation for the rest of our lives, but generally the unstressed prefixes *de- / di-* and *in- / en-* sound much the same. It is also extremely difficult to detect differences in meaning between the two members of each pair.

SPELLINGS WHICH FOLLOW SMALL PATTERNS

In addition to the spellings which diverge from dominant patterns listed so far, there are another 98 words which follow 10 separate small patterns, and a further 16 words which disobey them. It is perhaps more accurate to say that there is another list of 114 words with idiosyncratic spellings which need to be memorised.

All the words are set out in table S 42 below. Their patterns are also explained in more detail on the next two pages.

<u>Table S 42</u>. 114 words which obey or disobey **10 small spelling patterns**.

almost	already	also	altogether	always
altar	alter	alternate	alternative	
award	dwarf	reward		
walk	wall	walnut	walrus	waltz
war	warble	ward	wardrobe	warm
warn	warp	wart	water	
wore	*(worn)*			
quart	quarters	quartet	quartz	
allow	bow	brow	cow	how	miaow
now	row	sow	vow	wow	
bough	*plough*	*slough*	*thou*	
annoy	boy	convoy	corduroy	coy	destroy
employ	enjoy	hoy	joy	ploy	toy
	buoy				
to				
accuracy	agency	aristocracy	conspiracy	democracy
delicacy	diplomacy	emergency	fancy	frequency
juicy	mercy	policy	tendency	urgency
vacancy				
controversy	*courtesy*	*gypsy*	*topsy-turvy*	*embassy*
beautician		electrician	Grecian	logician	magician
mathematician		musician	optician	physician	politician
statistician		tactician		*gentian*	
zap	zeal	zealous	zebra	zero
zest	zigzag	zinc	zip	zodiac
zone	zoo	zoom	zulu	*xylophone*
buzz	jazz		*quiz*	*whiz*

Fuller explanations of the 10 patterns listed in table S 42 (on the previous page) **which are followed by fewer than 20 words**

1. An initial **AUL-** sound which is followed by another consonant is spelt *al-*.

| almost | already | also | altogether | always |
| altar | alter | alternate | alternative | |

2. *After w,* an **AU**-sound is spelt mainly *a,* except in *wore* and *worn*.

award	dwarf	reward		
walk	wall	walnut	walrus	waltz
war	warble	ward	wardrobe	warm
warn	warp	wart	water	

3. This pattern extends to 4 words which begin with *qu*: **qua**rt, **qua**rters, **qua**rtet, **qua**rtz.

4. At the end of words the *OU-sound* is spelt predominantly as *ow*, with 4 exceptions.

allow	bow*	brow	cow	how	miaow
now	row*	sow*	vow	wow	
bough	plough	slough	thou		

*The spellings 'bow', 'row' and 'sow' can have different pronunciations [bo, ro, so] or [bou, rou, sou] and different meanings.

5. *At the end of words* the **OI**-sound is spelt *-oy*, with the exception of b*uoy*.

| annoy | boy | convoy | corduroy | coy | destroy |
| employ | enjoy | hoy | joy | ploy | toy |

6. The infinitive marker *to*, as in '*to go*' or '*to see*' has a unique sound, with the *o* barely audible, pronounced more like [t'go, t'see] and occurring in just this one word.

The word *to* has a different pronunciation and meaning in '*to him*' or '*to London*'. In such cases it sounds like the other two spellings for the same word (*two* and *too*). - This helps to explain why confusion between *to, too* and *two* is one of the main sources of English spelling errors.

7. The dominant spelling for the unstressed ending with the sound of **SEE** is
-*cy*, with 5 exceptions.

accura**cy**	agen**cy**	aristocra**cy**	conspira**cy**	democra**cy**
delica**cy**	diploma**cy**	emergen**cy**	fan**cy**	frequen**cy**
jui**cy**	mer**cy**	poli**cy**	tenden**cy**	urgen**cy**
vacan**cy**				
controversy	courtesy	gypsy	topsy-turvy	embassy

8. A final -**SHAN** / -**SHN** sound is spelt -*cian*, except in *gentian*.

beauti**cian**	electri**cian**	Gre**cian**	logi**cian**	magi**cian**
mathemati**cian**	musi**cian**	opti**cian**	physi**cian**	politi**cian**
statisti**cian**	tacti**cian**			

9. At the beginning of words the **Z**-sound is spelt *z*, except in *xylophone*.

zap	zeal	zealous	zebra	zero
zest	zigzag	zinc	zip	zodiac
zone	zoo	zoom	zulu	

10. After a short vowel, at the end of words, the *final -z* may be *doubled or not doubled*.

buzz	jazz	quiz	whiz

11. The 22 words with a **ZH**-sound should perhaps also be listed among these small patterns, although this group is slightly bigger than the other 10. The ZH-sound is spelt predominantly with -*si*-, but 7 words spell it with just -*s*-, one with -*z*- and one with -*ss*-.

Asia	division	occasion	exposure	casual	azure
conclusion	explosion	precision	leisure	usual	
confusion	illusion	vision	measure		fissure
decision	Indonesian	*and derivatives*:	pleasure		
diffusion	invasion	supervision	treasure		
		provision			
		television			

227

Words with week spellings - as explained in chapter 4

The **EE-sound** has seven unpredictable spelling patterns.

Table S 43. 152 words spell the **EE**-sound with *ea*.

appeal	dean	heath	peanut	sneak	yeast
appear	dear	heathen	peat	speak	zeal
beach	decrease	heave	plea	spear	
beacon	defeat	increase	plead	squeak	
bead	disease	jeans	please	squeal	
beak	dream	knead	pleat	squeamish	
beam	dreary	leach	preach	steal	
bean	each	lead*	queasy	steam	
beard	eager	leaf	reach	streak	
beast	eagle	league	read*	stream	
beat	ear	leak	real	tea	
beaver	ease	lean	really	teach	
beneath	east	leap	reap	teak	
bleach	Easter	lease	rear	team	
bleak	eat	leash	reason	tear*	
bleat	eaves	least	release	tease	
breathe	fear	leave	repeat	treacle	
cease	feast	meagre	retreat	treason	
cheap	feat	meal	reveal	treat	
cheat	feature	mean	scream	treaty	
clean	flea	measles	sea	veal	
clear	freak	meat	seal	weak	
colleague	gear	near	seam	wean	
conceal	gleam	neat	sear	weary	
congeal	glean	ordeal	season	weasel	
creak	grease	pea	seat	weave	
cream	heal	peace	sheaf	wheat	
crease	heap	peach	shear	wreak	
creature	hear	peak	sheath	wreath	
deal	heat	peal	smear	year	

228

Table S 44. 133 words spell the **EE-sound** with *ee*.

agree	employee	kneel	seem	three
bee	engineer	lee	seen	tree
beech	exceed	leek	seep	trustee
beef	fee	marquee	seesaw	tweed
been	feeble	meek	settee	tweezers
beer	feed	meet	sheep	volunteer
beet	feel	need	sheer	weed
beetle	feet	needle	sheet	week
between	flee	pedigree	sleek	weep
bleed	fleece	peek	sleep	wheedle
bleep	fleet	peel	sleet	wheel
breed	free	peep	sleeve	wheeze
breeze	freeze	peer	smithereens	wildebeest
career	geese	pioneer	sneer	
cheek	glee	preen	sneeze	
cheer	greed	proceed*	speech	* NB:
cheese	green	proceedings*	speed	precede
cheetah	greet	proceeds*	squeeze	and
chimpanzee	guarantee	queen	steel	proceed
creek	heel	queer	steep	
creep	indeed	reed	steeple	
deed	interviewee	reef	steer	
deep	jamboree	reel	street	
deer	jeep	referee	succeed	
degree	jeer	refugee	sweep	
discreet	jubilee	screech	sweet	
domineer	keel	screen	teem	
dungarees	keen	see	teeth	
eel	keep	seed	teetotal	
eerie	knee	seek	thirteen	

229

Table S 45. 86 words spell the __EE-sound__ on the pattern of *eve*, or as in *legal, legion* and *torpedo* - with *'magic e'*, or by the *'open vowel'* method.

adhere	fever	persevere	swede
adhesive	frequent	peter	tedious
arena	genie	polythene	theatre
cafeteria	genius	precede	theme
cedar	here	previous	theory
cereal	hero	query	these
chameleon	hyena	recent	torpedo
Chinese	imperial	recess	trapeze
comedian	inferior	region	vehicle
compete	ingredient	relay	Venus
complete	interfere	scene	zero
concrete	intermediate	scheme	
convene	legal	sequence	
convenient	legion	sequin	
decent	lenient	series	
demon	lever	serious	
equal	material	serum	
era	medium	severe	
eve	mere	sincere	
even	meteor	species	
evil	meter	sphere	
experience	millipede	stampede	
exterior	mysterious	strategic	
extreme	obedient	superior	
female	period	supreme	

Table S 46. 31 words spell the **EE-sound** with *ie* and 12 with *ei*.

achieve	field	medieval	relief	thieve	frontier
belief	fiend	niece	relieve	tier	
believe	fierce	piece	shield	wield	
brief	grief	pier	shriek	yield	
chief	grieve	pierce	siege	cavalier	
diesel	hygienic	priest	thief	chandelier	
ceiling	conceit	conceive	deceit	deceive	receipt
receive*					
	protein	seize	sheikh	weir	weird*

*The words above and in the other five tables for the EE-sound make it clear that, in the whole context of learning to spell the EE-sound, the mnemonic *"I before e, except after c"* is of very limited use.

Table S 47. 29 words spell the **EE-sound** with an *open i*.

albino	guillotine	marine	ravine	tangerine
antique	kiosk	mosquito	regime	trampoline
aubergine	kiwi	pizza	routine	trio
bikini	machine	plasticine	sardine	unique
clementine	magazine	police	suite	vaseline
fatigue	margarine	prestige	tambourine	

Table S 48. 7 words spell the **EE-sound** with *e* and another *6 words have various spellings*.

be	me	we	cathedral	debris	quay	people
he	she		secret	key	ski	souvenir

THE SHORT AND LONG OO-SOUNDS

The grapheme *oo* spells predominantly the **long OO**-sound of *'room, school'* and *'spoon'*, but it is also used for the **short OO**-sound in *'good wood'*.

Scottish and Northern English accents use predominantly just the long OO-sound, pronouncing the *'oo'* in *'good'* and *'mood'* with the same sound. In American English the short OO-sound of standard UK English is also pronounced somewhat longer.

In some parts of England words which usually have the standard sound of *'but, cut'* and *'nut'* are pronounced with the same sound as *'pull, push, put'* and *'foot'*.

These pronunciation differences may all stem from the fact that *the short OO-sound does not have a clearly identifiable grapheme of its own.* The graphemes used for it - *oo, u, ou, oul, o* - are more often used to spell other sounds (e.g. b*oo*t, b*u*t, b*ou*t, sh*ou*lder, h*o*t).

Table S 49. The **short OO-sound** occurs in 36 common words:
   15 words spell it with *oo*,
   15 with **u** and
   6 with *other graphemes*.

book	look	good		
brook	rook	hood		
cook	shook	stood		
hook	took	wood		
wool	whoosh		foot	
bull	bush		put	cuckoo
full	push		butcher	pudding
pull	shush			pussy
bullet	cushion			sugar
bullion				
	wolf	could		courier
	woman	should		
		would		

Table S 50. The **long OO-sound** occurs in 131 common words (in the stem of words): 72 words spell it with *oo*, but 59 words spell it differently.

OO-sound spelt *oo*

baboon	goose	moor	shoot
balloon	groom	moot	smooth
bloom	groove	mushroom	snooker
boom	harpoon	noodle	soon
boon	hoof	noon	soothe
boost	hooligan	noose	spoof
boot	hoop	pontoon	spook
brood	hoot	poodle	spool
broom	lagoon	pool	spoon
cartoon	loom	proof	stool
choose	loop	roof	stoop
cocoon	loose	room	swoon
cool	loosen	root	swoop
doom	loot	saloon	tool
droop	macaroon	school	tooth
food	maroon	schooner	troop
fool	mood	scoop	whoop
gloom	moon	scooter	zoom

OO-sound spelt with *other graphemes*

brutal	fluent	acoustic	lose
brute	fluid	bivouac	move
crucial	fluke	boutique	prove
crude	flute	coupon	
frugal	glucose	group	cruise
intrude	lubricate	recoup	fruit
prune	ludicrous	toucan	bruise
ruby	ludo	tourist	recruit
rude	lukewarm	troupe	sluice
ruined	luminous	wound	
rule	lunar	youth	sleuth
rural	lunatic	soup	
truant	plural	route	shrewd
truce	recluse		gruesome
truly	secluded	tomb	manoeuvre
truth	zulu	womb	

233

Table S 51. The **AIR-sound** occurs in 58 common words:
31 words spell it with *are,* or with *ar* followed by another vowel (e.g M*ary*),
27 words spell it differently.

area	Mary	air	bear
aware	pare	chair	pear
bare	parent	dairy	tear*
blare	prepare	fair	swear
canary	rare	flair	wear
care	scare	hair	
compare	share	lair	aerial
dare	snare	pair	aeroplane
declare	spare	prairie	aerobatics
fare	square	stairs	
flare	stare		heir
glare	various	affair	their
hare	vegetarian	despair	
hilarious	wares	éclair	there
malaria	wary	repair	where
mare		questionnaire	

* *'tear'* has 2 different pronunciations.

234

Table S 52. The **AU-sound** occurs in 103 common words:
39 words spell the AU-sound with *au*,
64 words spell it differently.

applause	maul	bawl	all	caught
assault	nautical	brawl	ball	daughter
astronaut	Paul	crawl	call	haughty
auburn	pause	drawl	fall	naughty
auction	Santa-Claus	scrawl	gall	slaughter
audible	sauce	shawl	hall	taught
August	saucer	sprawl	install	
authentic	staunch	trawl	pall	
author	tarpaulin		recall	bought
authorise	taunt	awe	small	brought
automatic	taut		squall	fought
autonomy	vault*	awful	stall	nought
autumn		awkward	tall	ought
because *		awning	wall	sought
cauldron		brawn		thought
cause		dawdle	appal	
caution		dawn	bald	
cosmonaut		drawn	chalk	
daub		fawn	falter	broad
exhaust		hawk	halt	
fault		lawn	instalment	
gaudy		pawn	salt	poultry
haul		prawn	scald	
haunt		sawn	stalk	
jaunt		spawn	talk	
launch		squawk		
launder		yawn		

* In UK English, *because* and *vault* are increasingly being pronounced as [becoz] and [volt].

The **stressed ER-sound** (as distinct from the unstressed one in words like *ex_ercise* or *m_other*) occurs in 195 common words, but only

> 70 words spell it with *er*;
> 125 words spell it differently.

Table S 53. 70 words which spell the stressed **ER-sound** with *er*.

advertisement	external	perfect	universal
alert	fern	perfume	university
alternative	fertile	permanent	verb
anniversary	germinate	permit	verdict
assert	her	person	verge
berth	herb	pertinent	vermin
certain	herd	preserve	verse
commercial	hermit	refer	version
concern	impertinent	reserve	versus
confer	insert	reverse	vertical
conserve	interpret	sermon	
conversion	jerk	serpent	
deserve	jersey	serve	
dessert	kernel	stern	
detergent	merchant	swerve	
determine	mercury	term	
emerge	mercy	terminate	
eternal	nerve	termite	
exert	observe	thermal	
expert	perch	transfer*	

The verb ('to transf_er'*) and the noun (to make a *'tr_ansfer'*) are stressed differently.

Table S 54. 125 words which do *not use er* for the **ER-sound:**
      65 use **ur**, 36 **ir**, 11 **ear**, 9 **or**, 3 **our** and 1 **ere**.

absurd	purse	birch	earl
blur	return	bird	early
burden	slur	birth	earn
burglar	spur	chirp	earnest
burgle	spurn	circle	earth
burly	spurt	circuit	heard
burn	sturdy	circular	learn
burst	surf	circumstances	pearl
church	surface	circus	rehearse
churn	surge	dirt	search
curl	surgeon	fir	yearn
curse	surgery	firm	
curt	surname	first	attorney
curve	surplus	flirt	word
disturb	survey*	girder	work
excursion	Thursday	girdle	world
fur	topsy-turvy	girl	worm
furnish	turban	mirth	worse
further	turf	shirk	worship
gurgle	turkey	shirt	worst
hurdle	turmoil	sir	worth
hurl	turn	skirmish	
hurt	turnip	skirt	courtesy
hurtle	turtle	smirk	journal
lurch	urban	squirm	journey
lurk	urchin	squirt	
murder	urge	stir	
murmur	urn	swirl	were
nasturtium	yurt	third	
nurse		thirst	
nursery		thirty	
occur		twirl	
purchase		virtually	
purple		virtue	
purpose		whir	
purr		whirl	

* *Survey* is stressed on the first syllable when used as a noun [s<u>e</u>rvay], but as a verb it is stressed on the second [to serv<u>ay</u>].

237

Many word endings are spelt unpredictably

Table S 55. The *stressed* **IE-sound** occurs at the end of 31 one-syllable
words: 17 words spell it with -*y*; 14 spell it differently.

by	my	sly	why	die	high	bye	buy
cry	ply	spy	wry	lie	nigh	dye	guy
dry	pry	sty		pie	sigh	rye	
fly	shy	thy		tie	thigh		
fry	sky	try		vie			

(See also 2c and table R 37 on page 163.)

Table S 56. The **long OO-sound** occurs at the end of 52 common words, but
it is spelt very unpredictably:
18 use *oo*, 34 use different graphemes.

boo	bamboo	blew	slew	accrue	do	canoe
coo	cockatoo	brew	strew	blue	lasso	shoe
goo	hullabaloo	cashew	threw	clue	to*	
loo	igloo	crew		construe	two	choux
moo	kangaroo	drew		flue	who	pooh
shoo	shampoo	flew	flu	glue		through
too	tattoo	grew	gnu	rue		you
woo	voodoo	screw	guru	true		
zoo	yahoo	shrew				

* *'To'* can have a short vowel sound or a long one
(e.g. I have *to* go *to* London.).

Table S 57. The -*ue* *ending* is also unpredictable:
20 words use -*ue*, but 22 do not.

cue	devalue	statue	askew	interview	review	emu
due	imbue	subdue	chew	Jew	spew	menu
sue	issue	tissue	curfew	knew	stew	
argue	pursue	value	curlew	mildew	view	you*
avenue	queue	venue	dew	nephew	yew	
barbecue	rescue	virtue	ewe	new		
continue	revenue		few	pew		

*The word **you** follows neither the pattern of *cue, due* or *sue*, nor that of the
initial open *u* in *union* or *universe*. The simplest spelling for it would be *U*,
by analogy with *I*.

Table S 58. The *-ary ending,* with an *unstressed,* or *even silent a,* occurs in 92 words. It is spelt very unpredictably: 37 words spell this ending *-ary*, but 55 do not.

adversary	arch**ery**	categ**ory**	carpen**try**	cent**ury**
anniversary	art**ery**	dormit**ory**	chemis**try**	inj**ury**
arbitrary	artill**ery**	fact**ory**	coun**try**	lux**ury**
aviary	blust**ery**	hist**ory**	en**try**	Merc**ury**
boundary	cel**ery**	invent**ory**	gan**try**	treas**ury**
burglary	cemet**ery**	iv**ory**	indus**try**	
commentary	colli**ery**	laborat**ory**	infan**try**	
contemporary	crock**ery**	mem**ory**	pal**try**	sav**oury**
contrary	deliv**ery**	observat**ory**	pas**try**	
diary	discov**ery**	satisfact**ory**	poe**try**	
dictionary	drudg**ery**	territ**ory**	poul**try**	
elementary	ev**ery**	the**ory**	tapes**try**	
estuary	gall**ery**			
February	jewell**ery**			
January	lott**ery**			
library	machin**ery**			
literary	monast**ery**			
military	myst**ery**			
monetary	nurs**ery**			
necessary	pott**ery**			
ordinary	recov**ery**			
planetary	robb**ery**			
preliminary	scen**ery**			
primary	station**ery**			
pulmonary	surg**ery**			
reactionary				
revolutionary				
salary				
secondary				
secretary				
solitary				
stationary				
summary				
temporary				
veterinary				
vocabulary				
voluntary				

The **unstressed half-vowel before** *final -n* (as in *pollen* or *person*) occurs in 205 common words, but its spelling is not rule-governed. During the learning stage, pupils are usually encouraged to exaggerate the pronunciation of the different endings, to help them remember them. This can eventually make spellers think that they are able to hear slightly different vowels before the final *'n'*, but if they were all spelt with *'e'* instead, we would pronounce them all exactly as we do in normal speech now.

Table S 59. 73 words spell an *unstressed half-vowel before a final -n with an -e-.*

abdomen	forgotten	loosen	spoken
alien	frighten	madden	stamen
awaken	frozen	mitten	stolen
barren	garden	often	strengthen
bitten	given	omen	sudden
bracken	glisten	open	sullen
brazen	golden	oven	swollen
brighten	happen	oxygen	taken
chicken	heathen	pollen	threaten
children	heaven	raven	token
chosen	hidden	ridden	vixen
christen	hydrogen	ripen	warren
citizen	kindergarten	risen	women
delicatessen	kitchen	rotten	wooden
dozen	kitten	sadden	woollen
driven	laden	seven	written
eleven	lessen	sharpen*	
even	lichen	sodden	
fallen	listen	specimen	

* It is possible to create many more verbs from adjectives by adding *-en* to them: e.g. broad*en*, wid*en*, enlight*en*, height*en* - but *not all verbs* with an unstressed vowel before the final N-sound are spelt with *-en* endings (e.g. aband*on*, beck*on)*.

Table S 60. 131 words use spellings *other than* *e* for the unstressed half-vowel *before a final -n:*
63 use *o*, 34 *a*, 22 *i*, 7 *ai* and 6 *eo*.

abandon	nylon	Alsatian	aspirin*
apron	octagon	amphibian	basin
bacon	pardon	cardigan	bulletin
badminton	pentagon	Christian	cabin
baron	person	civilian	catkin
baton	phenomenon	comedian	coffin
beacon	piston	Dalmatian	cousin
beckon	poison	historian	dolphin
bison	prison	hooligan	gherkin
carbon	pylon	Indonesian	goblin
carton	python	magician	javelin
cauldron	reason	metropolitan	origin
common	reckon	musician	paraffin
comparison	ribbon	ocean	penguin
cordon	salmon	optician	pumpkin
cotton	salon	organ	raisin
coupon	Saxon	orphan	robin
crayon	season	partisan	satin
crimson	sermon	pedestrian	sequin
damson	siphon	pelican	tarpaulin
demon	skeleton	republican	urchin
dragon	summon	Roman	vermin
electron	talon	rowan	
flagon	treason	ruffian	
gallon	venison	slogan	bargain
heron	wagon	suburban	captain
horizon	wanton	tartan	certain
iron	weapon	toucan	fountain
jettison		turban	mountain
lemon	chameleon	urban	porcelain
lesson	dungeon	utopian	villain
mason	luncheon	vegetarian	
matron	pigeon	veteran	
melon	surgeon	woman	
mutton	truncheon		

* Most of the words with *-in* endings are pronounced with a fairly audible short I-sound before the final *n*, unlike the other words in this table.

241

The **final S-sound** *after an unstressed vowel* is spelt predictably in the suffixes *-less* and *-ness*, and *some female nouns*, e.g. *helpless, jobless, firmness, wittiness; actress, lioness.*

In 55 words with almost identical unstressed endings the *spelling of the S-sound <u>and</u> the vowel before it* are *both erratic*. Among them is the notorious *practice / practise* differentiation which is a well-known spelling problem in the UK. (In American English the verb and noun are both spelt *practice*.)

<u>Table S 61</u>. This shows the different spellings which are used for word endings in which a *<u>final</u>* **S**-sound is *<u>preceded by an unstressed vowel</u>*. Precise speakers of English manage to pronounce some of the unstressed vowels slightly differently, but even then the differences are minimal. In more ordinary speech they are imperceptible.

abs**cess**	analy**sis**	atlas	appren**tice**	men**ace**
ac**cess**	a**xis**	can**vas**	armis**tice**	neck**lace**
con**gress**	ba**sis**	Christmas	cop**pice**	pa**lace**
cy**press**	bron**chitis**	pam**pas**	cre**vice**	sur**face**
for**tress**	chry**salis**	py**jamas**	jus**tice**	ter**race**
mat**tress**	cri**sis**		no**tice**	
pro**cess**	empha**sis**		no**vice**	
pro**gress**	hypothe**sis**	*prac**tise***	of**fice**	let**tuce**
re**cess**	i**ris**	pre**mise**	*prac**tice***	
har**ness***	oa**sis**	pro**mise**	preci**pice**	
wit**ness***	pel**vis**		ser**vice**	
	probo**scis**	pur**chase**		
car**cass**	synthe**sis**			
com**pass**	ten**nis**	pur**pose**		
embar**rass**	tonsil**litis**			
tres**pass**	trel**lis**	tor**toise**		

* In *harness* and *witness* the *-ness* endings are not suffixes, like in firm*ness*.

Twelve common words may give the misleading impression that the purpose of a final *-ss* is to indicate a stressed last syllable:

abyss, across, address (stressed on the 1st syllable in the US), *amiss, caress, confess, discuss, excess, express, impress, possess, success.*

The fifteen words in the first column above, with *-ss endings* and *stress on the first syllable*, (and the American pronunciation of *address*) show that this is not a reliable pattern.

The endings *-tial / -cial* and *-cious / -tious* are also unpredictable. The spellings of *facial, financial* and *glacial* at first seem logical derivations from *face, finance* and *glacier*, until one realises that this rule does not apply consistently: *space - spatial, palace - palatial, essence - essential*. Learners once again have to learn word by word when to use *-ci-* and when *-ti-* for the **SH**-sound *before -al and -ous*.

Table S 62. This shows the use of *-tial / -cial* and *-cious / -tious* (as well as *-sial, scious* and *xious*) in commonly occurring words.

circumstantial	artificial	atrocious	ambitious
credential	beneficial	avaricious	cautious
existential	commercial	judicious	conscientious
palatial	crucial	pernicious	contentious
preferential	facial	pugnacious	facetious
reverential	financial	suspicious	fictitious
substantial	glacial	vivacious	licentious
confidential	judicial	audacious	nutritious
differential	official	delicious	pretentious
infuential	racial	malicious	propitious
penitential	sacrificial	precious	superstitious
presidential	social	rapacious	surreptitious
sequential	special	tenacious	
torrential	superficial	voracious	
consequential		auspicious	conscious
essential		ferocious	luscious
initial		officious	
potential		precocious	
residential	controversial	spacious	anxious
spatial		vicious	

Only 22 common English words have a medial SH-sound. This is also spelt very unpredictably.

bishop	ancient	pressure	crochet
cashew	appreciate	assure	machine
marshal	associated	issue	parachute
mushroom	efficient	tissue	
usher	ocean		
	species	conscience	patient
	sufficient	fascism	

Words which _obey_ the English consonant doubling rule - (Chapter 4.3.)

380 common words of more than one syllable (and which are not created by adding suffixes to one-syllable words) have _a short, stressed vowel which is followed by a doubled consonant_; or by _tch_, _dge_ and _ck_ (e.g. _hatchet, budget, pocket_). But because more multi-syllable words fail to double a consonant after a short vowel than do double them, learners have to memorise the words which double them and those which do not - word by word.

In the following tables the words are grouped by doubled consonant and the vowels which precede them.

Table S 63. 61 words in which **bb**, **dd**, **ff** and **gg** _follow a short stressed vowel._

abbey		ribbon	hobby	chubby
cabbage			lobby	rubber
jabber				rubbish
rabbit				stubborn
Sabbath				stubby
shabby				
adder	eddy	giddy	shoddy	pudding
caddie	teddy	hidden	sodden	rudder
caddy	wedding	ridden		shudder
daddy				sudden
ladder				
daffodil	effigy	different	coffee	buffalo
scaffold	effort	difficult	coffin	buffer
traffic		jiffy	offer	buffet
			office	chuffed
				ruffian
				suffer
				suffocate
baggage				
jagged				
maggot	beggar	snigger	soggy	
scraggy		trigger		luggage
stagger				nugget
swagger				rugged

Table S 64. 84 words in which *ll* and 25 in which *mm* marks a short, stressed vowel.

alley	bellow	armadillo	collar	lullaby
alligator	belly	artillery	colleague	sullen
ally	cellar	billiard	college	
ballast	cello	billion	collie	**with a short**
ballet	cellophane	billow	colliery	**OO-sound:**
ballot	fellow	billy	dollar	bullet
challenge	intelligent	brilliant	follow	bulletin
gallant	jelly	frilly	hollow	bullion
gallery	pellet	gorilla	holly	bullock
allon	rebellion	guerrillas	jolly	bully
gallop	sellotape	guillotine	lollipop	pulley
gallows	trellis	illustrate	lolly	pullover
mallet	umbrella	milligrams	mollusc	
rally	yellow	million	pollen	
shallow		pillar	pollinate	
stallion		pillow	trolley	
valley		silly	volley	
		vanilla		syllable
		villa		
with O-sound:		village		
swallow		villain		
wallaby				
wallet				
wallop				
wallow				

ammonite	dilemma	glimmer	comment	dummy
clammy		simmer	commentary	mummy
hammer			commerce	rummage
inflammable			common	summary
mammal			communism	summer
mammoth			communist	summit
stammer				summon
				tummy
		symmetry		

Table S 65. 20 word with ***nn***, 18 with ***pp*** and 51 ***rr*** *after a short and stressed vowel.*

annual	antenna	dinner	bonnet	
banner	pennant	inner		
cannot	penny	innocence		
granny	tennis	innocent		
manner		spinnaker		
nanny				
pannier				
savannah				
spanner				
uncanny				

appetite	pepper	flipper	copper	puppet
happen		kipper	coppice	puppy
happy		skipper	opposite	supper
nappy		slippers	poppy	upper
			sloppy	

arrow	berry	irritable	borrow	burrow
barren	cherry	mirror	corridor	current
barrier	errand	squirrel	horrible	furrowed
barrister	error	stirrup	lorry	furry
barrow	ferry		sorrow	hurricane
carrot	herring		sorry	hurry
carry	interrogate		tomorrow	scurry
garret	merry		torrent	turret
marrow	sherry			
marry	terrace		worry	
narrative	terrible			
narrow	territory			
parrot	terror			
quarry				
sparrow				
warrant				
warren				

Table S 66. 23 words with *ss*, 52 *tt* and 4 *zz* as short, stressed vowel markers.

ambassador	delicatessen	missile	blossom	
casserole	essay	narcissus	colossal	
classic	essence	rissole	fossil	
massacre	lesson	scissors	gossip	
massive	message		possible	
passage	necessity			
passenger	professor			
attic	better	bitten	bottom	butter
attitude	confetti	bitter	cottage	button
batter	jettison	glitter	cotton	clutter
battery	jetty	kitten	forgotten	gutter
chatter	letter	litter	lottery	mutter
clatter	lettuce	mitten	motto	mutton
fatty	pretty	sitter	otter	putty
latter	spaghetti	titter	potter	shutter
matter		twitter		splutter
patter		written		stutter
pattern				utter
regatta				
scatter				
shatter		blizzard		buzzard
tatter		dizzy		fuzzy

Table S 67. 25 words with *short vowels followed by ck*, 8 by *tch* and 8 by *dge* .

bracken	reckon	bicker	wicker	cockerel	socket	bucket
bracket		chicken	wicket	crockery	sprocket	
packet		cricket		hockey	stocking	
jacket		rickety		jockey		cuckoo (short oo)
racket		ticket		pocket		
		wicked		rocket		
despatch	ketchup		kitchen			crutches
hatchet			pitcher			butcher (short oo)
satchel						
badger	fledgeling	midget		dodgems		budget
				podgy		budgie
						drudgery

397 words have *'missing'* doubled consonants.

The words in the following tables would have doubled consonants if the doubling rule applied consistently, but they are spelt with just a single consonant after a short, stressed vowel. They undermine the consonant doubling rule and help to ensure that it cannot be applied logically, as a matter of course, and that the 380 words with doubled consonants (in tables S 63-7) have to be individually memorised.

Table S 68. 13 words with a ***single b***, 21 ***d***, 6 *f* and 7 *g after a short, stressed vowel.*

cabinet	nebula	liberal	probable	
cabaret	treble	liberty	robin	
cabin		tribute		
elaborate				
fabulous				
habit				
academy	credit	hideous	body	study
adequate	dedicated	video	model	
radical	edible		modern	
radish	edit		modest	
	educate		produce	
	federal			
	medical			
	pedal			
	pedigree			
café	refuge	magnificent	profit	
	refuse (noun)	significant		
agony	negative	brigand		
dragon		frigate		
flagon				
hexagonal				

248

Table S 69. 55 words with a *single l* and *33 m* after a short, stressed vowel.

analysis	celery	ability	abolish
balance	delegate	bilious	colony
battalion	delicacy	military	column
calendar	deluge	ventriloquist	demolish
chalet	develop		holiday
galaxy	element		olive
italic	eligible		policy
morality	helicopter		politics
palace	melody		polythene
palate	melon		solemn
palette	pelican		solid
reality	relevant		tolerate
salad	relic		volume
salary	skeleton		voluntary
salon	telescope		
talent			
talon			
valentine			
valiant			
valid			
value			
vitality			

amateur	cemetery	criminal	abominable
camel	chemical	eliminate	comet
camera	democrat	limit	comic
damage	emerald	timid	dominate
dynamic	epidemic	image	domino
enamel	memory		economic
famished	remedy		prominent
laminate	lemon		promise
	feminine		vomit
	premise		
	semi		

Table S 70. 42 words with a *single n*, 19 *p* and 48 *r after short, stressed vowels.*

animal	benefit	aluminium	astonish
anorak	enemy	cinema	conifer
banish	energy	clinical	economy
banister	menace	continue	electronic
canopy	penetrate	finish	monastery
manage	venison	linear	monarch
manor	lieutenant	minimal	monument
organic		minister	supersonic
panel		minute	tonic
panic		opinion	
spaniel		sinister	
vanish		spinach	
manual		vinegar	

rapid	leper	triple	copy
tapestry	tepid		opera
capita	epic		operate
capital	separate		proper
capitol			property
chapel			topic
			popular
			tropics

Arab	America	conspiracy	authority
arable	beret	empirical	coral
arid	ceremony	miracle	florist
asparagus	cherish	spirit	forest
baron	derelict		historic
caramel	herald		horoscope
caravan	heritage		majority
chariot	heroine		minority
charity	heron		moral
caricature	merit		orange
carol	peril		priority
clarity	perish		
comparison	sincerity		
garage	sterilise		
parasol	therapist		
parish	very		
transparent			

Table S 71. 22 words do *not* use the expected *ss* *after a short, stressed vowel* (e.g. *massive, lesson, missile, gossip*): 17 use just *c* and 5 *sc*.

acid	decimal	electricity	solicitor	adolescent
capacity	precipice	explicit		crescent
glacier	recipe	municipal	velocity	discipline
pacifist	specify	participate		fascinate
	specimen	publicity		convalescence
		simplicity		

Table S 72. 28 words use a *single t* *instead of a doubled t*.

atom	athletic	British	botany
baton	magnetic	citizen	
catalogue	metal	city	
catapult	petal	critical	
category	tetanus	pity	
compatible	veteran	literally	
lateral	yeti	obliterate	
latitude	competitive		
platinum			
platypus			
satin			
strategy			

Table S 73. 5 words use a *single z*, 16 a *single s* and 1 *ss where one would logically expect zz* (as in *blizzard*).

		wizard	lozenge
		wizened	
hazard		lizard	
	desert	chisel	closet
	designate	miserable	deposit
	desolate	prison	positive
	hesitate	risen	
	present	visible	
	president	visit	
	resident		
	scissors		

251

Table S 74. 32 words *fail to mark a short vowel* with **tch**, **dg** and **ck**:

2 words use just **ch** *instead of tch* (as in *kitchen*);
11 use **g** and 1 **gg** *instead of dg* (as in *badger*);
20 words with a K-sound after a short vowel do *not* mark this with **ck**
    (as in *ticket* and *pocket)* : 9 words use **c**, 5 **cc**, 2 **ch**, 3 **qu** and 1 **cqu**.

atta**ch**		li**ch**en		
exa**gg**erate	le**g**end le**g**islate re**g**iment re**g**ister ve**g**etable	pi**g**eon ri**g**id reli**g**ion	lo**g**ic	
va**cu**um	de**c**ade exe**c**utive re**c**ognise re**c**ord (noun) se**c**ond se**c**ular		cro**c**odile do**c**uments	
a**cc**urate toba**cc**o		pi**cc**olo	o**cc**upy	su**cc**ulent
	che**qu**ered	li**qu**or li**qu**orice		
la**cqu**er				
	e**ch**o me**ch**anism			

Words with *'missing'* and *'surplus'* doubled consonants are problematic for readering as well as spelling. They have therefore also been listed in alphabetical order in tables R 59 - 64 in Appendix R. Some spellers will perhaps find them easier to memorise that way, instead of the current listings in tables S 68 - 79.

Table S 75. 47 words are particularly hard for learners because they have *unpredictably spelt short vowels* <u>and</u> *do not double the following consonant.*

with short *E*-sound	short *I*-sound	short *O*-sound	short *U*-sound
			double trouble
already meadow ready steady			
heifer			
jealous zealous	cylinder	quality knowledge	colour
	women		stomach plumber
any many	cynical synagogue synonym		honey money onion
weapon jeopardy leopard	typical		couple
bury	lyric syrup tyranny	laurel quarantine	thorough courage nourish
	chrysalis	sausage	
peasant pheasant pleasant	physics busy		dozen cousin

'Surplus' or *unpredictably doubled* consonants

159 multi-syllable words have doubled consonants which do not keep a stressed vowel short. They all need to be learned word by word too, and they are likely to cause reading difficulties as well (See tables R 63 and R 64 on pages 184-5).

Table S 76. 14 words have a *surplus c*, 3 a *surplus d*, 15 a *surplus f* and
3 a *surplus g* .
(The stressed vowels in the listed words are underlined.)

acc<u>o</u>mmodate			occ<u>a</u>sion	succ<u>u</u>mb
accommod<u>a</u>tion			occup<u>a</u>tion	
acc<u>o</u>mpany			occ<u>u</u>rrence	
acc<u>o</u>mplish				
acc<u>o</u>rd				
acc<u>o</u>rdion				
acc<u>ou</u>nt				
acc<u>u</u>mulate				
acc<u>u</u>se				
acc<u>u</u>stom				
add		mi<u>dd</u>a<u>y</u>	**odd**	
aff<u>ai</u>r	eff<u>e</u>ct	diff<u>e</u>rential	off<u>e</u>nd	suff<u>i</u>cient
aff<u>e</u>ct	eff<u>i</u>cient	diff<u>u</u>sion	off<u>i</u>cial	
aff<u>e</u>ction	e<u>ff</u>luent*			
aff<u>o</u>rd				
p<u>a</u>raffin				
staff*				chauff<u>eu</u>r*

* In *staff* the vowel is long;
in *chauffeur* the stress varies, but the *au* always has a long sound;
in *effluent* the *f* is followed by another consonant and no doubling is needed to keep the *e* short.

a<u>gg</u>ravate	*compare:*	sugg<u>e</u>st*	
aggr<u>e</u>ssive	*a<u>g</u>riculture*		
		suggest is often pronounced *sugjest* in the US	

254

Table S 77. 23 words have a *surplus l*, 20 a *surplus m* and 7 a *surplus n*.

parallel	excellent	caterpillar	collage	
	hello	illegible	collapse	
	jewellery	illiterate	collect	
llama	marvellous	illusion	collide	
	satellite	illustration		
	constellation	illuminate	controlled*	* with 'll' after
		pastille	roller*	a long vowel
		tonsillitis	swollen*	
ammunition		immediate	accommodation	
programme*		immense	command	
		immortal	commemorate	
		immune	commence	
			commercial	
			commit	
			commodities	
			commotion	
			communication	
			communion	
			community	
			commuter	
			committee	
			recommend	
anniversary			mayonnaise	
announce			personnel	
annoy			questionnaire	
			connect	

* In computer terminology this word is universally spelt *program*; and US English makes no distinction between a *computer program* and a *radio programme*, as is this the case in the UK.

Table S 78. 21 words have a *surplus p*, 19 a *surplus r* and 19 a *surplus s*.

appal		hippopotamus	opportunity	supply
apparatus			oppose	support
apparent				suppose
appeal				
appear				
appendix				
applaud				
apply				
appoint				
appreciate				
apprentice				
approach				
appropriate				
approve				
approximate				
arrange	erratic	irregular	torrential	surrender
array	interrupt	irrigation	correspond	surround
arrest	serrated		correct	curriculum
arrive	terrific		correlation	hurrah
barricade				
assail	dessert		possess	
assassin	essential		possibility	
assault	necessary			
assemble				
assert				
assessment				
assign				
assist				
associate				
assort				
assume				
cassette				
embassy				
cf. diplomacy passport*				

* In *passport* the *ss* follows a long vowel. The word is a compound of the words *pass* and *port*. There are no clear rules in English about keeping and losing doubled consonants in compounds (e.g. well + come = welcome; fare + well = farewell; full + fill = fulfil).

Table S 79. 14 words have a *needlessly doubled t*.

att<u>a</u>ch	<u>o</u>melette*
att<u>ai</u>n	p<u>a</u>lette*
att<u>e</u>mpt	
att<u>e</u>nd	sett<u>ee</u>
att<u>e</u>ntion	
att<u>o</u>rney	
attr<u>a</u>ct	
attr<u>i</u>buted	
batt<u>a</u>lion	
m<u>a</u>ttress	– In *'mattres'* there are now 3 consonants after *'a'*;
tatt<u>oo</u>	two are sufficient to keep a stressed vowel short.

* *omelette* and *palette* were once probably stressed in the French manner, before *tt*, as *ros<u>e</u>tte* and *servi<u>e</u>tte* still are nowadays. When <u>o</u>melette and p<u>a</u>lette became stressed in the more usual English style, on the first syllable, the doubling of the *t* became redundant.

This is now happening with *cigarette* and *s<u>i</u>lhouette*, although some people still stress these words in the French manner. As foreign imports become part of common English vocabulary, they gradually acquire an English stress, but often retain their foreign spelling.

This is particularly unhelpful to French learners of English who then naturally enough tend to continue pronouncing such words in the French manner. The spelling gives them no indication that this should no longer be the case.

Predictable *-dge -tch, -ck,* **and** *-ll* **in word endings**

One-syllable words with a K-sound, L-sound, CH-sound or J-sound after a short vowel are nearly all spelt with *-ck, -ll, -tch* or *-dge* endings (e.g. *stick, bill, hitch, badge*). Many young learners take a long time to get used to them, even though they are relatively predictable.

This is partly because many others consonants, in similar words, are not doubled (e.g. *fib, lid, big, him, bin, sip, sit*). Spellings like *fulfil* and *instil*, or *much* and *rich* also show that doubling a final *-l* or inserting a *t before a ch* is of doubtful value. Furthermore, recently introduced words like *mac, rec* and *vac* end simply with *-c*.

Not so very long ago many multi-syllable words ended in *-ck* too. *Music* used to be spelt *musick* and *traffic* as *traffick*. Now such words are all spelt with just a final *-c* (e.g. *lilac, comic, havoc*).

Only the *-dge* endings serve a clearly useful purpose. They differentiate between words with a long vowel and those with a short one (e.g. *badge* [baj] - *cage* [kaij]).

Table S 80. Below are 17 one-syllable words with *-dge endings*.

badge	dredge	bridge	dodge	grudge
cadge	edge	fridge	lodge	judge
	hedge	ridge		nudge
	ledge			smudge
	sledge			trudge

Table S 81. 23 one-syllable words *end in -tch*, but *four much used words* are *spelt with just -ch*.

catch	sketch	ditch	notch	hutch
hatch	stretch	hitch	watch	Dutch
latch	wretch	itch		
match		pitch		**exceptions:**
patch		stitch		*rich*
scratch		switch		*which*
snatch		twitch		*much*
thatch		witch		*such*

258

Table S 82. 62 common one-syllable word*s* *end in* *-ck*.

back	stack	check	brick	block	buck
black	track	deck	click	clock	cluck
crack	whack	neck	flick	cock	duck
hack		peck	kick	dock	luck
jack		speck	lick	flock	pluck
knack		wreck	nick	knock	struck
lack			pick	lock	stuck
pack			prick	mock	suck
quack			quick	rock	truck
rack			sick	shock	tuck
sack			slick	smock	
shack			stick	sock	
slack			thick	stock	
smack			tick		
snack			trick		

Table S 83. 43 one-syllable words with short vowels have *-ll endings*;
but an *o before ll* is *mostly not short,* and a *final -all* has the
sound of aul (see also table R 65 for more on the uncertain role
of *l*-doubling).

bell	bill	doll	dull
cell	drill	loll	gull
dwell	fill		hull
fell	gill		lull
hell	grill		scull
quell	hill		skull
sell	ill		bull* *these have
shell	kill		full* the short OO-sound
smell	mill		pull*
spell	pill		
swell	quill	**oll = ole**	**all = aul**
tell	shrill	poll	all small
well	skill	roll	ball squall
yell	spill	scroll	call stall
	still	stroll	fall tall
	thrill	toll	gall wall
	till	troll	hall
	will		pall

Table S 84. A further 87 one-syllable words with a *final* **L-sound** have the endings *-bble*, *-ddle*, *-ffle*, *-ggle*, *-pple*, *-ssle*, *-ttle*, *-zzle* and *-ckle*.

These *seem* to follow a regular *doubling pattern* and a regular *final -le* spelling, but 38 words *diverge from this mo**del*** in various ways.

babble	baffle	*camel*	hassle	battle
bubble	muffle			bottle
cobble	raffle	*pommel*	*apostle*	cattle
dabble	ruffle	*pummel*	*bristle*	kettle
double	scuffle	*channel*	*bustle*	little
dribble	shuffle	*flannel*	*gristle*	nettle
gabble	sniffle	*funnel*	*hustle*	rattle
gobble		*kennel*	*jostle*	scuttle
hobble	giggle			settle
nibble	goggle	*panel*	*muscle*	skittle
pebble	haggle		*mussel*	*subtle*
quibble	niggle	*tunnel*		throttle
rubble	smuggle		*rustle*	wattle
scribble	snuggle			
squabble	straggle	apple	*tassel*	
treble	struggle	*chapel*		*chisel*
trouble	wiggle	*couple*	*thistle*	
wobble	wriggle	cripple	*trestle*	dazzle
		grapple		drizzle
cuddle	buckle	ripple	tussle	grizzle
fiddle	cackle	supple		guzzle
huddle	chuckle	tipple	*vessel*	muzzle
meddle	crackle	topple		nozzle
middle	fickle	*triple*	*whistle*	nuzzle
model	knuckle		*wrestle*	puzzle
muddle	*nickel*			sizzle
paddle	pickle	*barrel*		
peddle	prickle			
puddle	speckle	*laurel*		
riddle	suckle			
saddle	tackle	*quarrel*		
toddle	tickle	*squirrel*		
waddle				

Doubling of a final *f* or *s* follows no regular pattern. Both are unpredictable.

Table S 85. 10 words with a short vowel end with *-ff* but 7 do not.

chef	cliff if sniff stiff whiff	off cough trough	cuff duff gruff puff stuff	rough slough tough

It is even more difficult to be certain when to double a final *-s*, or to understand what purpose *s*-doubling is meant to serve.

Table S 86. 22 one-syllable words with a final **S**-sound *after a short vowel*
end in *-ss*, but
6 *very frequently used words do not*, and in
6 others the *vowel before ss is long*,
while *mass* has two different pronunciations in standard UK English.

ass gas lass	bless yes chess dress	hiss this kiss miss	boss cross gloss	fuss bus puss plus truss us
brass *class* *glass* *grass* *mass** *pass*	guess less mess press stress		loss moss toss *gross*	

  In longer words the purpose of a final *-ss* is even more obscure:
12 words with *-ss* are stressed on the last syllable (e.g. *confess, discuss*), while 15 others are not (e.g. *fortress, mattress*), and 44 other words with identically sounding endings use *s* , *ce* or *se* (e.g. *crisis, office, promise*). (See table S 61 on page 242 for complete lists of these multi-syllable words.)

3695 common English words containing one or more *graphemes* that are *not predictable* or *rule-governed*

Highlighted in **bold** are the graphemes which are likely to give learners trouble. (Words with several unpredictable elements in them may not always have all their difficulties picked out.)

* Words which have more than one pronunciation have been marked with an asterisk (e.g. bow*).

Common words with doubled consonants which obey the basic consonant doubling principle (e.g. *pollen*) have been included because many more words fail to follow this rule (e.g. *abolish*).

abandon abbey abdomen ability abolish abominable above abscess absent abstain absurd abyss academy accelerate accent accept access accident accommodate accommodation accompany accomplish accord accordance accordion account accrue accumulate accurate accuse accustom ache achieve acid acoustic acquaint acquire acquit actor add adder adequate adhere adhesive adjective admission adolescent adore advance adventure adversary advertisement advisor aerial aerobatics aeroplane affair affect affection afford afloat afraid after against aggravate agony agree agriculture ah aid ail aim ain't air albino alcohol alert algebra alien alight all alley alliance alligator allowance ally almond almost alphabet already Alsatian also altar alter alternate alternative altogether aluminium always amateur amaze ambassador ambitious America ammonite ammunition among amphibian analysis ancestors anchor ancient anemone anger angular animal anniversary announce annoy annual anorak answer antenna antique anvil anxiety anxious any apostle appal apparatus apparent appeal appear appearance appendix appetite applaud applause appliance applicant apply appoint appreciate apprentice approach appropriate approve approximate apron Arab arable arbitrary archery architect architecture area arena argue arid armada armadillo armistice armour arrange array arrest arrive arrow arsenic artery artificial artillery ascertain Asia ask askew asparagus aspersion asphyxiate aspirin assail assassin assault assemble assert assessment assessor assign assist assistant associate assort assume assurance assure astonish astronaut asylum athletic atlas atom atrocious attach attack attain attempt attend attention attic attitude attorney attract attributed aubergine auburn auction audacious audible August aunt auspicious authentic author authorise authority automatic autonomy autumn avalanche avaricious avenue aviary awaken award aware awe awful awkward awning axis baa baboon bacon badger badminton baggage bail bait balance bald ball ballast ballet balloon ballot bamboo banana banish banister banner barbecue bare bargain barley baron barrack barrel barren barricade barrier barrister barrow base basic basin basis bask bath baton battalion batter battery bawl bazaar be beach beacon bead beak beam bean bear beard beast beat beautician beauty beaver because beckon bee beech beef been beer beet beetle before beggar begin behaviour behind belief believe bellow belly below beneath beneficial benefit beret berry berth better between bible bicker bicycle bikini bilious billiard billion billow billy bind birch bird birth bishop bison bitten bitter bivouac blare blast blaze +(blazer) bleach bleak bleat bleed bleep blew blight blind blizzard blood bloom blossom blow blown blue blur blustery boaconstrictor boar board boast boat body bogey bold bolt bomb bonnet boo book boom boon boost boot bore borrow botany both bottom bough bought boundary bouquet boutique bow * bowl bra bracken bracket braid brain branch brass brawl brawn brazen bread breadth break breakfast breast breath breathe breed breeze brew bridle brief brigand bright brilliant bristle British broad broccoli bronchial bronchitis bronze brooch brooding brook broom brother brought brown brownie browse bruise brutal brute bucket budget budgie buffalo buffer buffet build built bull bulldoze bullet bulletin bullion bullock bully bungalow buoy burden burglar burglary burgle burly burn burrow burst bury bus bush bustle busy butcher butter button buy buzz buzzard by bye

cabaret cabbage cabin cabinet caddie caddy café cafeteria calculator calendar calf call calm camel camera campaign canary cannot canoe canopy canvas capacity capita capital capitol capsize captain capture caramel caravan carbon carcass cardigan care career caricature carnivore carol carpentry carrot carry carton cartoon case cashew cask casserole cassette cast caste castor catalogue catapult catastrophe category caterpillar cathedral catkin caught cauldron cause caution cautious cavalier
cease cedar ceiling celebrate celery cell cellar cello cellophane cement cemetery cent centigrade central centre century cereal ceremony certain certificate
chain chair chalet chalk challenge chameleon champagne chance chandelier channel chant chaos chapel character charade chariot charity chase chasm chatter chauffeur cheap cheat cheek cheer cheese cheetah chef chemical chemistry cheque chequered cherish cherry chew chicken chief chilblain child children chimney chimpanzee china Chinese chirp chisel chivalrous chlorine chocolate choir cholesterol choose chore chorus chosen choux christen Christian Christmas chrome chrysalis chrysanthemum chubby chuffed church churn chute

cider cigar cigarette cinder cinema circle circuit circular circulate circumference circumstances circumstantial circus cistern cite citizen citrus city civic civil civilian civilisation civilise

claim clammy clarity clasp class classic clatter claw clean cleanliness cleanse clear clementine clerk cliff climb clinical cloak close* closet clown clue clutter coach coal coarse coast coat coax cobra cockatoo cockerel cockney cockroach cocktail cocoa cocoon coercion coffee coffin cold collage collapse collar colleague collect college collide collie colliery colonel colony colossal colour colt column combat come comedian comet comfort comic command commemorate commence comment commentary commerce commercial commission commit committee commodities common commotion communication communion communism communist community commuter company compare comparison compass compatible compete competitive complain complete composite comprehension conceal conceit conceive concern concrete condemn condescension conductor confer confetti confidential congeal congress conifer conjure connect conquer conscience conscientious conscious consent consequence consequential conservative conserve consider consist conspiracy constellation construe contain contemporary contentious continue contrary contrast control controlled controversial controversy convalescence convene convenient conversion convey conveyor coo cook cookie cool copper coppice copse copy coral cordon core corgi corps corpse correct correlation correspond corridor cosmonaut cottage cotton cough could council counsel country couple coupon courage courier course court courtesy cousin covenant cover covet covey coward craft crawl crayon craze +(crazy) creak cream crease creature credential credit creek creep crescent crevice crew cricket criminal crimson crisis critical croak crochet crockery crocodile crow crowd crown crucial crude cruel cruise crumb crutches cry crypt crystal cuckoo cue cuff culture curfew curl curlew current curriculum curse curt curve cushion

cycle cyclical cygnet cylinder cymbals cynical cypress cyst

daddy daffodil daft dahlia daily dainty dairy daisy Dalmatian damage damn damson dance dare data* daub daughter dawdle dawn dead deaf deal dealt dean dear death debris debt decade deceit deceive decent decimal decipher declare decorator decrease dedicated deed deep deer defeat defiant definite degree deign delegate delicacy delicatessen delicious delight delivery deluge democrat demolish demon demonstrator dense departure deposit depot derelict descant desert deserve designate desolate despair despatch dessert detail detain detergent determine devalue develop devil dew dialogue diary dictionary die diesel different differential difficult diffusion dilapidated dilemma dimension dinghy dinner diploma diplomatic director dirt disappear disaster disc discharge disciple discipline discover discovery discreet discuss discussion disease disguise disgust dismantle dismay dispersion displace display dispose dispute distant distinct distribute disturb diversion divide divine division divorce dizzy do doctor documents dodgems doe does dollar dolphin dolt dominant dominate domineer domino done donkey doom door dormitory dose double doubt dough dove down doze dozen draft dragon drain drama draught draw drawl drawn dread dream dreamt dreary drew drivel droop drown drowse drudgery dry due duel duff dumb dummy dungarees dungeon duvet dwarf dye dyke dynamic dynamite dynamo

each eager eagle ear earl early earn earnest earth ease easel east Easter eat eaves eccentric echo éclair eclipse economic economy ecstatic eddy edible edit editor educate eel eerie effect efficient effigy effluent effort eider-down eight either elaborate elapse elbow electrician electricity electron electronic element elementary elephant elevator eleven eligible eliminate else embarrass embassy emerald emerge emission emperor emphasis emphasise empirical emu enable enamel encamp enchant encircle enclose encounter encourage encrusted endanger endeavour endurance endure enemy energy enforce engage engineer English engrave engulf enhance enjoy enlarge enlist enough enquire enrage enrol entangle entertain enthusiastic entire entitled environment epic epidemic epilogue equal equator era errand erratic error escalator essay essence essential estuary eternal eucalyptus eve even every evil ewe exact exaggerate examine example exasperate exceed excellent except excess excite exclaim excursion excuse* executive exert exhaust exhibition exist existential expanse expansion expenditure expense experience expert explain explicit exposure exquisite extension exterior external extra extravagant extreme eye

fabulous facetious facial factor factory Fahrenheit fail faint fair faith fall fallen falter familiar famine famished fare fascinate fascism fashion fast father fatigue fatty fault favour favourite fawn fear feasible feast feat feather feature February federal fee feeble feed feel feet feign fellow female feminine fern ferocious ferry fertile fete feud feudal fever few fibre fictitious field fiend fierce fight finance financial find finger finish fir firm first fishmonger fission fissure flabbergast flagon flair flannel flare flask flavour flaw flea fledgling flee fleece fleet flew flexible flight flipper flirt floe flood floor florist flow flower flu flue fluent fluid fluke flute fly foal foam foe fold folk folklore follow food fool foot fore foreign forest forget forgotten formula fortress fossil fought fountain four fourth fracture fragrant freak free freeze freight frequent friend frigate frighten frilly front frontier frown froze frozen frugal fruit fry fuel full funnel fur furnish furniture furrowed furry further fuselage fuss future fuzzy

gaily gain gala galaxy gall gallant gallery gallon gallop gallows gantry garage garden garret gas gasp gaudy gaze gazelle gear geese gem general generation generous genie genius gentian gentle genuine geography geranium germ germinate gesture get geyser

ghastly gherkin ghost ghoulish

giant giddy giggle gild gills gilt gin ginger gipsy giraffe girder girdle girl give glacial glacier gladiator glamour glance glare glass gleam glean glee glimmer glimpse glisten glitter gloat gloom glove glow glucose glue gnash gnat gnaw gnome gnu goat goblin goes gold golden gondola gone goo good goose gore gorilla gorse gossip govern governor gown graffiti graft grain grammar granite granny graph grasp grass gravel graze grease great Grecian greed green greet grew grey grief grieve grind gristle groan groom groove gross group grow growl grown growth gruesome gruff guarantee guard guerrillas guess guest guidance guide guillotine guilt guinea-pig guitar gurgle guru gutter guy gym gymkhana gyp gypsy gyroscope

habit hail hair half halfpenny hall halt halve hamburger hammer happen happy harbour hare harness* harpoon hatchet haughty haul haunt hawk hazard haze hazel he head heal health heap hear heard heat heath heathen heather heave heaven heavy heel heifer height heir helicopter hello her herald herb herd here heritage hermit hero heroine heron herring hesitate hexagonal hey hiccough hidden hideous high hilarious hind hippopotamus historian historic history hoard hoarse hobby hockey hoe hold holey holiday hollow holly holster honey honour hood hoof hook hooligan hoop hoot horizon horoscope horrible horse host hostel house* howl hullabaloo humour hunger hurdle hurl hurrah hurricane hurry hurt hurtle hustle hyacinth hydrangea hydrogen hyena hygienic hygrometer hymn hypnotise hypothesis hysterical

idea idle idol if igloo ignorant ignore illegible illiterate illuminate illusion illustrate illustration image imagine imbue immediate immense immersion immortal immune imperial impertinent implore important impulse increase incredible incursion indeed indicator indict indignant Indonesian industry infant infantry inferior infinite inflammable influential ingredient initial inject injure injury inner innocence innocent insect insert insist install instalment instant instead insurance intelligent intense interfere interior intermediate interpret interrogate interrupt interview intrude inventor inventory inversion investors invisible iris iron irregular irrigation irritable island issue italic ivory

jabber jacket jagged jaguar jail jamboree January jaunt javelin jaw jazz jealous jeans jeep jeer jelly jeopardy jerk jersey jest jet jettison jetty Jew jewel jewellery jiffy jig jigsaw jilt jingle jive jockey jodhpurs jolly jolt Joseph jostle journal journey jubilant jubilee judicial judicious juice junior juror justice kaleidoscope kangaroo karate kayak keel keen keep kennel kernel kestrel ketchup key kidney kilometre kind kindergarten kiosk kipper kitchen kitten kiwi knack knave knead knee kneel knew knife knight knit knob knobbly knock knoll knot know knowledge known knuckle

la label laboratory labour lacquer ladder laden lagoon laid lair lamb laminate lance lapse lasso last lateral lather latitude latter laugh launch launder laurel lava law lawn laze leach lead* leaf league leak lean leant leap leapt learn lease leash least leather leave lecture lee leek legal legend legion legislate legislator legislature leisure lemon lenient leopard leper lessen lesson letter lettuce lever lewd liar liberal liberty library license licentious lichen lie lieutenant light lightning limb limit linear linger liquor liquorice listen literally literary literature litter lizard llama load loaf loan loathe lobby logic logician lollipop lolly longitude loo look loom loop loose loot lorry lose lottery love low lozenge lubricate ludicrous ludo luggage lukewarm lullaby luminous lunar lunatic luncheon lurch lurk luscious luxury lynch lynx lyric

ma mac macaroon machine machinery mackerel madden magazine maggot magician magnetic magnificent maid mail maim main maintain maintenance majestic major majority malaria malicious mallet mammal mammoth manage manner manoeuvre manor mansion manual manufacture many mare margarine marine maroon marquee marrow marry marshal martyr marvellous Mary masculine mask mason mass* massacre massive mast material mathematician matinee matron matter mattress maul mauve mayonnaise mayor maze me meadow meagre meal mean meant measles measure meat mechanism medical medicine medieval medium medley meek meet melody melon memory menace menu merchant mercury mercy mere meringue merit merry message metal meteor meter metre metropolitan microfiche midday midget might mighty mild mildew military militia milligrams million millipede mind miniature minimal minister minor minority minute miracle mirror mirth miserable missile mission mitten mixture moan model modern modest mollusc monarch monastery Monday monetary money monger mongrel monitor monk monkey month monument moo mood moon moor moot moral morality more morsel mosque mosquito most mother motor motto mould moult mountain mourn mouse moustache move movie mow mown much mummy municipal murder murmur muscle muscular mushroom musician mussel mutter mutton my mysterious mystery myth

nail nanny nappy narcissus narrative narrow nasturtium nature naughty nautical navigator near neat nebula necessary necessity necklace nectar need needle negative neigh neighbour neither nephew nerve neutral new newt nickel niece nigh night ninth none nonsense noodle noon noose nostril nothing notice nought nourish novel novice nuclear nugget nuisance numb nurse nursery nutritious nylon nymph

oaf oak oar oasis oath oats obedient obey object objection obliterate oboe observatory observe obtain occasion occupation occupy occur occurrence ocean octagon odd odour off offend offer office official officious often ogre oh old olive Olympics omelette omen once one onion only opaque open opera operate operator opinion opportunity oppose opposite optician orange orator orchestra orchid ordeal ordinary ore organ organic origin orphan other otter ought oven overwhelm owe owl own oxygen

pa pacifist packet pageant paid pail pain paint pair palace palate palatial palette pall palm paltry pampas pamphlet panda panel panic pannier panorama parachute paraffin parallel paralyse parasol parcel pardon pare parent parish parlour parrot parsley participate particular partisan pass passage passenger passion passport past pastille pastry path patient patrol patter pattern Paul pause paw pawn pea peace peach peak peal peanut pear pearl peasant peat peculiar pedal pedestrian pedigree peek peel peep peer pelican pellet pelvis pencil penetrate penguin penitential pennant penny pension pentagon people pepper perch percussion perfect performance perfume peril period perish permanent permissible permission permit pernicious persevere persistent person personnel pertinent petal peter petrol pew pewter

phantom pharaoh phase pheasant phenomena phenomenon philosophy phone photograph phrase physician physics physiological

piano piazza piccolo picture picturesque pie piece pier pierce pigeon pillar pillow pint pioneer piranha pistol piston pitcher pity pixie pizza plague plaice plain planetary plant plasticine platinum platypus plea plead pleasant please pleasure pleat plough plumber plural plus ply pneumatic pneumonia poach pocket podgy poetry poison polar police policy politician politics poll pollen pollinate polythene pommel pontoon poodle pooh pool poplar poppy popular porcelain pore positive possess possibility possible post poster potential potter pottery poultry pour powder power practice practise prairie praise prance prawn preach precede precious precipice precise precocious preen preferential prehensile preliminary premise prepare present preserve president presidential pressure prestige pretentious pretty prevail previous priest primary prior priority prison prize probable proboscis procedure proceed proceedings proceeds process proclaim produce professor profit programme progress project promenade prominent promise proof propaganda proper property prophet propitious proprietor prosecute protein protestant prove prowl prune pry pseudo psychological psychology pterodactyl publicity pudding puff pugnacious pull pulley pullover pulmonary pulse pummel pumpkin puncture pupa pupil puppet puppy purchase purple purpose purr purse pursue push puss pussy put putty pyjamas pylon python

quadrangle quaint quality quantity quarantine quarrel quarry quart quarter quartet quartz quay queasy queen queer query questionnaire queue quiz quoit quota

rabbit racial racket radar radiator radical radish raft raid rail rain raise raisin rally ransack rapacious rapid rare rascal rather raven ravine raw razor reach reactionary read ready real reality really realm reap rear reason rebellion rec recall receipt receive recent recess recipe reckon recluse recognise recommend record(noun) recoup recovery recruit rector reed reef reel refer referee refrain refrigerator refuge refuse(noun) regatta regime regiment region register regular rehearse reign reindeer reins reject relay release relevant relic relief relieve religion remain remedy remnant repair repeat replica republican rescue reserve resident residential resign resources respirator response responsible restaurant retail retain retreat return reveal revenue reverential reverse review revolt revolutionary reward rheumatism rhinoceros rhododendron rhubarb rhyme rhythm ribbon rich rickety ridden right rigid rind rinse ripen risen rissole road roam roar roast robbery robin rocket roe rogue roller Roman roof rook room root rotor rotten rough route routine rowan rubber rubbish ruby rucksack rudder rude rue ruffian rugged ruined rule rummage rumour rural rustle rye

Sabbath sabre sac sacrificial sadden safari said sail saint salad salami salary salmon salon saloon salt sandwich Santa-Claus sapphire sardine satchel satellite satin satisfactory sauce saucer sausage savannah saviour savour savoury saw sawn Saxon says scaffold scald scare scatter scene scenery scent scheme scholar school schooner science scissors scold scone scoop scooter score scoundrel scowl scraggy scrawl scream screech screen screw scripture scroll scurry scythe sea seal seam sear search season seat secluded second secondary secret secretary secular see seed seek seem seen seep seesaw seize sellotape semi senator senior sense sensible sensors separate sequence sequential sequin sergeant series serious sermon serpent serrated serum servant serve service settee seven severe sew sewage sewn sextant shabby shadow shaft shah shallow shampoo share sharpen shatter shawl she sheaf shear sheath sheep sheer sheet sheikh sherry shield shirk shirt shoal shoddy shoe shone shoo shook shoot shore should shoulder shove shovel show shower shown shrew shrewd shriek shudder shush shutter shuttlecock shy siege sieve sigh sight sign signature significant silly similar simile simmer simplicity sincere sincerity sinister siphon sir sitar sitter size skein skeleton ski skipper skirmish skirt sky slain slant slaughter sleek sleep sleet sleeve sleigh sleight sleuth slew slight slippers sloe slogan sloppy sloth slough slovenly slow sluice slur sly small smear smirk

269

smithereens smother smoulder snail snare sneak sneer sneeze sniff snigger snore snow soak soap soar soccer social socket sodden soggy solar sold solder soldier solemn solicitor solid solitary some son soon soothe sophisticated soprano sore sorrow sorry sought soul soup source southern souvenir sovereign sow* sown spa spacious spaghetti spaniel spanner spare sparrow spatial spawn speak spear special species specify specimen spectacular spectator spectra speech speed spew sphere spinach spinnaker spirit splendour splutter spoken sponge sponsor spoof spook spool spoon sprain sprawl spread sprocket spur spurn spurt spy squabble squad squall squander square squash squat squawk squeak squeal squeamish squeeze squirm squirrel squirt staff stagger stain stairs stalk stall stallion stammer stampede stance stare stationary stationery statistician statue staunch steady steak steal stealthy steam steel steep steeple steer stencil sterilise stern stew steward stiff stifle stigma stir stirrup stoat stocking stolen stomach stood stool stoop store storey stow straight strain straits strata strategic strategy straw streak stream street strengthen strew stroll structure stubborn stubby study stuff sturdy stutter sty style subdue subject substantial subtle suburban subversion succeed successor succulent succumb such sudden sue suffer sufficient suffocate sugar suggest suicide suitable suitcase suite sullen summary summer summit summon superficial superior supersonic superstitious supervisor supper supply support suppose supreme sure surf surface surge surgeon surgery surname surplus surrender surreptitious surround survey surveyor survivor suspense suspension suspicion suspicious sustain swagger swallow swamp swan swap swear sweat swede sweep sweet swerve swirl swollen swoon swoop swore syllable symbol symmetry sympathy symphony symptom synagogue synchronise syndicate syndrome synonym synopsis synthesis syringe syrup system

tactician tail tailor taken talent talk tall talon tambourine tangerine tangible tapestry tarantula target tarpaulin tartan task tassel tatter tattoo taught taunt taut taxi tea teach teak team tear* tease technical technique teddy tedious teem teeth teetotal telescope temperature temporary tenacious tennis tenor tense tension tepid term terminate termite terrace terrible terrific territory terror tetanus   thaw theatre their theme theory therapist there thermal these they thief thieve thigh third thirst thirteen thirty this thistle thorough those thou though thought thread threat three threw throat through throw thrown thumb Thursday thy thyroid   tiara tie tier tiger tight timid tissue titter to* toad toast tobacco toe together token told tolerate toll tomb tomorrow ton tongue tonic tonsil tonsillitis too took tool tooth topic topsy-turvy tore torpedo torrent torrential tortoise torture toucan touch tough tour tourist tournament tow towel tower town tractor traffic trail trailer train trainer traitor trampoline trance transfer* transmission transparent trapeze trawl treacherous treacle treadmill treason treasure treasury treat treaty treble tree trek trellis trespass trestle tribute trifle trigger trio triple triumph troll trolley troop trophy tropics trouble trough troupe truant truce true truly truncheon truss truth try Tuesday tummy tumour tundra tunnel turban turf turkey turmoil turn turnip turquoise turret turtle tutor tweed tweezers twirl twitter two type typhoon typical tyranny tyrant tyre

umbrella uncanny uncle unique universal universe university upper urban urchin urge urn us use* usher utensil utopia utopian utter

vacant vacuum vague vain valentine valiant valid valley value vanilla vanish various vase vaseline vast vault veal vegetable vegetarian vehicle veil vein velocity venison ventriloquist venture venue Venus veranda verb verdict verge vermin verse version versus vertical very vessel veteran veterinary via vicar vicious victor video vie view villa village villain vinegar vineyard virtually virtue visible visit visitor vitality vivacious vixen vocabulary volley volume voluntary vomit voodoo voracious vowel vulgar vulture

waft wagon wail waist wait waiter walk wall wallaby wallet wallop wallow walnut walrus waltz wan wand wander want wanton war warble ward wardrobe wares warm warn warp warrant warren warrior wart
wary was wash wasp watch water watt wattle we weak wealth wean weapon wear weary weasel weather weave wedding Wednesday weed week weep weigh weight weir weird were whack whale wharf what wheat wheedle wheel wheelie wheeze whelk when where whether whey which whiff while whilst whimper whine whip whir whirl whirring whisk whiskers whiskey whisky whisper whistle white whiz who wholly whoop whoosh why wicked wicker wicket widow wield wild wildebeest willow winding witness wizard wizened woe wolf woman womb women won wonder woo wood wooden wool woollen word wore work world worm worn worry worse worship worst worth would wound wrangle wrap wrath wreak wreath wreck wren wrench wrestle wretch wriggle wring wrinkle wrist write writhe written wrong wrote wrung wry

xylophone

yahoo yak yawn year yearn yeast yellow yes yeti yew yield yoga yoghurt yolk you young your youth yurt

zeal zealous zebra zero zoo zulu

Bibliography

Ackroyd, P. 2001. London, the biography. Vintage.
Amery, H & Cartwright S. 1992. The Usborne First Thousand Words. Usborne.
    2001. The Usborne First Hundred Words. Usborne.
Barber, C. 2000. The English language. Cambridge UP.
Boswell, J. 1791 The Life of Samuel Johnson. Wordsworth Editions, 1999.
Bryson, B. 1991. Mother Tongue. Penguin.
Carney, E. 1993. A survey of English spelling. Routledge.
    " 1997. English spelling. Routledge.
Chapman, J., Tunmer W. & Prochnow. J. 1999. Success in Reading Recovery
    Depends on the Development of Phonological Processing Skills.
    Report for NZ Ministry of Education.
Chaucer, G. The Canterbury Tales. The Wordsworth Poetry Library, 1995.
Chruchill, W. 1998, A history of the English-speaking peoples, Cassell.
Collins Publishers. Cobuild Corpus of 50 000 most frequently used English words.
    Electronic file.
Crystal, D. 1987c. The Cambridge Encyclopedia of the English Language.
    Cambridge University Press.
Delaney, F. 1986. The Celts. Hodder and Stoughton / BBC Publication.
Dewey, G. 1963. English heterography. NY: Lake Placid Club Education
    Foundation.
Dewey, G. 1970. Relative frequency of English spellings. NY,
    Teachers College Press.
    1971. English spelling: Roadblock to reading. NY: Teachers College Press.
Downing, J. 1962. The augmented Roman alphabet. Cassell, London.
    1967. Evaluating the Initial Teaching Alphabet: A study of the influence of
    English orthography on learning to read and write. London: Cassell.
Feynman, R.P. 1998. The Meaning of It All. Helix books.
Fergusson, R. 1985. Rhyming dictionary. Penguin.
Frith, U., Wimmer, H. & Landerl, K. 1998. 'Differences in phonological decoding in
    German- and English-speaking children. Scientific Studies of Reading, 2(1).
Fowler, H. W. 1937. Fowler's Modern English usage.
    Revised by E. Gower. Oxford 1981.
Frazer, A. 1999. The six wives of Henry VIII. Weidenfeld.
Gee, R & Watson, C. 1992. The Usborne Book of English Spelling. Usborne.
Hanna, P.R., Hanna, J. S., Hodges, R. E. & Rudorf, E. H. 1966. Phoneme-grapheme
    correspondences as cues to spelling improvement.
    Washington: U.S. Government Printing Office.
Hawker, G.T. 1995. Spell it yourself! Oxford.
Honey, J. 1997. Language is power. Faber & Faber.
Hornsby, B and Shear, F. 1974. Alpha to omega. Heinemann.
Hunter B. P. 1991. An introduction to Anglo-Saxon England. Cambridge UP.
Hutton, W. 1996. The State We're in. Vintage.
James, Clive. 1997. The Silver Castle. Picador.
Johnson, Samuel. 1755 . Preface to A Dictionary of the English language: in which
    the words are deduced from their originals.

King, G. 2000. <u>Super Speller</u>. Collins.

Kipling , Rudyard. <u>Just-so Stories</u>. How the alphabet was made.

Lamb, B. 1992., <u>A national survey of UK undergraduates' standard of English</u>.
The Queen's English Society.

1994. <u>A national survey of communication skills of young entrants to
industry and commerce.</u> The QES.

1997. <u>The opinions and practices of teachers of English</u>. The QES.

Landerl, K., Wimmer, F & Frith, U. 1997. <u>The impact of orthographic consistency
on dyslexia:</u> A German-English comparison. Cognition, 63.

Literacy Task Force, U.K. 1996. <u>The Implementation of the National Literacy
Strategy</u>. Dept. for Education and Employment, London.

Lee, C. 1997. <u>This sceptred isle</u>. Penguin/BBC.

Lindgren, Harry. 1969. <u>Spelling Reform: a new approach.</u> Sydney: Alpha Books.

McGuinness, Diane. 1998. <u>Why children can't read</u>. Penguin.

McNally,J& Murray,W. 1968. <u>Key words to literacy and the teaching of reading</u>.
Schoolmaster Publishing Co.

Mencken, H. L. 1963. <u>The American Language</u>. Abridged edition, NY: Knopf.

Michael, I. 1987. <u>The teaching of English from the sixteenth century to 1870</u>.
Cambridge UP.

Moser, C. 1999. <u>Improving literacy and numeracy</u>. A fresh start. Department of
Education and Employment Publications.

New York Times.18/12/2001. <u>Report on Education Bill passed by Senate</u>.

OECD. 2002. <u>Programme for International Student Assessment</u>. www.pisa.oecd.org.
(Organisation for Economic Cooperation and Development)

Ogden, C. K. 1930. <u>The general Basic English Dictionary</u>. Evans Brothers.

Oney, B. & Goldman, S. 1984. <u>Decoding and comprehension skills in Turkish and
English: effects of regularity of grapheme-phoneme correspondence</u>.
Journal of Educational Psychology

Oxford. 1999. <u>My first Oxford book of words</u>.
<u>Oxford Concise Dictionary</u> . 1926, 1935, 1980.
<u>Oxford Concise Companion to the English Language</u>. 1998. Ed. McArthur.

Paulesu, E and 11 others (from Italy, France, England and Quebec), 2001, Science
291, March 16. <u>Dyslexia: Cultural diversity and biological unity</u>.

Paxman, J. 1999. <u>The English</u>. Penguin.

*Pei, Mario.*1968. Preface to A. Tauber's <u>A history of spelling reform</u>.
Reprinted in Spelling Progress Bulletin <u>8</u>.

Qualifications and Curriculum Authority (QCA).1999. <u>Improving writing at key
stages 3 and 4.</u>

Richards, B. 1998. <u>Oxford Spelling</u>. The Oxford Magazine, noughth week, Hilary
term.

Ripman, W. & Archer, W. 1948. <u>New Spelling.</u> London: Pitman.

Ross, J. 1982. <u>Kings & Queens of Britain</u>. Artus Books.

Russell, Bertrand. 1946. Preface to <u>History of Western philosophy.</u> London: Allen
& Unwin.

Sampson, G. 1985. <u>Writing systems.</u> Stanford UP.

Schiffman, Lana (illustrator). 1992. <u>My first book of words</u>:
1000 words every child should know. Cartwheel Co.

Schonell, Fred. J. 1932 and 25 reprints up to 1966. The essential spelling list. Melbourne: Macmillan.

Scragg, D. G. 1974, A history of English spelling. Manchester University Press.

Seymour, P. H. K. 2001. Is English more difficult than other languages? Lecture at the B.A. Festival of Science in Glasgow.

Shakespeare, W. 1594. Complete works. Quarto Edition in British Library. 1625. Complete works. Folio Edition in British Library.

Spencer, K. A. 2002. English spelling and its contribution to illiteracy: word difficulty for common English words. Journal of Reading, 36 (1).

Thorstad, G. 1991. The effect of orthography on the acquisition of literacy skills. British Journal of Psychology, 82, 527-537.

Twain, M. Simplified Spelling in Ancient Egypt. reprinted in Spelling Progress Bulletin 15.3.1975. 1906. Spelling and Pictures. In The Works of Mark Twain, vol 18, Gabriel Wells.

Venezky. R. L. 1999. The American Way of Spelling. Guilford Press.

Vernon, M. D. 1971. Reading and its difficulties. Cambridge University Press.

Viking project (Anglo-Danish), 1981. Vikings in England.

Vikla, M. 1963. On Czechoslovak learning. Spelling Progress Bulletin 3.4: 14.

Webster, N. New International Dictionary of the English Language. (prior to 1957)

Wijk, Axel. 1959. Regularized English. Almqvist-Wiksell.

Wimmer, H. & Goswami, U. 1994. The influence of orthographic consistency on reading development: Word recognition in English and German children.

Yule, V. 1991. Orthography and Reading: Spelling and Society. Doctoral thesis, Monash University, Australia.

Index to graphemes - (letter combinations used for spelling English sounds.)

Index to graphemes *o* to *z*

Index to sounds

Index to names - for subjects see next page

Subject index